Read, REMEMBER, Recommend FOR TEENS

A Reading Journal for Book Lovers

D1469278

CREATED BY
RACHELLE ROGERS KNIGHT

For my parents, Jim and Shirley. Thank you for everything.

Published by Sourcebooks, Inc.
P.O. Box 4410, Naperville, Illinois 60567-4410
(630) 961-3900
Fax: (630) 961-2168
www.sourcebooks.com

Originally published in 2008 by Bibliopages.

CIP data on file with the publisher.

Printed and bound in China.
OGP 10 9 8 7 6 5 4 3 2 1

Contents

Miscellaneous Lists

Read-Alikes

Mysteries, Thrillers, Crime, and Paranormal

Fantasy and Science Fiction

Romance

Westerns

Folklore and Fairy Tales

Comics, Graphic Novels, and Manga

GLBTQ

Poetry

College Bound

Biographies and Autobiographies

Nonfiction, Science, and Social Studies

Other Countries and Cultures

State Awards

Introduction

Welcome to the young adult version of the Read, Remember, Recommend journal series.

The journal was created to provide young adults with thousands of reading suggestions—in all different genres of literature. There are lists for those who love fiction, graphic novels (manga), romance, westerns, crime novels, and poetry. There are nonfiction selections to help with homework assignments as well as expand interests—in the nonfiction, historical fiction, biography, and autobiography genres. College bound readers will find a section to help guide their reading selections for the preparation of a secondary education.

Teens

Explore new genres you might never have tried. Make it a goal to read at least one book from each list. Tell your friends about what you are reading and get their suggestions. Keep track of what genres and authors you like. Make sure to write down how you feel about each book you read.

Each suggested title has the beginning age group number listed in the column next to the title. Don't let the age turn you away from a title, as this is a minimum age. In other words, the age is the youngest suggested age for reading the title—not the oldest. The category of young adult is one of the most popular groups of books for both adults as well as teens. All of the selections mentioned are sure to provide some great reading, so don't miss out on anything! Get reading!

Parents

This journal is guaranteed to provide you and your kids (ages twelve to eighteen) with thousands of wonderful reading suggestions. While a list may have been provided by a national or state institution—all of which have the best interest of the child at heart and the goal to encourage literary development—not all titles may be appropriate for your teen. Please make sure you are aware of what your children are reading, and use this journal as an opportunity to engage them and spark their interest in further titles. While the young adult genre spans six years (ages twelve to eighteen), there can be vast differences between the development of teens, and not all titles may be appropriate. Please peruse these lists with your kids and help them choose what is appropriate for their age. Every effort has been made to make the publisher-suggested age group visible for each title. If you are at all unsure of a title, please ask your local bookstore or librarian—or better yet, read it first!

The main objective of this journal is to provide a resource for young adults and their parents to find valuable, engaging reading material. The second goal of this publication is to encourage parents to read with their teens. The quality and amount of reading material available for young adults is staggering. These suggestions are wonderful—and not meant just for teens. Many of the suggestions in this journal will be found on adult book club reading lists and are national best sellers. Don't miss out on a great opportunity to read some great books—and discuss them with your kids. Have a mini book group in your own home and engage those budding bibliophiles. These books offer some great opportunities to get to know your child, as well as exchange feelings about different subjects. Is there a better way to get conversation flowing than with a great book?

Some of the titles might fall into a lower age group than was intended for this journal, but because they are part of a list that is applicable to this group, they have been included. Some lists were intentionally left out because the majority of the titles were below the age group for this journal. If you find a list that you feel is appropriate for the journal but wasn't included in this edition, contact BiblioBabe (suggestions@bibliobabe.com), and we'll review it for future editions.

The Boxes

Own	Recommend	To Read	Want
X			
		/	

Throughout this journal, you will find boxes similar to these. They are designed to help you keep track of what you have read, what you want to read, what you want to recommend for someone else to read, what you own, and what you would like to buy or borrow. The following is an explanation of each of the boxes and how to use them.

Own: Use a check in this box to indicate if you own the book. This will help you organize your personal library. It can also assist you when you desire to loan a particular selection.

Recommend: If you have read the book, use this box to indicate whether or not you would recommend the selection to someone in the future. If you wouldn't recommend it, leave the box blank. Remember, to recommend a particular work, you don't have to love it. It just has to be a story someone in your reading circle would be interested in.

To Read: Use this box to indicate whether you have read the book, using an X; or would like to read the book, using a /. After you have read the selection, come back and finish marking with a \. This is a great method to quickly indicate what you have already read and to help you find your next book.

Want: Scan this column, on the right-hand side, to find those works you would like to buy or check out from the library. Use a / to indicate a book you want. After acquiring the selection, use a \ to complete the X.

Read

The Lists

It's late at night and you've just finished a great book. Ahhhhh. What a feeling! The characters are still fresh in your imagination, friends you will keep and think back on from time to time. Questions and thoughts swirl in your mind.

As you reflect over the book's ending, a strange panic begins to form in your mind. What's next? It's too late to call a friend, and your bookshelf is empty.

The lists in this journal will help ensure that you never have that feeling again. They offer stacks of suggestions in all genres, across many interests.

Each list represents the inspiration and effort of an individual or group of people devoted to publicizing what they believe are examples of the world's greatest literature.

So, peruse, ponder, and plunge in!

Award Lists

Academic organizations, newspapers, library associations, and even states review hundreds of each year's most notable books. They reward what they deem the "best" book for their group, and by doing so help publicize works of literary merit. All the lists reflect the tastes and values of the organization or awarding group. An introduction to the organization and an explanation of the award purpose is provided.

Awards listed in this journal represent a sample of the great honors granted to young adult and children's books each year. Most major awards are included, along with some lesser-known prizes. At the beginning of each list, a brief explanation of the award is given. Space is provided so that you may enter the authors and titles of award winners for the next two years.

Each entry includes the year of the award, author, title, original publication year, and appropriate beginning age. In addition, there are patterned boxes indicating whether a title is fiction ▬▬, non-fiction ▬▬, juvenile fiction ▭▭, or juvenile nonfiction ▭▭. These indicators are publisher-assigned designations and are provided to help in title selection. Where data was not available, a strike-through appears ⬚.

One goal of publishing this journal is to promote great works of literature; therefore, every effort has been made to note all the awards a particular author or work has been granted and to emphasize accu-mulated awards whenever an author or work is listed. This is accom-plished through the use of footnotes. Each award has a corresponding footnote symbol, and when a particular title is listed, the additional awards it has won are footnoted.

Notable Lists

If you check online or with your local library, you will find countless reading lists available for all genres, interests, and age groups. Along with the awards lists, this journal contains notable lists that offer a wide selection of well-considered, noteworthy reading suggestions.

Blank Lists

Blank lists have been provided at the back of the lists section, start-ing on page 191. Use these pages to record your own personal best lists, book club lists (past and present), and other lists that aren't represented in this journal.

Remember

Books To Read

Use this section to keep track of all the books you want to read. Whenever you hear of a book through a recommendation, an assignment, or your own research, make sure to record the title and author. The resulting list will be a great resource when it's time to shop for books. Mark books you want to buy or borrow, and check them off as you acquire them; then, as you finish each book, complete the check mark to record and remember what you have read.

Journal Pages

At the beginning of this section are several pages to record each title you have read. If you journal about the book, enter the page number of the journal entry. If not, enter the date you finished reading the title. Use the journal pages to record information about what you have read, including the following elements:

Title, author, and date you started the book, along with a **check box** for noting whether you would **recommend** the book to others.

Who recommended the book? A book you choose to record may be a gift, an award winner, a recommendation from a friend or publication, an assignment, or a book written by an author whose previous books you've enjoyed.

Reason for reading the book. Are you reading this book for fun, for an assignment, or for a book club discussion? Or was it on one of the lists?

Words you don't know. Include the word, definition, and page number on which you found it.

Passages to remember. Sometimes sections in a book capture your interest or intrigue you. They might make you say, "I wish I'd said that!" or "Wow, I've definitely felt that way before." Make sure to remember these segments by including them in your journal entries.

Include the passage, the page, and, if you wish, how you feel about the passage or why you want to remember it. Such passages can be great to read to a discussion group, send to a friend, tape to your refrigerator, or use as future inspiration.

Comments. This is the most important space in your reading journal. Use it to record comments about the book itself, the characters, the plot, how specific events or characters made you feel, the dialogue, the narration, and parts you don't like or don't understand. You might also wish to record how this book compares to other books you've read by the same author. Are you more or less inclined to seek out additional works? If you are reading this book as a book club selection or for an assignment that will be discussed in class, jot down discussion points and questions throughout your reading. Don't forget to record highlights from the group discussion itself. It's interesting to note how others experienced the book. Did they share similar thoughts and feelings? Did you change any of your conclusions about the book after discussing it? What did you learn about yourself, the book, and other members of the group from the discussion? What insights did you gain?

A Note on Journaling

Although it may take some time to develop the habit, journaling throughout the course of reading a book can leave you feeling as though you've truly experienced the work. Jot down your thoughts and feelings as you experience them to ensure you capture the moment. Keep your journal with you on the bus, subway, in car trips, and at the doctor's office. Take it in your backpack or purse and put it on your nightstand—anywhere you read. Next to your treasured books, your journal will become your greatest friend. With this friend you can browse back and reminisce. Looking back over past journal entries and remembering a book—and who you were when you read it—offers great opportunity for reflection and insight.

Books have the capacity to transform us—how we feel, think, and perceive our world. We may be as changed by reading a book as are the characters who live in its pages.

Books also have the ability to help us reason and sort through past experiences and present challenges in our lives. Allow this journal to act as a good listener and communicate the way you feel while recollecting these people and events. Make the journal yours. Don't worry about complete sentences, your handwriting, whether something makes sense or not—*if you feel it, write it down.*

Recommend

Recommendation List

The only thing better than reading a good book is sharing it. Your recommendations can enrich the reading lives of those in your reading circle. Use the Recommendation list to record the books you would recommend. Keep in mind that a book doesn't have to be a favorite to be recommended. Jot down selections you know someone else would enjoy. There is room to keep recommendations for different people and groups.

Loaner Lists

These lists are designed to help you keep track of books you've shared. Record the names of the books you've loaned and the persons who borrowed them, as well as when they were borrowed and returned. Similar lists will remind you to read and return books others have loaned to you.

Award and Blog Links

The References and Resources section includes the names and websites of most national and international book awards not given list space in the journal. The websites for the author awards are also listed.

A myriad of book-related blogs are also referenced. All of these blogs contain a wealth of book-related information from reviews, opinions, news on new books, author interviews, and reading challenges.

Literary Terms

The next step in appreciating and enjoying great literature is to understand the methods writers employ in crafting their stories. Becoming familiar with their tools will help you understand works better from the writer's perspective.

The literary term definitions in the References and Resources section will help you recognize not only different types of fiction, but also how the stories themselves are constructed. Stories are assembled using a large and intricate structure involving characters, their relationships to each other, settings, plots, themes, and narration. Authors use these literary tools to turn a simple narrative into a complex, memorable experience for their readers.

As you become familiar with the terms, you will be able to point out specific literary techniques an author has used. Make sure to journal about these devices as you discover them.

Reflect

As humans, we were born to gather. And we love to look at what we've collected. We bibliophiles (book lovers) need to gather books. We can't deny it—and shouldn't try. And who among us can resist a good annotated list? It is wonderful to turn over the pages of a reading journal—your personal bookshelf in miniature—to see what you have assembled. This journal was created with the book lover in mind. We hope that its size, its ease of use, and the information contained within it will inspire active and involved reading.

We also hope it will help you savor your reading accomplishments. When you've scrutinized the lists, go back, note the check marks, check your notes, and celebrate! What you have read will be yours forever.

Awards and Notable Lists

I've traveled the world twice over,
Met the famous, saints and sinners,
Poets and artists, kings and queens,
Old stars and hopeful beginners,
I've been where no one's been before,
Learned secrets from writers and cooks
All with one literary ticket
To the wonderful world of books.

—Anonymous

National Book Award—Young People's Literature *

The National Book Awards are given annually in October to American authors for books published the prior year. The purpose of these awards, created in 1950 by a group of publishers, is "to enhance the public's awareness of exceptional books...and to increase the popularity of reading in general." Award categories have varied over the years, but now include fiction, nonfiction, poetry, and young people's literature. For each genre, an independent five-judge panel selects the winner. Each winner receives a crystal sculpture and $10,000. More information can be found at http://www.nationalbook.org/nba.html.

Year	Author	Title	Age	Own	Recommend	To Read	Want
2010							
2009	Phillip M. Hoose	*Claudette Colvin: Twice Toward Justice*	9				
2008	Judy Blundell	*What I Saw and How I Lied*	12				
2007	Sherman Alexie	*The Absolutely True Diary of a Part-Time Indian* ᵃᵃᵃ,♥♥♥,♪♪♪	12				
2006	M. T. Anderson	*The Astonishing Life of Octavian Nothing: Traitor to the Nation, Vol. 1: The Pox Party* ᵃᵃᵃ	15				
2005	Jeanne Birdsall	*The Penderwicks: A Summer Tale Of Four Sisters Two Rabbits And A Very Interesting Boy*	9				
2004	Pete Hautman	*Godless* ££	12				
2003	Polly Horvath	*The Canning Season* $$$	15				
2002	Nancy Farmer	*The House of the Scorpion* ##,♦♦♦,¶¶¶,o,¿,oo,3	12				
2001	Virginia Euwer Wolff	*True Believer*	12				
2000	Gloria Whelan	*Homeless Bird*	12				
1999	Kimberly Willis Holt	*When Zachary Beaver Came to Town*	9				
1998	Louis Sachar	*Holes* ᵃᵃᵃ,##,♦♦♦,♪♪,iii,ᵃᵃᵃ,∩,¿¿¿,¿,∩∩	9				
1997	Han Nolan	*Dancing on the Edge*	15				
1996	Victor Martínez	*Parrot in the Oven* ♦♦,♥♥	12				

□ Juvenile Nonfiction ▨ Juvenile Fiction ■ Fiction ■ Nonfiction

Carnegie Medal **

The Carnegie Medal is awarded annually to the writer of an outstanding book for children. Established by the Library Association (Great Britain) in 1936 to honor the nineteenth-century philanthropist Andrew Carnegie, the medal is now awarded by the Chartered Institute of Library and Information Professionals (CILIP), an organization formed in 2002 by combining the Institute of Information Scientists and the Library Association. The Scottish-born Carnegie, who made his fortune in the United States, set up more than 2,800 libraries across the English-speaking world. By the time he died, over half the library authorities in Great Britain had Carnegie libraries. The winner receives a golden medal and £500 worth of books to donate to a library of his or her choice. For more information, go to www.carnegiegreenaway.org.uk/carnegie.

Year	Author	Title	Age	Own	Recommend	To Read	Want
2011							
2010							
2009	Siobhan Dowd	*Bog Child*	12				
2008	Philip Reeve	*Here Lies Arthur*	15				
2007	Meg Rosoff	*Just in Case*	15				
2005	Mal Peet	*Tamar*	15				
2004	Frank Cottrell Boyce	*Millions*	9				
2003	Jennifer Donnelly	*A Gathering Light*	12				
2002	Sharon Creech	*Ruby Holler* iii	9				
2001	Terry Pratchett	*The Amazing Maurice and His Educated Rodents*	12				
2000	Beverly Naidoo	*The Other Side of Truth*	12				
1999	Aidan Chambers	*Postcards from No Man's Land* ii	15				
1998	David Almond	*Skellig* ii	9				
1997	Tim Bowler	*River Boy*	12				
1996	Melvin Burgess	*Junk*	12				
1995	Philip Pullman	*His Dark Materials: Book 1 Northern Lights*	12				
1994	Theresa Breslin	*Whispers in the Graveyard*	9				
1993	Robert Swindells	*Stone Cold*	8				

Carnegie Medal **			Age	Own	Recommend	To Read	Want
Year	Author	Title					
1992	Anne Fine	*Flour Babies*	12				
1991	Berlie Doherty	*Dear Nobody*	12				
1990	Gillian Cross	*Wolf*	12				
1989	Anne Fine	*Goggle-Eyes*	12				
1988	Geraldine McCaughrean	*A Pack of Lies*	12				
1987	Susan Price	*The Ghost Drum*	12				
1986	Berlie Doherty	*Granny Was a Buffer Girl*	12				
1985	Kevin Crossley-Holland	*Storm*	8				
1984	Margaret Mahy	*The Changeover*	12				
1983	Jan Mark	*Handles*	12				
1982	Margaret Mahy	*The Haunting*	15				
1981	Robert Westall	*The Scarecrows*					
1980	Peter Dickinson	*City of Gold*	15				
1979	Peter Dickinson	*Tulku*	12				
1978	David Rees	*The Exeter Blitz*	12				
1977	Gene Kemp	*The Turbulent Term of Tyke Tiler*	9				
1976	Jan Mark	*Thunder and Lightnings*	12				
1975	Robert Westall	*The Machine Gunners*	12				
1974	Mollie Hunter	*The Stronghold*	15				
1973	Penelope Lively	*The Ghost of Thomas Kempe*	12				
1972	Richard Adams	*Watership Down* ♪	10				
1971	Ivan Southall	*Josh*	12				
1970	Leon Garfield and Edward Blishen	*The God Beneath the Sea*	12				
1969	Kathleen Peyton	*The Edge of the Cloud*	12				
1968	Rosemary Harris	*The Moon in the Cloud*	12				
1967	Alan Garner	*The Owl Service*	12				
1966	Prize Withheld as No Book Considered Suitable						
1965	Philip Turner	*The Grange at High Force*	12				

▢ Juvenile Nonfiction   ▨ Juvenile Fiction   ▰ Fiction   ▰ Nonfiction

Carnegie Medal **			Age	Own	Recommend	To Read	Want
Year	Author	Title					
1964	Sheena Porter	*Nordy Bank*	8				
1963	Hester Burton	*Time of Trial*					
1962	Pauline Clarke	*The Twelve and the Genii*	9				
1961	Lucy M. Boston	*A Stranger at Green Knowe*	8				
1960	Ian Wolfram Cornwall	*The Making of Man*					
1959	Rosemary Sutcliff	*The Lantern Bearers*	12				
1958	Philippa Pearce	*Tom's Midnight Garden*	10				
1957	William Mayne	*A Grass Rope*	12				
1956	C. S. Lewis	*The Last Battle*	9				
1955	Eleanor Farjeon	*The Little Bookroom*	8				
1954	Ronald Welch	*Knight Crusader*	15				
1953	Edward Osmond	*A Valley Grows Up*					
1952	Mary Norton	*The Borrowers*	9				
1951	Cynthia Harnett	*The Woolpack*					
1950	Elfrida Vipont Foulds	*The Lark on the Wing*	10				
1949	Agnes Allen	*The Story of Your Home*					
1948	Richard Armstrong	*Sea Change*					
1947	Walter de la Mare	*Collected Stories for Children*					
1946	Elizabeth Goudge	*The Little White Horse*	12				
1944	Eric Linklater	*The Wind on the Moon*	10				
1943	No Award Given						
1942	BB	*The Little Grey Men*	10				
1941	Mary Treadgold	*We Couldn't Leave Dinah*					
1940	Kitty Barne	*Visitors from London*					
1939	Eleanor Doorly	*Radium Woman*					
1938	Noel Streatfeild	*The Circus is Coming*					
1937	Eve Garnett	*The Family from One End Street*	12				
1936	Arthur Ransome	*Pigeon Post*					

Boston Globe-Horn Book Award ***

The Boston Globe-Horn Book Award is presented annually and was first presented in 1967. The Boston Globe-Horn Book Award is are among the most prestigious awards given in the field of children's and young adult literature. Winners are named by an independent panel of three judges, appointed by the editor of Horn Book, in three categories: picture book, fiction and poetry, and nonfiction. In addition, two honorary books may also be selected in each category, and special citations for high quality and overall creative excellence are occasionally awarded. Winning titles must be published in the United States, but they may be written or illustrated by non-U.S. citizens. The fiction and nonfiction categories are listed here.

Year	Author	Title	Age	Own	Recommend	To Read	Want
Fiction							
2011							
2010							
2009	Terry Pratchett	*Nation* !	12				
2008	Sherman Alexie	*The Absolutely True Diary of a Part-Time Indian* *,▼▼▼,♫♫	12				
2007	M. T. Anderson	*The Astonishing Life of Octavian Nothing: Traitor to the Nation, Vol. 1: The Pox Party* *	15				
2006	Kate Dicamillo	*The Miraculous Journey of Edward Tulane*	8				
2005	Neal Shusterman	*The Schwa was Here* ♪	12				
2004	David Almond	*The Fire-Eaters*	8				
2003	Anne Fine	*The Jamie and Angus Stories*	5				
2002	Graham Salisbury	*Lord of the Deep*	7				
2001	Marilyn Nelson	*Carver: A Life in Poems*	12				
2000	Franny Billingsley	*The Folk Keeper* ᵛᵛᵛ	9				
1999	Louis Sachar	*Holes* *,##,♦♦♦,♫♫,ⅲ,•••,∩,¿¿¿,¿,∩∩	9				
1998	Francisco Jiménez	*The Circuit: Stories from the Life of a Migrant Child* ▼▼	12				
1997	Kazumi Yumoto	*The Friends*	9				

☐ Juvenile Nonfiction　　☐ Juvenile Fiction　　■ Fiction　　■ Nonfiction

Boston Globe-Horn Book Award ***			Age	Own	Recommend	To Read	Want
Year	Author	Title					
1996	Avi	*Poppy*	8				
1995	Tim Wynne-Jones	*Some of the Kinder Planets*	9				
1994	Vera Williams	*Scooter*	8				
1993	James Berry	*Ajeemah and His Son*	12				
1992	Cynthia Rylant	*Missing May*	12				
1991	Avi	*The True Confessions of Charlotte Doyle* [33],***	12				
1990	Jerry Spinelli	*Maniac Magee* ♪♪♪,**	9				
1989	Paula Fox	*The Village by the Sea*	9				
1988	Mildred D. Taylor	*The Friendship*	8				
1987	Lois Lowry	*Rabble Starkey*	12				
1986	Zibby Oneal	*In Summer Light*	12				
1985	Bruce Brooks	*The Moves Make the Man*	15				
1984	Patricia Wrightson	*A Little Fear*	12				
1983	Virginia Hamilton	*Sweet Whispers, Brother Rush*	12				
1982	Ruth Park	*Playing Beatie Bow*	12				
1981	Lynn Hall	*The Leaving*	12				
1980	Andrew Davies	*Conrad's War*	9				
1979	Sid Fleischman	*Humbug Mountain*	9				
1978	Ellen Raskin	*The Westing Game* **	12				
1977	Laurence Yep	*Child of the Owl*	12				
1976	Jill Paton Walsh	*Unleaving*	12				
1975	Tuti Degens	*Transport 7-41-R* ~~~	12				
1974	Virginia Hamilton	*M. C. Higgins the Great*	9				
1973	Susan Cooper	*The Dark is Rising*	9				
1972	Rosemary Sutcliff	*Tristan and Iseult*	9				
1971	Eleanor Cameron	*A Room Made of Windows*	12				
1970	John Rowe Townsend	*The Intruder*	9				
1969	Ursula K. Le Guin	*A Wizard of Earthsea*	9				

Year	Author	Title	Age	Own	Recommend	To Read	Want
1969	John Lawson	*The Spring Rider*	7				
1967	Erik Christian Haugaard	*The Little Fishes*	12				
Nonfiction							
2011							
2010							
2009	Candace Fleming	*The Lincolns: A Scrapbook Look at Abraham and Mary*	9				
2008	Peter Sis	*The Wall: Growing Up Behind the Iron Curtain* ♦♦	8				
2007	Nicolas Debon	*The Strongest Man in the World: Louis Cyr*	6				
2006	Faith McNulty	*If You Decide to Go to the Moon*	5				
2005	Phillip M. Hoose	*The Race to Save the Lord God Bird*	12				
2004	Jim Murphy	*An American Plague: The True and Terrifying Story of the Yellow Fever Epidemic of 1793* ♦♦	9				
2003	Maira Kalman	*Fireboat: The Heroic Adventures of the John J. Harvey*	7				
2002	Elizabeth Partridge	*This Land Was Made For You and Me: The Life and Songs of Woody Guthrie*	12				
2001	Joan Dash	*The Longitude Prize*	9				
2000	Marc Aronson	*Sir Walter Ralegh and the Quest for El Dorado* ♦♦	12				
1999	Steve Jenkins	*The Top of the World: Climbing Mount Everest*	7				
1998	Leon Walter Tillage	*Leon's Story* %%%	8				
1997	Walter Wick	*A Drop of Water: A Book of Science and Wonder*	8				
1996	Andrea Warren	*Orphan Train Rider: One Boy's True Story*	8				
1995	Natalie S. Bober	*Abigail Adams: Witness to a Revolution*	12				

⬜ Juvenile Nonfiction　⬜ Juvenile Fiction　⬛ Fiction　⬛ Nonfiction

Boston Globe-Horn Book Award ***			Age	Own	Recommend	To Read	Want
Year	**Author**	**Title**					
1994	Russell Freedman	*Eleanor Roosevelt: A Life of Discovery*	7				
1993	Patricia C. and Fredrick McKissack	*Sojourner Truth: Ain't I a Woman?*	9				
1992	Pat Cummings	*Talking with Artists*	8				
1991	Cynthia Rylant	*Appalachia: The Voices of Sleeping Birds*	8				
1990	Jean Fritz	*The Great Little Madison*	9				
1989	David Macaulay	*The Way Things Work*	12				
1988	Virginia Hamilton	*Anthony Burns: The Defeat and Triumph of a Fugitive Slave* %%%	9				
1987	Marcia Sewall	*The Pilgrims of Plimoth*	6				
1986	Peggy Thomson	*Auks Rocks and the Odd Dinosaur*	9				
1985	Rhoda Blumberg	*Commodore Perry in the Land of the Shogun*	9				
1984	Jean Fritz	*The Double Life of Pocahontas*	9				
1983	Daniel S. Davis	*Behind Barbed Wire*	9				
1982	Aranka Siegal	*Upon the Head of the Goat*	12				
1981	Kathryn Lasky	*The Weaver's Gift*	9				
1980	Mario Salvadori	*Building: The Fight Against Gravity*					
1979	David Kherdian	*The Road from Home*	12				
1978	Ilse Koehn	*Mischling Second Degree*	12				
1977	Peter Dickinson	*Chance Luck and Destiny*					
1976	Alfred Tamarin and Shirley Glubok	*Voyaging to Cathay*					

Alex Award ~

The Alex Award was first given in 1998 to honor Margaret Alexander Edwards, called "Alex" by friends, a legendary young adult librarian at the Enoch Pratt Free Library in Baltimore. When Ms. Edwards began her career in the 1930s, young people were forbidden or discouraged from visiting public libraries, a practice she deplored. She described her efforts to develop services specifically for young adults in her book *Fair Garden and the Swarm of Beasts*, which has inspired subsequent generations of young adult librarians. The Alex Award is given annually to ten books written for adults that have special appeal to young adults, ages twelve through eighteen. The winning titles are selected from the previous year's publishing lists. Sponsored by the Margaret Alexander Edwards Trust and Booklist, the award became an official American Library Association (ALA) award in 2002, through its subsidiary organization Young Adult Library Services Association (YALSA). For more information, see www.ala.org/yalsa/booklists/alex.

Year	Author	Title	Age	Own	Recommend	To Read	Want
2011							
2011							
2011							
2011							
2011							
2011							
2011							
2011							
2011							
2011							
2010							
2010							
2010							
2010							
2010							
2010							
2010							

☐ Juvenile Nonfiction   ☐ Juvenile Fiction   ■ Fiction   ■ Nonfiction

Alex Award ~			Age	Own	Recommend	To Read	Want
Year	Author	Title					
2010							
2010							
2010							
2009	David Benioff	City of Thieves					
2009	Michael Swanwick	The Dragons of Babel					
2009	Zoë Ferraris	Finding Nouf					
2009	Hannah Tinti	The Good Thief					
2009	Stephen King	Just After Sunset: Stories					
2009	Hillary Jordan	Mudbound					
2009	Todd Tucker	Over and Under					
2009	Stephen G. Bloom	The Oxford Project					
2009	Toby Barlow	Sharp Teeth					
2009	Theresa Rebeck	Three Girls and Their Brother					
2008	Ishmael Beah	A Long Way Gone: Memoirs of a Boy Soldier					
2008	Matt Ruff	Bad Monkeys					
2008	Jeff Lemire	Essex County Vol. 1: Tales from the Farm					
2008	Matthew Polly	American Shaolin: Flying Kicks, Buddhist Monks, and the Legend of Iron Crotch: An Odyssey in the New China					
2008	Conn Iggulden	Genghis: Birth of an Empire					
2008	Lisa Lutz	The Spellman Files					
2008	Lloyd Jones	Mister Pip					
2008	Aryn Kyle	The God of Animals					
2008	Patrick Rothfuss	The Name of the Wind					
2008	Thomas Maltman	The Night Birds					
2007	John Hamamura	Color of the Sea					
2007	Michael D'Orso	Eagle Blue: A Team, a Tribe, and a High School Basketball Season in Arctic Alaska					

Year	Author	Title	Age	Own	Recommend	To Read	Want
2007	Diane Setterfield	*The Thirteenth Tale*					
2007	Ivan Doig	*The Whistling Season* ♣					
2007	Pamela Carter Joern	*Floor of the Sky*					
2007	John Connolly	*The Book of Lost Things*					
2007	David Mitchell	*Black Swan Green*					
2007	Ron Rash	*The World Made Straight*					
2007	Michael Lewis	*The Blind Side: Evolution of the Game*					
2007	Sara Gruen	*Water for Elephants*					
2006	Gregory Galloway	*As Simple as Snow*					
2006	Julia Scheeres	*Jesus Land: A Memoir*					
2006	Kalisha Buckhanon	*Upstate*					
2006	Susan Palwick	*The Necessary Beggar*					
2006	Judy Fong Bates	*Midnight at the Dragon Cafe*					
2006	Nancy Rawles	*My Jim*					
2006	Jeannette Walls	*The Glass Castle* ˙˙					
2006	Kazuo Ishiguro	*Never Let Me Go*					
2006	A. Lee Martinez	*Gil's All Fright Diner*					
2006	Neil Gaiman	*Anansi Boys*					
2005	Kent Meyers	*Work of Wolves*					
2005	Jodi Picoult	*My Sister's Keeper* ˜˜,#,ΩΩΩ,˙˙,Σ					
2005	Lynne Cox	*Swimming to Antarctica: Tales of a Long-Distance Swimmer*					
2005	Steve Almond	*Candyfreak: A Journey Through the Chocolate Underbelly of America*					
2005	Brendan Halpin	*Donorboy*					
2005	Jim Shepard	*Project X*					
2005	Robert Sullivan	*Rats: Observations on the History and Habitat of the City's Most Unwanted Inhabitants*					

▢ Juvenile Nonfiction ▢ Juvenile Fiction ▮ Fiction ▮ Nonfiction

Alex Award ~			Age	Own	Recommend	To Read	Want
Year	Author	Title					
2005	Ann Patchett	Truth & Beauty: A Friendship					
2005	Robert Kurson	Shadow Divers					
2005	Kit Reed	Thinner Than Thou					
2004	Mark Haddon	The Curious Incident of the Dog in the Night-Time	12				
2004	Marjane Satrapi	Persepolis: The Story of a Childhood	15				
2004	Mary Roach	Stiff: The Curious Lives of Human Cadavers					
2004	Khaled Hosseini	The Kite Runner					
2004	Amanda Davis	Wonder When You'll Miss Me					
2004	Jacqueline Winspear	Maisie Dobbs					
2004	Mark Salzman	True Notebooks	12				
2004	Bart Yates	Leave Myself Behind					
2004	Audrey Niffeneger	The Time Traveler's Wife					
2004	Z. Z. Packer	Drinking Coffee Elsewhere					
2003	Timothy Ferris	Seeing in the Dark: How Backyard Stargazers Are Probing Deep Space and Guarding Earth From Interplanetary Peril					
2003	Julie Otsuka	When the Emperor Was Divine					
2003	Ann Packer	The Dive from Clausen's Pier					
2003	Jasper Fforde	The Eyre Affair					
2003	Lynda Barry	One Hundred Demons					
2003	Martha Southgate	The Fall of Rome	12				
2003	Joseph Weisberg	10th Grade					
2003	Mary Lawson	Crow Lake					
2003	Pat Conroy	My Losing Season					
2003	Brian Malloy	The Year of Ice					
2002	Mel Odom	The Rover					
2002	Kobie Kruger	The Wilderness Family: At Home with Africa's Wildlife	12				

Year	Author	Title	Age	Own	Recommend	To Read	Want
2002	Barbara Ehrenreich	Nickel and Dimed: On (Not) Getting by in America	12				
2002	Vineeta Vijayaraghavan	Motherland					
2002	Leif Enger	Peace Like a River					
2002	David Anthony Durham	Gabriel's Story					
2002	Rebecca Walker	Black, White and Jewish: An Autobiography of a Shifting Self	15				
2002	Donna Morrissey	Kit's Law					
2002	William Doyle	An American Insurrection: The Battle of Oxford Mississippi					
2002	Geraldine Brooks	Year of Wonders: A Novel of the Plague	15				
2001	Tracy Chevalier	Girl with a Pearl Earring					
2001	James Bradley and Ron Powers	Flags of Our Fathers	12				
2001	Nathaniel Philbrick	In the Heart of the Sea: The Tragedy of the Whaleship Essex					
2001	Alan Watt	Diamond Dogs	10				
2001	Juliet Marillier	Daughter of the Forest					
2001	Larry Colton	Counting Coup					
2001	Darin Strauss	Chang and Eng					
2000	Orson Scott Card	Ender's Shadow					
2000	David Breashears	High Exposure: An Enduring Passion for Everest and Unforgiving Places					
2000	Connie Rose Porter	Imani All Mine ‡					
2000	Elva Trevino Hart	Barefoot Heart					
2000	Esme Raji Codell	Educating Esme: Diary of a Teacher's First Year					
2000	Jonathon Scott Fuqua	The Reappearance of Sam Webber	9				
2000	Neil Gaiman	Stardust	12				
2000	Breena Clarke	River Cross My Heart					

☐ Juvenile Nonfiction   ☐ Juvenile Fiction   ■ Fiction   ■ Nonfiction

Alex Award ~			Age	Own	Recommend	To Read	Want
Year	Author	Title					
2000	Linda Greenlaw	*The Hungry Ocean: A Swordboat Captain's Journey*					
2000	Kent Haruf	*Plainsong*					

Heartland Award for Excellence in Young Adult Literature ~~

The Writing Conference, Inc., established the Heartland Award in 1996 to encourage young adults to read literature, middle and secondary schools to teach literature, and young adults to become lifelong readers. Nominations can be made by young adult literature enthusiasts. Winning titles are selected by students. Details can be found at www.writingconference.com/heartlan.htm.

Year	Author	Title	Age	Own	Recommend	To Read	Want
2011							
2010							
2009	Jay Asher	*Thirteen Reasons Why* Ω,‡‡‡	12				
2008	Will Hobbs	*Crossing the Wire*	12				
2007	Sharon M. Draper	*Copper Sun*	12				
2006	Jodi Picoult	*My Sister's Keeper* ~,#,ΩΩΩ,••,Σ					
2005	Sue Mayfield	*Drowning Anna*	12				
2004	Gordon Korman	*Son of the Mob* ##,•••,‡‡‡	12				
2003	Ann Brashares	*The Sisterhood of the Traveling Pants* ‡,‡‡,Σ,¶,ii,•••,3	15				
2002	Phyllis Reynolds Naylor	*Jade Green*	12				
2001	Laurie Halse Anderson	*Speak* ‡‡‡,ii,•••,¿,oo,3	15				
2000	Robert Cormier	*Heroes*	15				
1999	Alden R. Carter	*Bull Catcher*	12				
1998	Karen Hesse	*Phoenix Rising* •••,oo	12				
1997	Sharon Creech	*Walk Two Moons* ¿,••	12				

IRA Award—Intermediate and Young Adult ~~~

The International Reading Association (IRA), established in 1956, is a nonprofit, global network of individuals and institutions committed to worldwide literacy. The IRA grants children's and young adult's book awards for an author's first or second published book written for children or young adults (birth to 17 years). Awards, which include a monetary stipend, may go to works of fiction or nonfiction in each of three categories: primary, intermediate, and young adult. Books from any country and in any language published for the first time during the preceding calendar year will be considered. Winning titles in the intermediate and young adult categories are listed here. For more information about the award or the International Reading Association, go to www.reading.org.

Year	Author	Title	Age	Own	Recommend	To Read	Want
Intermediate Nonfiction							
2011							
2010							
2009	Carlyn Beccia	*The Raucous Royals*	7				
2008	Loree Griffin Burns	*Tracking Trash: Flotsam, Jetsam, and the Science of Ocean Motion*	9				
2007	Carla Killough McClafferty	*Something Out of Nothing: Marie Curie and Radium*	9				
2006	Robert Shetterly	*Americans Who Tell the Truth*	12				
2004	Penelope Niven	*Carl Sandburg: Adventures of a Poet*					
2003	David J. Smith	*If the World Were a Village: A Book About the World's People*	8				
2002	Dorinda Makanaonalani Nicholson And Larry Nicholson	*Pearl Harbor Warriors*	12				
Intermediate Fiction							
2011							
2010							
2009	K. A. Nuzum	*The Leanin' Dog*	9				
2008	Constance Leeds	*The Silver Cup*	12				
2007	Joyce Moyer Hostetter	*Blue*	9				

⬜ Juvenile Nonfiction ⬜ Juvenile Fiction ⬛ Fiction ⬛ Nonfiction

Year	Author	Title	Age	Own	Recommend	To Read	Want
IRA Award—Intermediate and Young Adult ~~~							
2006	David L. Dudley	*The Bicycle Man*	12				
2005	Joan Marie Arbogast	*Buildings in Disguise*	8				
2005	Maiya Williams	*The Golden Hour*	9				
2004	Esme Raji Codell	*Sahara Special*	9				
2003	Marlene Carvell	*Who Will Tell My Brother?*	12				
2002	Yin	*Coolies*	6				
Young Adult Nonfiction							
2011							
2010							
2009	Moying Li	*Snow Falling in Spring*	12				
2008	Ibtisam Barakat	*Tasting the Sky: A Palestinian Childhood* ###	12				
2007	Margarita Engle	*The Poet Slave of Cuba: A Biography of Juan Francisco Manzano* ♥♥	9				
2006	Wynton Marsalis and Paul Rogers	*Jazz Abz: An A to Z Collection of Jazz Portraits*					
2005	Brent Runyon	*The Burn Journals*	15				
2004	Miriam Stone	*At the End of Words: A Daughter's Memoir*	12				
2003	Duane Damon	*Headin' For Better Times: The Arts of the Great Depression*	12				
2002	Wilborn Hampton	*Meltdown: A Race Against Nuclear Disaster at Three Mile Island*	10				
Young Adult Fiction							
2011							
2010							
2009	Heidi Ayarbe	*Freeze Frame*	12				
2008	Laura Resau	*Red Glass* ♥♥	12				
2007	Christopher Grey	*Leonardo's Shadow: Or My Astonishing Life as Leonardo Da Vinci's Servant*	12				
2006	Paul Volponi	*Black and White*	15				

Year	Author	Title	Age	Own	Recommend	To Read	Want
2005	Brenda Woods	*Emako Blue*	12				
2004	Kathe Koja	*Buddha Boy*	12				
2003	Chris Crowe	*Mississippi Trial 1955* %%%,¶¶	12				
2002	An Na	*A Step from Heaven* ‖,♦	12				
Younger Reader							
2001	Carl R. Sams and Jean Stoick	*Stranger in the Woods*	9				
2001	Sophie Webb	*My Season with Penguins*	7				
2000	Alice McGill	*Molly Bannaky*	7				
2000	Sy Montgomery	*The Snake Scientist*	9				
1999	Frances and Ginger Park	*My Freedom Trip: A Child's Escape from North Korea*	10				
1998	Milly Lee and Yangsook Choi	*Nim and the War Effort*	7				
1997	Ingrid Slyder	*The Fabulous Flying Fandinis*	12				
1996	Marie Bradby and Chris K. Soentpiet	*More Than Anything Else*	7				
1995	Gay Matthaei Jewel Grutman and Adam Cvijanovic	*The Ledgerbook of Thomas Blue Eagle*					
1994	Deborah Hopkinson	*Sweet Clara and the Freedom Quilt*	7				
1993	Douglas Wood and Cheng-Khee Chee	*Old Turtle*	10				
1992	Virginia Grossman and Sylvia Long	*Ten Little Rabbits*	10				
1991	Megan McDonald	*Is this a House for Hermit Crabs?*	12				
1990	Anna Egan Smucker And Steve Johnson	*No Star Nights*	7				
1989	Patricia Polacco	*Rechenka's Eggs*	7				
1988	Leslie Baker	*The Third-Story Cat*	7				
1987	Marisabina Russo	*The Line Up Book*	6				

☐ Juvenile Nonfiction   ☐ Juvenile Fiction   ▨ Fiction   ■ Nonfiction

IRA Award—Intermediate and Young Adult ~~~			Age	Own	Recommend	To Read	Want
Year	**Author**	**Title**					
Older Reader							
2001	Peggy Brooke	*Jake's Orphan*	9				
2001	Catherine Thimmesh and Melissa Sweet	*Girls Think of Everything*	8				
2000	Christopher Paul Curtis	*Bud, Not Buddy* ♦♦♦,iii	12				
2000	Eleanor Ramrath Garner	*Eleanor's Story: An American Girl in Hitler's Germany*	12				
1999	John H. Ritter	*Choosing Up Sides*	12				
1998	Ronder Thomas Young	*Moving Mama to Town*	8				
1997	Margaret Peterson Haddix	*Don't You Dare Read This, Mrs. Dunphrey* ¶¶	12				
1996	Elizabeth Alder	*The King's Shadow*	12				
1995	Trudy Krisher	*Spite Fences*	12				
1994	Nelly S. Toll	*Behind the Secret Window*	9				
1993	Karen Hesse	*Letters from Rifka*	9				
1992	Ben Mikaelson	*Rescue Josh McGuire* xxx,♪	12				
1991	Marita Conlon-Mckenna	*Under the Hawthorn Tree*	9				
1990	Linda Crew	*Children of the River*	3				
1989	Virginia Euwer Wolff	*Probably Still Nick Swansen*	12				
1988	Philip Pullman	*The Ruby in the Smoke*	12				
1987	Margaret I. Rostkowski	*After the Dancing Days* %%%	12				
Informational Reader							
1999	Derek T. Dingle	*First in the Field: Baseball Hero Jackie Robinson*	9				
1998	Brandon Marie Miller	*Just What the Doctor Ordered: The History of American Medicine*	9				
1997	Elizabeth Mann	*The Brooklyn Bridge*	7				
1996	Susan E. Quinlan	*The Case of the Mummified Pigs and Other Mysteries in Nature*					
1995	Gary Bowen	*Stranded at Plimoth Plantation 1626*					
No categories before 1986							
1986	Pam Conrad	*Prairie Songs* xxx,†	12				

Year	Author	Title	Age	Own	Recommend	To Read	Want
1985	Janni Howker	*Badger on the Barge*	12				
1984	Clare Bell	*Ratha's Creature*	12				
1983	Meredith Ann Pierce	*The Darkangel* ♪	12				
1982	Michelle Magorian	*Good Night, Mr. Tom* **	12				
1981	Delores Beckman	*My Own Private Sky*	9				
1980	Ouida Sebestyen	*Words by Heart*	9				
1979	Alison Smith	*Reserved for Mark Anthony Crowder*	9				
1978	Lois Lowry	*A Summer to Die* ♪	9				
1977	Nancy Bond	*A String in the Harp*	9				
1976	Laurence Yep	*Dragonwings* $,♦♦♦	12				
1975	Tuti Degens	*Transport 7-41-R* ***	12				

Los Angeles Times Book Award for Young Adult Fiction !

The *Los Angeles Times* has awarded a set of book prizes annually since 1980. To be eligible, a book must be published in the United States during the preceding calendar year. English does not have to be the original language of the work, but its first American publication must be in English. Authors may be of any nationality, but they need to be alive at the time of their book's qualifying U.S. publication, unless the book is a significant new translation of a dead writer's work. Eight panels of three judges, who typically serve two-year terms, nominate books for consideration, name the finalists, and decide the ultimate winners, who are announced each April at the *Los Angeles Times* Festival of Books. The winners in the young adult category are listed here. For more information about the award or the festival, visit www.latimes.com/extras/bookprizes.

Year	Author	Title	Age	Own	Recommend	To Read	Want
2010							
2009							

☐ Juvenile Nonfiction   ☐ Juvenile Fiction   ■ Fiction   ■ Nonfiction

Los Angeles Times Book Award for Young Adult Fiction !			Age	Own	Recommend	To Read	Want
Year	Author	Title					
2008	Terry Pratchett	*Nation* ***	12				
2007	Philip Reeve	*A Darkling Plain*	12				
2006	Coe Booth	*Tyrell*	15				
2005	Per Nilsson	*You & You & You*	15				
2004	Melvin Burgess	*Doing It*	15				
2003	Jennifer Donnelly	*A Northern Light*	15				
2002	M. T. Anderson	*Feed* ˣ	12				
2001	Mildred D. Taylor	*The Land* ˆ	12				
2000	Jacqueline Woodson	*Miracle's Boys*	12				
1999	Robert Cormier	*Frenchtown Summer*	12				
1998	Joan Bauer	*Rules of the Road*	15				

Michael L. Printz Award ‼

The Michael L. Printz Award is given for a young adult book that exemplifies literary excellence. It is named for a school librarian in Topeka, Kansas, who was also a long-time active member of the Young Adult Library Services Association (YALSA). *Booklist*, a publication of the American Library Association, sponsors the award. YALSA produces Printz Award seals, gold for the winning book and silver for the honor books, which can be placed on library or bookstore copies. See www.ala.org/yalsa/printz for more information.

Year	Author	Title	Age	Own	Recommend	To Read	Want
2011							
2010							
2009	Melina Marchetta	*Jellicoe Road*	12				
2008	Geraldine McCaughrean	*The White Darkness*	12				
2007	Gene Luen Yang and Lark Pien	*American Born Chinese* ###	12				
2006	John Green	*Looking for Alaska* #,‡‡‡,•	15				

Year	Author	Title	Age	Own	Recommend	To Read	Want
2005	Meg Rosoff	*How I Live Now*	12				
2004	Angela Johnson	*The First Part Last* #,ΩΩ,•	12				
2003	Aidan Chambers	*Postcards from No Man's Land* **	15				
2002	An Na	*A Step from Heaven* ~~~,♦	12				
2001	David Almond	*Kit's Wilderness*	12				
2000	Walter Dean Myers	*Monster* ‡‡‡	12				

Schneider Family Book Award !!!

The Schneider Family Book Award of the American Library Association honors authors or illustrators of books that embody an artistic expression of the disability experience for children and adolescents. Three annual awards, each consisting of $5,000 and a framed plaque, are given annually in each of the following categories: birth through grade school (ages 0–8), middle school (ages 9–13), and teens (ages 14–18). The book must portray some aspect of living with a disability, whether physical, mental, or emotional. The nominated novel, biography, and/or picture book must be published during the preceding two years. The middle school and teen category winners are listed here. For more information about the Schneider Award or the ALA, visit www.ala.org.

Year	Author	Title	Age	Own	Recommend	To Read	Want
Middle School							
2011							
2010							
2009	Leslie Conner	*Waiting for Normal*	9				
2008	Vaughn Zimmer	*Reaching for Sun*	9				
2007	Cynthia Lord	*Rules* ‡‡‡	9				
2006	Kimberly Newton Fusco	*Tending to Grace*	12				
2005	Pam Muñoz Ryan	*Becoming Naomi León*	9				

⬜ Juvenile Nonfiction ⬜ Juvenile Fiction ⬛ Fiction ⬛ Nonfiction

Schneider Family Book Award !!!

Year	Author	Title	Age	Own	Recommend	To Read	Want
2004	Wendy Mass	*A Mango-Shaped Space*	12				
Teens							
2011							
2010							
2009	Jonathan Friesen	*Jerk, California*	12				
2008	Ginny Rorb	*Hurt Go Happy*	9				
2007	Louis Sachar	*Small Steps*	15				
2006	Adam Rapp	*Under the Wolf, Under the Dog*	15				
2005	Samantha Abeel	*My Thirteenth Winter: A Memoir*	12				
2004	Andrew Clements	*Things Not Seen* ♪,£££	12				

YALSA Teen Top Ten Award

The Young Adult Library Services Association's Teen Top Ten Award is a teen choice list. Teens nominate and vote on their favorite books of the previous year. More information can be found and votes can be placed at: www.ala .org/teenstopten.

Year	Author	Title	Age	Own	Recommend	To Read	Want
2011							
2011							
2011							
2011							
2011							
2011							
2011							
2011							
2011							
2011							

Year	Author	Title	Age	Own	Recommend	To Read	Want
2010							
2010							
2010							
2010							
2010							
2010							
2010							
2010							
2010							
2010							
2009	John Green	Paper Towns ▼	15				
2009	Stephenie Meyer	Breaking Dawn	15				
2009	Suzanne Collins	The Hunger Games ###,x	15				
2009	Cassandra Clare	City of Ashes	15				
2009	Ellen Hopkins	Identical	9				
2009	Neil Gaiman	The Graveyard Book ᵛᵛ	9				
2009	Lisa McMann	Wake	12				
2009	P. C. and Kristin Cast	Untamed	12				
2009	E. Lockhart	The Disreputable History of Frankie Landau-Banks ###	15				
2009	Kristin Cashore	Graceling ᵛᵛᵛ	15				
2008	Laurie Halse Anderson	Twisted ‡	15				
2008	Stephenie Meyer	Eclipse ♫,±,±±	12				
2008	J. K. Rowling	Harry Potter and the Deathly Hallows ˣˣ	9				
2008	Richelle Mead	Vampire Academy	12				
2008	James Patterson	Maximum Ride: Saving the World and Other Extreme Sports	15				
2008	Cassandra Clare	City of Bones	15				

☐ Juvenile Nonfiction   ▨ Juvenile Fiction   ▧ Fiction   ■ Nonfiction

YALSA Teen Top Ten Award #			Age	Own	Recommend	To Read	Want
Year	Author	Title					
2008	Jeff Kinney	*Diary of a Wimpy Kid*	9				
2008	Jenny Downham	*Before I Die*	12				
2008	Libba Bray	*The Sweet Far Thing*	12				
2008	Scott Westerfeld	*Extras*	15				
2007	Shannon Hale	*River Secrets*	12				
2007	James Patterson	*Maximum Ride: School's Out Forever*	12				
2007	Kevin Brooks	*Road of the Dead*					
2007	Sarah Dessen	*Just Listen* ‡‡,¶	15				
2007	Tony Abbott	*Firegirl*	9				
2007	Vivian Vande Velde	*All Hallows Eve (13 Stories)*	10				
2007	Susan Beth Pfeffer	*Life As We Knew It* Σ,ii,•••	12				
2007	Simone Elkeles	*How to Ruin a Summer Vacation*	15				
2007	Michele Jaffe	*Bad Kitty* 33	12				
2007	Stephenie Meyer	*New Moon* ##,oo,i	15				
2006	Libba Bray	*Rebel Angels*	12				
2006	Chris Wooding	*Poison*	12				
2006	Scott Westerfeld	*Peeps*	15				
2006	Maureen Johnson	*13 Little Blue Envelopes*	15				
2006	Melissa Kantor	*If I Have a Wicked Stepmother Where's My Prince?*	10				
2006	J. K. Rowling	*Harry Potter and the Half Blood Prince* ♪♪,∩	9				
2006	Gabrielle Zevin	*Elsewhere*	12				
2006	Christopher Paolini	*Eldest* ♪♪,∩∩,±±	12				
2006	J. V. Hart	*Captain Hook: The Adventures of a Notorious Youth*	9				
2006	Stephenie Meyer	*Twilight* •••,♪♪♪,Ω,ΩΩ,ΩΩΩ,‡,‡‡‡,¶,¶¶,¶¶¶,ii,•••,¿¿¿,◊,∩∩,3,¡,Σ	15				
2005	John Green	*Looking for Alaska* ‖,‡‡‡,•	15				

Year	Author	Title	Age	Own	Recommend	To Read	Want
2005	James Patterson	Maximum Ride: The Angel Experiment	12				
2005	Jordan Sonnenblick	Drums, Girls and Dangerous Pie £££,¿¿¿	12				
2005	Ann Brashares	Girls in Pants: The Third Summer of the Sisterhood	12				
2005	Meg Cabot	Teen Idol	12				
2005	Benjamin Zephaniah	The Gangsta Rap	14				
2005	Jodi Picoult	My Sister's Keeper ˜,˜˜,ΩΩΩ,••,Σ	12				
2005	Elise Aidinoff	The Garden	7				
2005	Marc Acito	How I Paid for College: A Novel of Sex, Theft, Friendship & Musical Theater	14				
2005	Sarah Dessen	The Truth About Forever ºº	15				
2004	Carolyn Mackler	The Earth, My Butt and Other Big Round Things	10				
2004	Cornelia Funke	Inkheart	9				
2004	J. K. Rowling	Harry Potter and the Order of the Phoenix ♪♪,∩	9				
2004	Celia Rees	Pirates! The True and Remarkable Adventures of Minerva Sharpe and Nancy Kington Female Pirates £	12				
2004	Meg Cabot	Princess in Pink	9				
2004	L. A. Meyer	Curse of the Blue Tattoo	12				
2004	Shannon Hale	The Goose Girl	12				
2004	Libba Bray	A Great and Terrible Beauty ‡‡	12				
2004	Tamora Pierce	Trickster's Choice	12				
2004	Christopher Paolini	Eragon ##,♦♦♦,♪♪,Ω,‡,¶,33,•••,∩,¿¿¿,º,¿,∩∩,ºº,3,••	12				
2003	Carol Plum-Ucci	What Happened to Lani Garver?	12				
2003	Herbie Brennan	Faerie Wars	12				
2003	Garth Nix	Abhorsen	12				

☐ Juvenile Nonfiction ☐ Juvenile Fiction ■ Fiction ■ Nonfiction

YALSA Teen Top Ten Award

Year	Author	Title	Age	Own	Recommend	To Read	Want
2003	Jean Ferris	*Once Upon a Marigold*	9				
2003	Tim Bowler	*Storm Catchers*	12				
2003	Francine Prose	*After* ♪	12				
2003	Ann Brashares	*The Second Summer of the Sisterhood*	12				
2003	Cornelia Funke	*The Thief Lord* ♦♦♦,ii	12				
2003	Holly Black	*Tithe: A Modern Faerie Tale*	12				
2003	Angela Johnson	*The First Part Last* ‖,ΩΩ,•	12				

Young Reader's Choice Award

The Pacific Northwest Library Association's Young Reader's Choice Award is the oldest children's choice award in North America. The awards were established in 1940 by a Seattle bookseller, the late Harry Hartman, who believed every student should have an opportunity to select a book for pleasure. The following policy, congruent with Hartman's values, was adopted by the Board of the Pacific Northwest Library Association in 2006: nominations are taken only from children, teachers, parents, and librarians in the Pacific Northwest—Alaska, Alberta, British Columbia, Idaho, Montana, Oregon, and Washington. The winners in the senior and intermediate categories are listed here. See www .pnla.org/yrca/ for more information.

Year	Author	Title	Age	Own	Recommend	To Read	Want
Senior							
2011							
2010							
2009	Stephenie Meyer	*New Moon* #,oo,i	15				
2008	Jodi Lynn Anderson	*Peaches*	12				
2007	Terry Pratchett	*A Hat Full of Sky*	15				
2006	K. L. Going	*Fat Kid Rules the World*	12				

Year	Author	Title	Age	Own	Recommend	To Read	Want
2005	Nancy Farmer	The House of the Scorpion •,♦♦♦,¶¶¶,o,¿,oo,3	12				
2004	Ann Brashares	Sisterhood of the Traveling Pants °,¿	15				
2003	Joan Bauer	Hope was Here £	12				
2002	William Sleator	Rewind	9				
2001	William Sleator	The Boxes	9				
2000	Mel Glenn	The Taking of Room 114	12				
Intermediate							
2011							
2010							
2009	John Boyne	Boy in the Striped Pajamas	12				
2008	Rick Riordan	The Lightning Thief ♦♦♦,‡‡,£££,¶¶,33,¿¿¿,¿, 3,••	9				
2007	Eoin Colfer	The Supernaturalist •••	12				
2006	Christopher Paolini	Eragon #,♦♦♦,♫♫,Ω,‡,¶,33,•••,∩,¿¿¿,o,¿,∩∩ ,oo,3,••	12				
2005	Gordon Korman	Son of the Mob ~~,♦♦♦,‡‡‡	12				
2004	Eoin Colfer	Artemis Fowl ii	12				
2003	Gordon Korman	No More Dead Dogs ••	12				
2002	Carolyn Meyer	Mary, Bloody Mary	12				
2001	Louis Sachar	Holes •,••••,♦♦♦,♫♫,iii,•••,∩,¿¿¿,¿,∩∩	9				
2000	Dick King-Smith	A Mouse Called Wolf	8				

▢ Juvenile Nonfiction ▢ Juvenile Fiction ▪ Fiction ▪ Nonfiction

Cybils—Children's and Young Adult Blogger's Literary Award

In the words of Anne Levy, contest administrator of the Children's and Young Adult Blogger's Literary Awards, the purpose the award is to "Reward the children's and young adult authors…whose books combine the highest literary merit and 'kid appeal' and to foster a sense of community among bloggers who write about children's and YA literature, highlight our best reviewers…(blogs) and provide a forum for the similarly obsessed." The winners of the Cybils Award, which started in 2006, are announced annually on Valentine's Day. Listed here are middle grade (MG) and young adult (YA) winners in all categories. For more information and to view future winners, go to www.dadtalk.typepad.com/cybils.

Year	Author	Title	Age	Own	Recommend	To Read	Want
Fiction							
2010							
2009							
2008-MG	Siobhan Dowd	The London Eye Mystery	9				
2008-YA	E. Lockhart	The Disreputable History of Frankie Landau-Banks #	15				
2007-MG	Linda Urban	A Crooked Kind of Perfect	9				
2007-YA	Barry Lyga	Boy Toy	12				
2006-MG	Laura Amy Schlitz	A Drowned Maiden's Hair: A Melodrama	12				
2006-YA	Rachel Cohn and David Levithan	Nick and Norah's Infinite Playlist	15				
Nonfiction							
2010							
2009							
2008-MG&YA	Cylin Busby and John Busby	The Year We Disappeared: A Father-Daughter Memoir	12				
2007-MG&YA	Ibtisam Barakat	Tasting the Sky: A Palestinian Childhood ~~~	12				
2006-MG&YA	Russell Freedman	Freedom Walkers	9				

Year	Author	Title	Age	Own	Recommend	To Read	Want
Fantasy and Science Fiction							
2010							
2009							
2008-MG	Neil Gaiman	*The Graveyard Book* #	9				
2008-YA	Suzanne Collins	*The Hunger Games* x,#	15				
2007-MG	Adam Rex	*The True Meaning of Smekday*	9				
2007-YA	Shannon Hale	*Book of a Thousand Days (Maid Maleen)*	12				
2006-YA	Jonathan Stroud	*Ptolemy's Gate*	9				
Graphic Novels							
2010							
2009							
2008-MG&YA	Shannon Hale and Dean Hale	*Rapunzel's Revenge*	9				
2008-YA	Mariko Tamaki	*Emiko Superstar*	12				
2007-MG	Eoin Colfer and Andrew Donkin	*Artemis Fowl: The Graphic Novel*	9				
2007-YA	Joann Sfar	*The Professor's Daughter*	15				
2006-MG&YA	Gene Luen Yang and Lark Pien	*American Born Chinese* !!	12				

☐ Juvenile Nonfiction   ☐ Juvenile Fiction   ■ Fiction   ■ Nonfiction

Phoenix Award $

The Children's Literature Association, "an organization of teachers, scholars, librarians, editors, writers, illustrators, and parents interested in encouraging the serious study of children's literature," has awarded the Phoenix Award since its inception in 1985. The award is given to a book published twenty years previously that did not receive a major award at the time of its publication. "The Phoenix Award is named after the fabled bird who rose from its ashes with renewed life and beauty. Phoenix books also rise from the ashes of neglect and obscurity and once again touch the imaginations and enrich the lives of those who read them." For more information see www.childlitassn.org/phoenix_award.html.

Year	Author	Title	Age	Own	Recommend	To Read	Want
2012							
2011							
2010	Rosemary Sutcliff	The Shining Company	9				
2009	Francesca Lia Block	Weetzie Bat	15				
2008	Peter Dickinson	Eva	12				
2007	Margaret Mahy	Memory	15				
2006	Diana Wynne Jones	Howl's Moving Castle	12				
2005	Margaret Mahy	The Catalogue of the Universe	12				
2004	Berlie Doherty	White Peak Farm	12				
2003	Ivan Southall	Long Night Watch	9				
2002	Zibby Oneal	A Formal Feeling	12				
2001	Peter Dickinson	The Seventh Raven	15				
2000	Monica Hughes	Keeper of the Isis Light	9				
1999	E. L. Konigsburg	Throwing Shadows	9				
1998	Jill Paton Walsh	A Chance Child	12				
1997	Robert Cormier	I Am the Cheese	12				
1996	Alan Garner	The Stone Book					
1995	Laurence Yep	Dragonwings ~~~,♦♦♦	12				
1994	Katherine Paterson	Of Nightingales That Weep	12				
1993	Nina Bawden	Carrie's War					

Year	Author	Title	Age	Own	Recommend	To Read	Want
1992	Mollie Hunter	A Sound of Chariots	9				
1991	Jane Gardam	A Long Way from Verona					
1990	Sylvia Louise Engdahl	Enchantress from the Stars	12				
1989	Helen Cresswell	The Night Watchmen					
1988	Erik Christian Haugaard	The Rider and His Horse					
1987	Leon Garfield	Smith	9				
1986	Robert Burch	Queenie Peavy	9				
1985	Rosemary Sutcliff	The Mark of the Horse Lord	12				

White Pine Award $$

The White Pine Award™ is a provincial reading program for high school students sponsored by the Ontario Library Association. Students read ten nominated Canadian young adult books and vote for their favorites. Based on student voting across the province, the most popular book is selected and the author honored. The goals of the White Pine Award™ program are to promote reading for enjoyment among high school students, to make students aware of quality Canadian young adult books, and to provide opportunities for students to discuss the nominated titles in an authentic manner. The official site of the White Pine Award™ is www.accessola.com/ola/bins/content_page.asp?cid=92-263.

Year	Author	Title	Age	Own	Recommend	To Read	Want
2011							
2010							
2009	Cory Doctorow	Little Brother ˣ	12				
2008	Martine Leavitt	Keturah and Lord Death	12				
2007	Eric Walters	Shattered					
2006	Charles De Lint	The Blue Girl					
2005	Marnelle Tokio	More Than You Can Chew	12				

☐ Juvenile Nonfiction ☐ Juvenile Fiction ■ Fiction ■ Nonfiction

White Pine Award $$

Year	Author	Title	Age	Own	Recommend	To Read	Want
2004	Don Aker	*The First Stone*					
2003	Gillian Chan	*A Foreign Field*	12				
2002	Shelley Hrdlitschka	*Dancing Naked*	12				

Canadian Library Association Award $$$

The Canadian Library Association (CLA) Young Adult Canadian Book Award was established in 1980 by the Young Adult Caucus of the Saskatchewan Library Association and is administered by the Young Adult Services Group (YASG). The prize is awarded to the author of an outstanding English language book for young adults (ages 13–18) published in the preceding calendar year. The winning title is a work of fiction (novel or collection of short stories) written by a Canadian citizen or landed immigrant published in Canada. The winner receives a leather bound book with the award seal embossed on the cover in gold. Visit www.bookcentre.ca for more information.

Year	Author	Title	Age	Own	Recommend	To Read	Want
2011							
2010							
2009	Allan Stratton	*Chanda's Wars*	12				
2008	Martha Brooks	*Mistik Lake*	12				
2007	William Bell	*The Blue Helmet*					
2006	Shyam Selvadurai	*Swimming in the Monsoon Sea*	15				
2005	Miriam Toews	*A Complicated Kindness*					
2004	Polly Horvath	*The Canning Season* *	15				
2003	Martha Brooks	*True Confessions of a Heartless Girl*	15				
2002	William Bell	*Stones*	12				
2001	Beth Goobie	*Before Wings*	12				
2000	Katherine Holubitsky	*Alone at Ninety Foot*	9				
1999	Gayle Friesen	*Janey's Girl*	12				

Year	Author	Title	Age	Own	Recommend	To Read	Want
1998	Martha Brooks	*Bone Dance*	12				
1997	R. P. MacIntyre, ed.	*Takes: Stories for Young Adults*					
1996	Tim Wynne-Jones	*The Maestro*	9				
1995	Julie Johnston	*Adam and Eve and Pinch-Me*	7				
1994	Sean Stewart	*Nobody's Son*	12				
1993	Karleen Bradford	*There Will be Wolves*	12				
1992	Susan Lynn Reynolds	*Strandia*	12				
1991	Budge Wilson	*The Leaving*	12				
1990	Diana J. Wieler	*Bad Boy*	12				
1989	Helen Fogwell Porter	*January, February, June or July*					
1988	Margaret Buffie	*Who is Frances Rain?*	12				
1987	Janet Lunn	*Shadow in Hawthorn Bay*	15				
1986	Marianne Brandis	*The Quarter-Pie Window*	15				
1985	Mary Ellen Lang-Collura	*Winners*	12				
1984	O. R. Melling	*The Druid's Tune*	12				
1983	Monica Hughes	*Hunter in the Dark*	15				
1982	Jamie Brown	*Superbike!*					
1981	Kevin Major	*Far from Shore*	12				

☐ Juvenile Nonfiction ☐ Juvenile Fiction ■ Fiction ■ Nonfiction

Norma Fleck Award for Nonfiction %

"The Norma Fleck Award for Canadian Children's Nonfiction was established by the Fleck Family Foundation and the Canadian Children's Book Centre on May 17, 1999, to recognize and raise the profile of these exceptional nonfiction books. The $10,000 Norma Fleck Award is the largest of its kind in Canadian children's books and is considered to be one of Canada's most prestigious literary prizes." For more information, see the Canadian Children's Book Centre at www.bookcentre.ca/awards/norma_fleck_award_canadian_childrens_nonfiction.

Year	Author	Title	Age	Own	Recommend	To Read	Want
2010							
2009							
2008	Hugh Brewster	*At Vimy Ridge: Canada's Greatest World War I Victory*					
2007	Jan Thornhill	*I Found a Dead Bird: The Kids' Guide to the Cycle of Life & Death*					
2006	Bill Slavin with Jim Slavin	*Transformed: How Everyday Things are Made*					
2005	Shari Graydon	*In Your Face: The Culture of Beauty and You*					
2004	Val Ross	*The Road to There: Mapmakers and their Stories*					
2003	Larry Loyie with Constance Brissenden	*As Long as the Rivers Flow*	9				
2002	Jack Batten	*The Man Who Ran Faster Than Everyone: The Story of Tom Longboat*					
2001	Gena K. Gorrell	*Heart and Soul: The Story of Florence Nightingale*					
2000	Simon Tookoome with Sheldon Oberman	*The Shaman's Nephew: A Life Far North*					
1999	Andy Turnbull and Debora Pearson	*By Truck to the North: My Arctic Adventure*					

Willow Award—Snow Willow %%

The Saskatchewan Young Readers' Choice Award (the Willow Award) promotes reading by granting an award to the Canadian books voted by students to be the best of those nominated in three categories: Shining Willow (K–3), Diamond Willow (4–6) and Snow Willow (7–9). The Snow Willow award recipients are listed here. View all the winners at www.willowawards.ca/home.

Year	Author	Title	Age	Own	Recommend	To Read	Want
2010							
2009							
2008	Gordon Korman	*Schooled*	8				
2007	Arthur Slade	*Megiddo's Shadow*	12				
2006	Sheree Fitch	*The Gravesavers*					
2005	Allan Stratton	*Chanda's Secrets*	15				
2004	Barbara Haworth-Attard	*Theories of Relativity*	15				
2003	Cathy Beveridge	*Offside*	12				
2002	Eric Walters	*Rebound*	12				

Jefferson Cup %%%

Originated in 1983, the Jefferson Cup honors a distinguished biography, historical fiction, or U.S. history book for young people. The goal of the award is "to promote reading about America's past; to encourage the quality writing of United States history, biography and historical fiction for young people and to recognize authors in these disciplines." Named after Thomas Jefferson, the award is administered by the Youth Services Forum of the Virgina Library Association. For more information and upcoming winners, visit www.vla.org/demo/Youth-Serv/cyart/jefferson_cup/Jeffersoncup_index.html.

Year	Author	Title	Age	Own	Recommend	To Read	Want
2010							
2009							

☐ Juvenile Nonfiction ☐ Juvenile Fiction ■ Fiction ■ Nonfiction

Year	Author	Title	Age	Own	Recommend	To Read	Want
2008	Carole Boston Weatherford	Birmingham, 1963	9				
2007	Elisa Carbone	Blood on the River: James Town 1607	12				
2006	Marlene Carvell	Sweetgrass Basket	9				
2005	Patricia Reilly Giff	A House of Tailors	9				
2004	Kristine L. Franklin	Grape Thief	9				
2003	Chris Crowe	Mississippi Trial 1955 ~~~,¶¶	12				
2002	Elisa Carbone	Storm Warriors	9				
2001	Jim Murphy	Blizzard: The Storm That Changed America	9				
2000	Katherine Paterson	Preacher's Boy	9				
1999	Gary Paulsen	Soldier's Heart: A Novel of the Civil War	15				
1998	Leon Walter Tillage	Leon's Story ***	8				
1997	Jean Thesman	The Ornament Tree	10				
1996	Jim Murphy	The Great Fire	9				
1995	Patricia Polacco	Pink and Say	7				
1994	Jim Murphy	Across America on an Emigrant Train	9				
1993	Jerry Stanley	Children of the Dust Bowl: The True Story of the School at Weedpatch ˣˣˣ	9				
1992	Russell Freedman	The Wright Brothers: How They Invented the Airplane	9				
1991	Russell Freedman	Franklin Delano Roosevelt	12				
1990	Carolyn Reeder	Shades of Gray ^	8				
1989	Virginia Hamilton	Anthony Burns: The Defeat and Triumph of a Fugitive Slave ***	9				
1988	Russell Freedman	Lincoln: A Photobiography	12				
1987	Margaret I. Rostkowski	After the Dancing Days ~~~	12				
1986	Patricia MacLachlan	Sarah Plain and Tall ^	12				

Jefferson Cup %%%

Year	Author	Title	Age	Own	Recommend	To Read	Want
1985	Bette Bao Lord	*In the Year of the Boar and Jackie Robinson*	9				
1984	Paula Underwood Spencer	*Who Speaks for Wolf?*					
1983	Milton Meltzer	*Jewish Americans: A History in Their Words*					

Scott O'Dell Historical Fiction Award ^

In 1982, Scott O'Dell established the Scott O'Dell Award for Historical Fiction. This annual award of $5,000 goes to a meritorious book published in the previous year for children or young adults. O'Dell, the acclaimed author of *Island of the Blue Dolphins* and many other books, sought to encourage other writers—particularly new authors—to focus on historical fiction. In this way, he hoped to increase young readers' interest in the history that has shaped their country and their world. For more information, see www.scottodell.com/odellaward.html.

Year	Author	Title	Age	Own	Recommend	To Read	Want
2011							
2010							
2009	Laurie Halse Anderson	*Chains*	9				
2008	Christopher Paul Curtis	*Elijah of Buxton* ^	9				
2007	Ellen Klages	*The Green Glass Sea*	9				
2006	Louise Erdrich	*The Game of Silence*	9				
2005	A. Lafaye	*Worth*	9				
2004	Richard Peck	*A River Between Us*	9				
2003	Shelley Pearsall	*Trouble Don't Last*	9				
2002	Mildred D. Taylor	*The Land* !	12				
2001	Janet Taylor Lisle	*The Art of Keeping Cool*	12				

☐ Juvenile Nonfiction ☐ Juvenile Fiction ■ Fiction ■ Nonfiction

Scott O'Dell Historical Fiction Award ^			Age	Own	Recommend	To Read	Want
Year	Author	Title					
2000	Miriam Bat-Ami	*Two Suns in the Sky*	12				
1999	Harriette Robinet	*Forty Acres and Maybe a Mule*	8				
1998	Karen Hesse	*Out of the Dust*	12				
1997	Katherine Paterson	*Jip: His Story*	8				
1996	Theodore Taylor	*The Bomb*	12				
1995	Graham Salisbury	*Under the Blood-Red Sun* ⁱ	9				
1994	Paul Fleischman	*Bull Run*	9				
1993	Michael Dorris	*Morning Girl*	9				
1992	Mary Downing Hahn	*Stepping on the Cracks* ᵒᵒ	9				
1991	Pieter Van Raven	*A Time of Trouble*	12				
1990	Carolyn Reeder	*Shades of Gray* %%%	8				
1989	Lyll Becerra De Jenkins	*The Honorable Prison*	12				
1988	Patricia Beatty	*Charley Skedaddle*	12				
1987	Scott O'Dell	*Streams to the River River to the Sea*	12				
1986	Patricia MacLachlan	*Sarah Plain and Tall* %%%	12				
1985	Avi	*The Fighting Ground*	12				
1984	Elizabeth George Speare	*The Sign of the Beaver*	12				

Geoffrey Bilson Award for Historical Fiction &

The Geoffrey Bilson Award for Historical Fiction for Young People, a $1,000 prize, is awarded annually for excellence in an outstanding work of historical fiction for young readers, by a Canadian author, published in the previous calendar year. The Canadian Children's Book Centre selects a jury that decides the winner. All books written by Canadian citizens or landed immigrants are eligible for consideration. The award's namesake, who died in 1987, taught history at the University of Saskatchewan and published historical novels for children. For more information, see www.bookcentre.ca/awards/geoffrey_bilson_award_historical_fiction_young_people.

Year	Author	Title	Age	Own	Recommend	To Read	Want
2011							
2010							
2009	Christopher Paul Curtis	*Elijah of Buxton* ^	9				
2007	Eva Wiseman	*Kanada*	9				
2006	Pamela Paige Porter	*The Crazy Man*	9				
2005	Michel Noel (Shelley Tanaka Trans.)	*Good for Nothing*	10				
2004	Brian Doyle	*Boy O'Boy*	12				
2003	Joan Clark	*The Word for Home*					
2002	Virginia Frances Schwartz	*If I Just Had Two Wings*	12				
2001	Sharon E. McKay	*Charlie Wilcox's Great War*	12				
2000	No Award Given						
1999	Iain Lawrence	*The Wreckers*	12				
1998	Irene N. Watts	*Good-Bye Marianne*	8				
1997	Janet Elizabeth Mc-Naughton	*To Dance at the Palais Royale*	12				
1996	Marianne Brandis	*Rebellion*	15				
1995	Joan Clark	*The Dream Carvers*					
1994	Kit Pearson	*The Lights Go on Again*	9				
1993	Celia Barker Lottridge	*Ticket to Curlew*	9				

☐ Juvenile Nonfiction   ☐ Juvenile Fiction   ■ Fiction   ■ Nonfiction

Geoffrey Bilson Award for Historical Fiction &			Age	Own	Recommend	To Read	Want
Year	Author	Title					
1991	Marianne Brandis	The Sign of the Scales	9				
1990	Kit Pearson	The Sky is Falling	12				
1989	Dorothy Perkyns	Rachel's Revolution					
1989	Martyn Godfrey	Mystery in the Frozen Lands	15				
1988	Carol Matas	Lisa's War	8				

Action and Adventure Novels from Marathon County Library

Marathon County Public Library (WI) created this list entitled "Action and Adventure." For more lists, homework help, teen book and game reviews, visit the Teenzone at www.mcpl.us/services/teenzone.

Author	Title	Year	Age	Own	Recommend	To Read	Want
Rick Riordan	The Lightning Thief ##,♦♦♦,‡‡,£££,¶¶,33,¿¿¿,¿,3,••	2005	9				
Graham McNamee	Acceleration &&&,▼,ΩΩ	2003	12				
Tom Clancy	Shadow of Honor	2000					
A. J. Butcher	The Serpent Scenario	2004	12				
Richard Yancey	The Extraordinary Adventures of Alfred Kropp	2005	12				
Riku Sanjo	Beet the Vandel Buster: Vol. 10	2006	9				
Shuichi Shigeno	Initial D Vol. 33	2009	12				
Daisuke Higuchi	Whistle! Vol. 20	2008	9				
Takeshi Konomi	The Prince of Tennis Vol. 31	2009	9				
Robb White	Deathwatch	1999	8				
Catherine Jinks	Evil Genius	2007	12				
Eoin Colfer	The Time Paradox	2008	9				
Michael Simmons	Finding Lubchenko	2006	12				
John Marsden	Tomorrow, When the War Began	1995	12				

Author	Title	Year	Age	Own	Recommend	To Read	Want
Robert Muchamore	*Divine Madness*	2006	15				
James Patterson	*The Final Warning*	2008	12				
Rick Riordan	*The Last Olympian*	2009	9				
Darren Shan	*Sons of Destiny*	2006	12				
Michael P. Spradlin	*To Hawaii, with Love: A Spy Goddess Novel*	2006	12				
Yozaburo Kanari	*Kindaichi Case Files Vol. 15: The Graveyard Isle*	2007	12				

Sports

The sports list assembled by the Plymouth District Library (MI) will keep sports enthusiasts busy when they aren't on the court, track, or field themselves. For more information, visit www.plymouthlibrary.org/yasportsbib.htm.

Author	Title	Year	Age	Own	Recommend	To Read	Want
General Sports and Athletics							
Cherie Bennett	*Girls in Love*	2002	12				
Chris Crutcher	*Athletic Shorts: Six Short Stories*	1991	12				
Alan Durant	*Sports Stories*	2003	9				
Donald R. Gallo ed.	*Ultimate Sports: Short Stories by Outstanding Writers for Young Adults*	1997	9				
Chris Lynch	*Iceman*	1995	13				
Chris Lynch	*Slot Machine* [ii]	1996	12				
Joyce Carol Oates	*Sexy*	2006	15				
Wendy Orr	*Peeling the Onion*	1999	12				
Patricia Rushford	*Dying to Win*	2006					
Tim Winton	*Lockie Leonard, Scumbuster*	1998					

☐ Juvenile Nonfiction   ☐ Juvenile Fiction   ■ Fiction   ■ Nonfiction

Sports				Age	Own	Recommend	To Read	Want
Author	Title	Year						
Baseball								
James Bennett	*Plunking Reggie Jackson*	2001	12					
Bruce Brooks	*Throwing Smoke*	2000	9					
Alden R. Carter	*Bull Catcher* ~~	2000	12					
Michael Chabon	*Summerland* ᵛᵛᵛ	2004	9					
Chris Crutcher	*The Crazy Horse Electric Game*	2003	12					
Carl Deuker	*Heart of a Champion* ¶¶.ἰἰἰ.3	2007	12					
Carl Deuker	*Painting the Black*	1999	6					
Scott Johnson	*Safe at Second*	2001	12					
Chris Lynch	*Gold Dust*	2008						
John H. Ritter	*The Boy who Saved Baseball*	2005	9					
John H. Ritter	*Over the Wall*	2003	12					
John H. Ritter	*Under the Baseball Moon*	2008	12					
Kristi Roberts	*My Thirteenth Season*	1996	9					
Jennifer E. Smith	*The Comeback Season*	2008	12					
Will Weaver	*Farm Team*	1999	12					
Will Weaver	*Hard Ball*	1999	12					
Basketball								
Larry Colton	*Counting Coup: A True Story of Basketball and Honor on the Little Big Horn*	2001	9					
Chris Crutcher	*Chinese Handcuffs*	2004	7					
Carl Deuker	*Night Hoops* ¶¶	2000	12					
Carl Deuker	*On the Devil's Court* ᵒᵒ	2008	15					
John Feinstein	*Last Shot: A Final Four Mystery* ▼	2005	9					
David Klass	*Danger Zone* Σ.¶¶.ἰ	1996	12					
Walter Dean Myers	*Hoops: A Novel*	1999	12					
Walter Dean Myers	*Slam!* ᵒᵒ	1999	12					
Matt de la Pena	*Ball Don't Lie*	2007	15					
Alan Lawrence Sitomer	*The Hoopster*	2006	15					

Author	Title	Year	Age	Own	Recommend	To Read	Want
Charles R. Smith Jr.	*Tall Tales*	2000	9				
Joyce Sweeney	*Players*	2005	12				
Rich Wallace	*Playing Without the Ball*	2003	15				
Football							
Margaret Bechard	*If It Doesn't Kill You*	1999	11				
H. G. Bissinger	*Friday Night Lights: A Town, a Team and a Dream*	2000					
Alden R. Carter	*Love, Football and Other Contact Sports*	1988					
Thomas Cochran	*Roughnecks*	1999	15				
Chris Crutcher	*Running Loose*	1983	12				
Thomas Dygard	*Backfield Package*	1992	9				
Thomas Dygard	*Forward Pass*	1990	9				
Thomas Dygard	*Running Wild*	1996	12				
A. M. Jenkins	*Damage*	2003	12				
Chris Lynch	*The Inexcusable*	2007	15				
Catherine Gilbert Murdock	*Dairy Queen* ⅈⅈⅈ	2007	12				
Jerry Spinelli	*Crash* ‡‡,£££,ⅈⅈⅈ,oo,••	1996	9				
Tim Tharp	*Knights of the Hill Country* ‡‡‡	2006	12				
Hockey							
Shelley Hrdlitschka	*Disconnected*	1998	12				
Pat Hughes	*Open Ice*	2007	12				
Diana J. Wieler	*Bad Boy* $$$	1997	12				
Rafting							
Will Hobbs	*River Thunder*	1999	12				
P. J. Petersen	*White Water*	1999	9				
S. L. Rottman	*Rough Waters*	1998	12				

☐ Juvenile Nonfiction   ☐ Juvenile Fiction   ■ Fiction   ■ Nonfiction

Sports			Age	Own	Recommend	To Read	Want
Author	Title	Year					
Soccer							
Edward Bloor	*Tangerine* £££,¶¶¶,ii,oo	1997	9				
Swimming							
Evelyn Coleman	*Born in Sin*	2003					
Chris Crutcher	*Staying Fat for Sarah Byrnes* ♪	2003	12				
Chris Crutcher	*Stotan!*	2003	12				
Chris Crutcher	*Whale Talk*	2009	12				
S. L. Rottman	*Head Above Water*	1999	15				
Track and Field							
Chris Crutcher	*Ironman* ♪	1995	12				
Anna Levine	*Running on Eggs*	1999	9				
Cynthia Voigt	*The Runner*	2005	12				
Wrestling/Boxing							
Michael Cadnum	*Redhanded*	2000	12				
Kathleen Karr	*The Boxer*	2004	12				
Robert Lipsyte	*The Brave*	1993	15				
Robert Lipsyte	*The Chief*	1995	12				
Robert Lipsyte	*The Contender*	1987	12				
Chris Lynch	*Shadow Boxer*	1997	12				
Alfred C. Martino	*Pinned*	2006	12				
Rich Wallace	*Wrestling Sturbridge*	1997	15				
Markus Zusak	*Fighting Ruben Wolfe*	2002	13				

Adventure and Survival

The APL ZONE, by Teens, 4Teens, portion of the Ames Public Library (IA) has lists related to fairy tales, science fiction, GLBT, fantasy, and horror. The Adventure and Survival list contains daring tales from all over the world. Visit www.amespubliclibrary.org/teens/youthHome.asp for homework help, teen advisory groups, and reviews of books, movies, and music.

Author	Title	Year	Age	Own	Recommend	To Read	Want
Caroline B. Cooney	*Flash Fire*	1995	12				
Nancy Farmer	*A Girl Named Disaster*	1998	12				
Will Hobbs	*Jason's Gold*	1999	12				
Anthony Horowitz	*Stormbreaker* ♪,‡‡,∩,oo	2006	9				
John Marsden	*Tomorrow, When the War Began*	1995	12				
Victoria McKernan	*Shackleton's Stowaway*	2006	12				
Ben Mikaelson	*Touching Spirit Bear* ♪,£££,¶¶,¶¶¶,33,∩,∩∩	2001	9				
James Patterson	*The Angel Experiment*	2006	12				
Gary Paulsen	*Hatchet* ‡‡,££,£££,¿,∩∩,••	2006	9				
Roland Smith	*Peak* ¶¶¶	2008	12				
Joyce Sweeney	*Free Fall*	1996	15				
Theodore Taylor	*Lord of the Kill*	2004	12				
Diane Tullson	*Red Sea*	2005	12				

Books by Teens for Teens

Did you know Christopher Paolini was only fifteen years old when he started writing *Eragon*? Ashley Darrow was just barely a teenager (thirteen) when she wrote *Beneath Minuela's Bed*. And the famous Mary Shelley, creator of *Frankenstein,* was nineteen when she penned her enduring gothic novel. If you're an aspiring author, or if you're interested in reading a novel written by someone your own age, check out the titles on this inspired list of teen books written by teen authors, compiled by the Appleton Public Library (WI). For more information and great lists, see www.teen.apl.org/bklists/index.asp.

Author	Title	Year	Age	Own	Recommend	To Read	Want
Anne Frank	*Anne Frank: Diary of a Young Girl*	1947	12				
Ashley Darrow	*Beneath Minuela's Bed*	2005					
Dave Lindsay	*Dave's Quick`n' Easy Web Pages: An Introductory Guide to Creating Web Sites*	2001	12				
Amelia Atwater-Rhodes	*Demon in My View*	2001	12				
Christopher Paolini	*Eragon* #,##,♦♦♦,♪♪,Ω,‡,¶,33,•••,∩,¿¿¿,◦,¿, ∩∩,oo,3,••	2003	12				
Mary Wollstonecraft Shelley	*Frankenstein or the Modern Prometheus*	1818	10				
Anonymous	*Go Ask Alice*	1971	15				
Jennifer Lynn Barnes	*Golden*	2006	12				
Amelia Atwater-Rhodes	*In the Forests of the Night*	2000	12				
Samantha Abeel	*My Thirteenth Winter: A Memoir* !!!	2004	12				
Megan McNeill Libby	*Postcards from France*	1996	12				
Lydia Omolola Okutoro	*Quiet Storm: Voices of Young Black Poets*	2002	12				
Maureen Daly	*Seventeenth Summer*	1942	12				
Amelia Atwater-Rhodes	*Shattered Mirror*	2003	12				
Bethany Hamilton	*Soul Surfer: A True Story of Faith Family and Fighting to Get Back on the Board*	2004	15				
Ned Vizzini	*Teen Angst? Naaah—A Quasi-Autobiography*	2002	12				

Author	Title	Year	Age	Own	Recommend	To Read	Want
Nora Coon	*Teen Dream Jobs: How to Get the Job You Really Want Now!*	2003	12				
Gil C. Alicea	*The Air Down Here: True Tales from a South Bronx Boyhood*	1995	12				
Latoya Hunter	*The Diary of Latoya Hunter: My First Year in Junior High*	1993	12				
S. E. Hinton	*The Outsiders* **	1997	12				
Esther Watson	*The Pain Tree and Other Teenage Angst-Ridden Poetry*	1967	12				
Flavia Bujor	*The Prophecy of the Stones*	2004	12				
Farah Ahmedi	*The Story of My Life: An Afghan Girl on the Other Side of the Sky*	2005					
Mark Pfetzer	*Within Reach: My Everest Story*	1998	12				
Zlata Filipovic	*Zlata's Diary: A Child's Life in Sarajevo*	1994	12				

Quick Picks for Reluctant Readers

Reluctant readers are kids who, for whatever reason, do not like to read. To help encourage 12–18-year-olds who may not be interested in reading for recreation, the Young Adult Library Services Association, part of the American Library Association, created the Quick Picks for Reluctant Readers list. The books are selected based on their catchy, action-oriented covers, high interest level or "hook" in first ten pages, well-defined characters, sufficient plot to sustain interest, clear writing, single point of view, and touches of humor when appropriate. The list is re-created each year. To view past lists, see www.ala .org/yalsa/booklists/quickpicks.

Author	Title	Year	Age	Own	Recommend	To Read	Want
S. A. Bodeen	*The Compound*	2008	12				
Coe Booth	*Kendra*	2008	15				
Suzanne Collins	*The Hunger Games* ˣ,#	2008	15				

☐ Juvenile Nonfiction   ▨ Juvenile Fiction   ■ Fiction   ■ Nonfiction

Author	Title	Year	Age	Own	Recommend	To Read	Want
Quick Picks for Reluctant Readers							
L. Divine	Drama High (Series)	2006	15				
Thomas Fahy	The Unspoken	2009	12				
Terri Fields	My Father's Son	2008	15				
Gail Giles	Right Behind You	2008	12				
Christopher Golden	Poison Ink	2008	12				
David Hernandez	Suckerpunch	2008	15				
Linda Oatman High	Planet Pregnancy	2008	15				
Ellen Hopkins	Identical #	2008	15				
Brian James	Thief	2008	15				
Dream Jordan	Hot Girl	2008	12				
Peggy Kern	No Way Out	2008	9				
Paul Kropp	Behind the Door	2008					
Christopher Krovatin	Venomous	2008	15				
Paul Langan	Schooled	2008	12				
Carrie Mac	Pain & Wastings	2008	12				
Mari Mancusi	Gamer Girl	2008	12				
Lurlene McDaniel	Prey	2008	12				
Margot McDonnell	Torn to Pieces	2008	12				
Lisa McMann	Wake #	2008	15				
Richelle Mead	Frostbite: A Vampire Academy Novel	2008	12				
Denene Millner and Mitzi Miller	Hotlanta (Series)	2008	12				
G. Neri	Chess Rumble	2007	8				
Sylvia Olsen	Middle Row	2008	12				
Kimberly Pauley	Sucks to Be Me: The All-True Confessions of Mina Hamilton, Teen Vampire (Maybe)	2008	12				
Marlene Perez	Dead is the New Black	2008	12				
Kristopher Reisz	Unleashed	2008	15				
Lisa Schroeder	I Heart You, You Haunt Me	2008	12				

Author	Title	Year	Age	Own	Recommend	To Read	Want
Julie Schumacher	Black Box	2009	12				
Elizabeth Scott	Living Dead Girl	2009	15				
Yasmin Shiraz	Retaliation	2007					
Alan Lawrence Sitomer	The Secret Story of Sonia Rodriguez	2010	12				
Carol Snow	Switch	2009	12				
Laurie Faria Stolarz	Project 17	2009	12				
Brooke Taylor	Undone	2008	15				
Lewis Trondheim	Kaput and Zosky	2008	9				
Tony Varrato	Fakie	2008	12				
Tony Varrato	Outrage	2008	12				
Will Weaver	Saturday Night Dirt	2009	12				
Nonfiction							
Jessica Abel and Gabriel Soria	Life Sucks	2008	12				
Steve Badillo and Steve Werner	Skateboarding: Legendary Tricks	2008					
Holly Black	Good Neighbors: Kin	2009	15				
Ben Boos	Swords: An Artist's Devotion	2008	9				
Crai S. Bower	Farts: A Spotter's Guide	2008					
Robin Bowman	It's Complicated: The American Teenager	2007					
Percy Carry and Ronald Wimberly	Sentences: The Life of M.F. Grimm	2007					
Comickers Magazine	Comickers Art 2: Create Amazing Manga Characters	2008					
Erin Elisabeth Conley	Uncool: A Girl's Guide to Misfitting In	2007	12				
Sean D'Arcy	Freestyle Soccer Tricks	2008					
Patrick Ecclesine	Faces of Sunset Boulevard	2008					
Editors of Cosmogirl	All the Questions About Hair, Makeup, Skin & More	2008					

Quick Picks for Reluctant Readers			Age	Own	Recommend	To Read	Want
Author	Title	Year					
Eminem	The Way I Am	2009					
John Fardon	Do Not Open: An Encyclopedia of the World's Best-Kept Secrets	2007	9				
Betsy Franco ed.	Falling Hard: 100 Love Poems by Teenagers	2008	15				
Michael Franzini	One Hundred Young Americans	2007					
Kip Fulbeck	Permanence	2008					
Mario Garza	More Stuff on My Cat: 2x the Stuff +2x the Cats = 4x the Awesome	2008					
Steve Greenberg	Gadget Nation: A Journey Through the Eccentric World of Invention	2008					
Christen Haden	Creepy Cute Crochet: Zombies, Ninjas, Robots, and More!	2008					
Michael Hague	In the Small	2008	12				
Ian Harrison	Take Me to Your Leader: Weird, Strange, and Totally Useless Information	2009					
Anthony Horowitz and Anthony Johnston	Point Blank: The Graphic Novel	2002	9				
Noel Hudson	The Band Name Book	2008					
Marina Khidekel	The Quiz Life	2008	12				
Kazu Kibuishi	Flight: Vol. 4	2007					
Dennis King	Art of Modern Rock: Mini #1: A-Z	2007					
Susan Kuklin	No Choirboy: Murder, Violence and Teenagers on Death Row	2008	15				
Yishan Li	500 Manga Creatures	2007					
The Manga University Culinary Institute and Chihiro Hattori	The Manga Cookbook	2007					
Karen Ngo	Indognito	2008					
Donna O'Meara	Volcano: A Visual Guide	2007					
Aaron Peckham	Mo'Urban Dictionary: Ridonkulous Street Slang Defined	2007					

Author	Title	Year	Age	Own	Recommend	To Read	Want
Ben Powell	Skateboarding Skills: The Reader's Guide	2008					
Deborah Reber	Chill: Stress-Reducing Techniques for a More Balanced, Peaceful You	2008	12				
Nancy Amanda Redd	Body Drama	2007					
Steve Saffel	Spider-Man, the Icon	2007					
Reymundo Sanchez and Sonia Rodriguez	Lady Q: The Rise and Fall of a Latin Queen	2008					
Noah Scalin	Skulls	2008					
Bill Shapiro	Other People's Love Letters: 150 Letters You Were Never Meant to See	2007					
Larry Smith and Rachel Fershleiser	Not Quite What I Was Planning: Six Word Memoirs by Writers Famous and Obscure	2008					
Kim Smits and Matthijs Maat	Custom Kicks	2008					
Rick and B. B. Spears	Black Metal, Vol. 1	2007					
Aimee Major Steinberger	Japan Ai: A Tall Girl's Adventures in Japan	2007	12				
Sloane Tanen and Stefan Hagen	Appetite for Detention	2008	12				
Melvyn Willin	Ghosts: Caught on Film	2007					
Daniel H. Wilson	How to Build a Robot Army: Tips on Defending the Earth Against Alien Invaders	2007					
David Zinczeko	Eat This, Not That!	2009					

Techies Not Trekkies

Compiled by Jamie Watson, literature adviser at AdLit.org (Adolescent Literacy), the titles on the Techies Not Trekkies list are full of computer- and technology-related stories ranging from blogs, video games, email, and websites to human brains implanted with "feeds." Check out more book lists at www.adlit.org/books_by_theme.

Author	Title	Year	Age	Own	Recommend	To Read	Want
Cory Doctorow	Little Brother [$$,x]	2008					
M. T. Anderson	Feed [!,x]	2002					
Meg Cabot	The Boy Next Door	2002					
Paula Danzinger and Ann M. Martin	Snail Mail No More	2000					
Lauren Myracle	TTYL	2004					
Janet Tasjian	The Gospel According to Larry	2001					
Judy Goldschmidt	The Secret Blog of Raisin Rodriguez	2005					
Aaron Ruby	Smartbomb: The Quest for Art, Entertainment, and Big Bucks in the Videogame Generation	2005					
Bob Pletka	My So Called Digital Life: 2,000 Teenagers, 200 Cameras and 30 Days to Document Their World	2005					
Sonya Sones	One of Those Hideous Books Where the Mother Dies [‡‡,o,3]	2005					

Humor

Being a teenager can be a stressful time; there are futures to plan, first dates to brave, tests to take, cars to drive, and parents to endure. Sometimes you need to indulge in some comedy to get through. This list represents the humorous choices of the Seattle Public Library (WA) and Carrolton City Library (TX), combined in a list that offers über-nerds, butt cheeks, chipmunk costumes, and body-possessing devils.

Author	Title	Year	Age	Own	Recommend	To Read	Want
A. M. Jenkins	Repossessed	2007	12				
Julie Linker	Disenchanted Princess	2007	12				
Kenjiro Hata	Hayate: Combat Butler	2007	15				
Louise Rennison	Angus, Thongs and Full-Frontal Snogging ii,**	2000	12				
M. T. Anderson	Burger Wuss	2008	12				
Marissa Walsh	A Field Guide to High School	2007	12				
Meg Cabot	All-American Girl ii,***	2003	12				
Michael Harmon	Last Exit to Normal	2008	12				
Ned Vizzini	It's Kind of a Funny Story	2006	12				
Ned Vizzini	Be More Chill	2005	12				
Neil Shusterman	The Schwa was Here ***,♪	2004	12				
Norma Howe	The Adventures of Blue Avenger	2000	12				
Randa Abdel-Fattah	Does My Head Look Big in This?	2007	12				
Stefan Petrucha	Teen, Inc.	2007	12				
Sue Limb	Girl, 15, Charming but Insane	2005	12				
Susan Juby	Miss Smithers	2004	12				
Terence Blacker	Boy2Girl	2005	12				
Jordan Sonnenblick	Notes from the Midnight Driver	2007	15				
John Van de Ruit	Spud	2008	12				
John Lekich	King of the Lost and Found	2007	12				
Adam Bagdasarian	First French Kiss: And Other Traumas	2002	12				

▢ Juvenile Nonfiction   ▣ Juvenile Fiction   ■ Fiction   ■ Nonfiction

Humor							
Author	Title	Year	Age	Own	Recommend	To Read	Want
Amber Kizer	One Butt Cheek at a Time	2008	15				
Andrew Peterson	On the Edge of the Dark Sea of Darkness	2008					
Brad Barkley and Heather Hepler	Dream Factory	2009	12				
Bryan Lee O'Malley	Scott Pilgrim's Precious Little Life	2004					
Dan Waters	Generation Dead	2009	12				
Daniel H. Wilson	How to Survive a Robot Uprising	2005					
David LaRochelle	Absolutely Positively Not	2005	15				
David Lubar	Sleeping Freshmen Never Lie £	2007	12				
Douglas Rees	Vampire High	2005	12				
Frank Portman	King Dork	2008	15				
Gennifer Choldenko	Al Capone Does My Shirts ♪,ii,	2004	9				
Gordon Korman	Son of the Mob ##,♦♦♦,‡‡‡,~~	2004	12				
Jean Ferris	Love Among the Walnuts	2008	9				
Jeff Smith	Out from Boneville	1995	9				
Jennifer Lynn Barnes	Squad: Perfect Cover	2008	12				
Warren Ellis	Nextwave: Agents of HATE	2007					

Amelia Bloomer Project

The Amelia Bloomer Project compiles an annual list of the best feminist books for young readers, ages birth through 18. The list is created by the Feminist Task Force of the Social Responsibilities Round Table of the American Library Association. According to the Amelia Bloomer Project website, the books on the list are chosen to "show girls and women—past and present, real and fictional—breaking stereotypes to follow their dreams and pursue their goals, challenging cultural and familial stereotypes to gain an education, taking charge and making plans for community, regional, national, and world change. We celebrate the history of feminism and highlight strides made in U.S. history in particular, and hope that these books inspire readers to make the world a better place for all." For more information, visit www.libr.org/ftf/bloomer.html.

Author	Title	Year	Age	Own	Recommend	To Read	Want
Middle Readers—Fiction							
Pat Murphy	*The Wild Girls*	2007	12				
Amjed Qamar	*Beneath My Mother's Feet*	2008	12				
Karen Schwabach	*The Hope Chest*	2008	9				
Kashmira Sheth	*Keeping Corner*	2009	12				
Nancy Springer	*The Case of the Peculiar Pink Fan*	2008	9				
Middle Readers—Nonfiction							
Michelle Benjamin and Maggie Mooney	*Nobel's Women of Peace*	2008	10				
Sandy Donovan	*Hypatia: Mathematician, Inventor, and Philosopher*	2008	9				
Donna Getzinger	*Triangle Shirtwaist Factory Fire*	2008	10				
Claire Mysko	*You're Amazing: A No-Pressure Guide to Being Your Best Self*	2008	9				
Suzanne Simoni	*Fantastic Female Filmmakers*	2008	11				
Young Adult—Fiction							
Susan Vaught	*Big Fat Manifesto*	2007	12				
Padma Venkatraman	*Climbing the Stairs*	2008	12				
Elizabeth C. Bunce	*A Curse Dark as Gold (Rumpelstiltskin)*	2008	12				

☐ Juvenile Nonfiction   ☐ Juvenile Fiction   ■ Fiction   ■ Nonfiction

Amelia Bloomer Project							
Author	Title	Year	Age	Own	Recommend	To Read	Want
E. Lockhart	The Disreputable History of Frankie Landau-Banks ###,#	2008	15				
Justina Chen Headley	Girl Overboard	2007	12				
Claire Dean	Girlwood	2008	12				
Kristin Cashore	Graceling vvv,#	2009	15				
Suzanne Collins	The Hunger Games ###,x,#	2009	15				
Sherri Winston	The Kayla Chronicles	2008	15				
Elizabeth Scott	Living Dead Girl	2009	15				
Nnedi Okorafor-Mbachu	The Shadow Speaker	2009	12				
Ellen Klages	White Sands, Red Menace	2008	9				
Young Adult—Nonfiction							
Jennifer Baumgardner	Abortion & Life	2008					
Heather Ball	Astonishing Women Artists	2007	12				
Jill Norgren	Belva Lockwood: Equal Rights Pioneer	2008	9				
Nancy Amanda Redd	Body Drama: Real Girls, Real Bodies, Real Issues, Real Answers	2007					
Sharon Rudahl	A Dangerous Woman: The Graphic Biography of Emma Goldman	2007	15				
Jessica Hein, Heather Holland, and Carol Kauppi ed.	GirlSpoken: From Pen, Brush, and Tongue	2008	12				
Gavin Mortimer	The Great Swim	2008					
Charlotte S. Waisman and Jill S. Tietjen	Her Story: A Timeline of the Women Who Changed America	2008					
Jessica Valenti	He's a Stud, She's a Slut and 49 Other Double Standards Every Woman Should Know	2008					
Catherine Gourley	Images and Issues of Women in the Twentieth Century Vol. 1–5						
Nadia Shivack	Inside Out: Portrait of an Eating Disorder	2007	12				

Author	Title	Year	Age	Own	Recommend	To Read	Want
Billie Jean King and Christine Brennan	*Pressure is a Privilege: Lessons I've Learned from Life and the Battle of the Sexes*	2008					
Gillian Greensite	*Rape at College: How to Help a Friend*	2008	15				
Marisa Anderson and Nicole Georges	*Rock 'n' Roll Camp for Girls: How to Start a Band, Write Songs, Record an Album, and Rock Out!*	2008	12				
Margarita Engle	*The Surrender Tree: Poems of Cuba's Struggle for Freedom* ♦♦,♥♥	2008	12				
Mabel Armstrong	*Women Astronomers: Reaching for the Stars*	2008	15				
Katherine Kiviat and Scott Heidler	*Women of Courage: Intimate Stories from Afghanistan*	2007					

Urban Lit

As defined by Molly Lindquist of Litlovers.com, urban lit, also known as street lit, "explores the dark, gritty environment of inner-city life. Primarily written by and for African-Americans, urban lit began as an outgrowth of the Black Power movement in the 1970s and, some believe, has continued in its new form as hip-hop music, as well as print." This list, a combination of urban lit selections from the Multnomah County Library (OR) and King County Library can be found at www.kcls.org/teens/booklist.cfm?booklistid=56 and www .multcolib.org/teens/urbanlit.html.

Author	Title	Year	Age	Own	Recommend	To Read	Want
Jessica Blank	*Almost Home*	2009	12				
Luis J. Rodriguez	*Always Running: La Vida Loca, Gang Days in L.A.*	2005					
Walter Dean Myers	*Autobiography of My Dead Brother*	2006	15				

☐ Juvenile Nonfiction   ☐ Juvenile Fiction   ■ Fiction   ■ Nonfiction

Urban Lit

Author	Title	Year	Age	Own	Recommend	To Read	Want
Lenora Adams	*Baby Girl*	2007	15				
Sharon G. Flake	*Bang*	2005	12				
Linda Glovach	*Beauty Queen*	1998	15				
Francisco X. Stork	*Behind the Eyes*	2006	12				
Paul Volponi	*Black and White* ~~~	2005	15				
Paul Langan and Anne E. Schraff	*Bluford High*	2006	12				
Nikki Grimes	*Bronx Masquerade*	2002	12				
Janet McDonald	*Brother Hood*	2004	12				
Kevin Brooks	*Candy*	2005	15				
Todd Strasser	*Can't Get There From Here*	2005	12				
Charles R. Smith Jr.	*Chameleon*	2008	12				
Janet McDonald	*Chill Wind*	2006	15				
Ellen Hopkins	*Crank* ΩΩΩ,¶,∴∩∩	2008	12				
Antonio Pagliarulo	*Different Kind of Heat*	2006	15				
L. Divine	*Drama High*	2006	15				
Manuel Luis Martinez	*Drift*	2003					
Todd Strasser	*Drift X*		12				
Brenda Woods	*Emako Blue* ~~~	2005	12				
Cassandra Carter	*Fast Life*						
Kate Wild	*Fight Game*	2009	12				
Angela Johnson	*The First Part Last*	2005	12				
Sherman Alexie	*Flight*	2007					
Walter Dean Myers	*Game*	2008	12				
Janet McDonald	*Harlem Hustle*	2006	15				
Alan Lawrence Sitomer	*Homeboyz*	2007	12				
Alan Lawrence Sitomer	*Hoopster*	2005	12				
Dream Jordan	*Hot Girl*	2008	12				
Denene Millner and Mitzi Miller	*Hotlanta*	2008	12				

Author	Title	Year	Age	Own	Recommend	To Read	Want
Paul Volponi	*Hurricane Song*	2009	9				
Earl Sewell	*If I Were Your Boyfriend*	2005	15				
Connie Rose Porter	*Imani All Mine* ~,‡	2000					
Monica McKayhan	*Indigo Summer*	2007					
Tia Williams	*It Chicks*	2007	12				
Dana Davidson	*Jason and Kyra*	2004	12				
Coe Booth	*Kendra*	2008	15				
Anne Schraff	*Lost and Found*	2007	12				
Virginia Euwer Wolff	*Make Lemonade* £	2009	12				
Sharon G. Flake	*Money Hungry*	2007	9				
Walter Dean Myers	*Monster* ‖,‡‡‡	1999	12				
Blake Nelson	*Paranoid Park*	2008	12				
Lynne Ewing	*Party Girl*	1999	15				
Dana Davidson	*Played*	2005	15				
Paul Volponi	*Response*	2009	12				
Katina King	*Ride Wit' Me*	2006					
Paul Volponi	*Rooftop*	2007	12				
Paul Volponi	*Rucker Park Setup*	2008	12				
K. L. Going	*Saint Iggy*	2006	15				
Walter Dean Myers	*Shooter*	2004	12				
Allison Van Diepen	*Snitch*	2007	15				
Allison Van Diepen	*Street Pharm*	2006	15				
Various Authors	*Teenage Bluez: A Collection of Urban Stories*	2005	9				
Derrick Barnes	*The Making of Dr. Truelove*	2006	15				
Monica McKayhan	*The Pact*	2008	15				
Thomas M. Yeahpau	*The X- Indian Chronicles: The Book of Mausape*	2006	15				
Barbara Haworth-Attard	*Theories of Relativity* %%	2005	15				

☐ Juvenile Nonfiction   ▨ Juvenile Fiction   ▧ Fiction   ■ Nonfiction

Urban Lit

Author	Title	Year	Age	Own	Recommend	To Read	Want
Coe Booth	*Tyrell* [1]	2006	15				
Beverly Naidoo	*Web of Lies*	2006	9				
Walter Dean Myers	*What They Found: Love on 145th Street*	2007	15				

Books for Guys

The Books for Guys list from the City of Carrolton Library (TX) contains titles from some of the most beloved authors in young adult literature: Chris Crutcher, M. T. Anderson, James Patterson, Carl Hiaasen, Ned Vizzini, and Gary Paulsen. Any guy will find great reads on the list. See www.cityofcarrollton.com/index .aspx?page=722 for more lists.

Author	Title	Year	Age	Own	Recommend	To Read	Want
M. T. Anderson	*Burger Wuss*	2008	12				
Ned Vizzini	*It's Kind of a Funny Story*	2006	15				
Rob Thomas	*Rats Saw God*	2007	12				
William Sleator	*The Boy Who Couldn't Die*	2005	12				
Aron Ralston	*Between a Rock and a Hard Place*	2005					
Gary Paulsen	*How Angel Peterson Got His Name*	2004	9				
James Patterson	*Maximum Ride: The Angel Experiment* [#]	2005	12				
Kenneth Oppel	*Airborn* [£,33,**]	2004	12				
David Lubar	*Hidden Talents*	2003	12				
Iain Lawrence	*The Cannibals*	2007	12				
Dorothy and Thomas Hoobler	*The Ghost in the Tokaido Inn*	1999	9				
Robert Heinlein	*Starship Troopers*	1999	12				
Carl Hiaasen	*Flush* ♥	2005	9				

Author	Title	Year	Age	Own	Recommend	To Read	Want
John Flanagan	The Ruins of Gorlan	2005	9				
Chris Crutcher	Whale Talk	2009	12				
Edward Bloor	Tangerine £££.¶¶¶.ii.oo	1997	9				
Paul Volponi	Black and White ~~~	2005	15				

Eragon Read-Alikes

If you liked Christopher Paolini's Inheritance trilogy, the fantasy novels *Eragon*, *Eldest*, and *Brisingr*, try some of the following suggested titles. This list was developed by the King Country Library in Washington state. This list and more great teen lists can be found at www.kcls.org/teens.

Author	Title	Year	Age	Own	Recommend	To Read	Want
Jonathan Stroud	Amulet of Samarkand	2003	9				
Susan Cooper	The Dark is Rising ***	1993	12				
Diana Wynne Jones	Dark Lord of Derkholm ᵛᵛᵛ	2001	9				
Patricia C. Wrede	Dealing with Dragons	1990	12				
Carole Wilkinson	Dragon Keeper	2007	9				
Cornelia Funke	Dragon Rider	2005	9				
Anne McCaffrey	Dragonflight	2002					
Vivian Vande Velde	Dragon's Bait	2003	9				
Jane Yolen	Dragon's Blood	2004	12				
Susan Fletcher	Dragon's Milk	1996	9				
Robert Jordan	Eye of the World	1990					
J. R. R. Tolkien	Fellowship of the Ring: Being the First Part of the Lord of the Rings	1988					
Chris D'Lacey	Fire Within	2001	9				
Robin McKinley	Hero and the Crown	1984	12				

Juvenile Nonfiction   Juvenile Fiction   Fiction   Nonfiction

Eragon Read-Alikes

Author	Title	Year	Age	Own	Recommend	To Read	Want
Naomi Novik	His Majesty's Dragon	2008					
MaryJanice Davidson	Jennifer Scales and the Ancient Furnace	2007					
Mercedes Lackey	Joust	2003					
T. A. Barron	Lost Years of Merlin	2002	15				
D. J. MacHale	Merchant of Death	2002	12				
Patrick Rothfuss	Name of the Wind	2007					
Alison Croggon	Naming	2005	12				
Patricia A. McKillip	Riddle-Master: The Complete Trilogy	1976	15				
John Flanagan	Ruins of Gorlan	2005	9				
Garth Nix	Sabriel	1997	15				
Ursula K. Le Guin	Wizard of Earthsea	1999	12				

Twilight Read-Alikes

Is there a reading life after *Twilight*? Even though there will always be just one Edward, the titles on this list will help introduce *Twilight* lovers to the larger world of vampires in print. The Denver Public Library (CO) has created an amazing list to satisfy even the most devoted Bella fans. For a complete synopsis of each title, see www.teens.denverlibrary.org/find/genre/twilight.html.

Author	Title	Year	Age	Own	Recommend	To Read	Want
M. T. Anderson	Thirsty	2008	12				
Amelia Atwater-Rhodes	Hawksong	2007	12				
Amelia Atwater-Rhodes	In the Forests of the Night	2000	12				
Holly Black	Tithe	2002	15				
Libba Bray	A Great and Terrible Beauty #,‡‡	2005	12				
Emma Bull	War for the Oaks	2001					
Meg Cabot	Shadowland	2005	12				

Author	Title	Year	Age	Own	Recommend	To Read	Want
Rachel Caine	*Glass Houses*	2006	12				
P. C. Cast	*Marked: A House of Night Novel*	2007	12				
Cassandra Clare	*City of Bones* #	2008	15				
Stephen Cole	*Wounded*	2005	15				
Liza Conrad	*High School Bites*	2005	15				
Melissa de la Cruz	*Blue Bloods*	2009	12				
Neil Gaiman	*Stardust* ˜	1999					
Claudia Gray	*Evernight*	2008	12				
Pete Hautman	*Sweetblood* ££	2004	15				
Simon Holt	*The Devouring*	2008	12				
A. M. Jenkins	*Beating Heart: A Ghost's Story*	2006	15				
Annette Curtis Klause	*Blood and Chocolate* ii,oo	2007	15				
Annette Curtis Klause	*The Silver Kiss* ♪,¿	2009	12				
Martine Leavitt	*Keturah and Lord Death* $$	2006	12				
Melissa Marr	*Wicked Lovely*	2007	12				
Katie Maxwell	*Got Fangs?*	2005	12				
Robin McKinley	*Sunshine*	2003					
Richelle Mead	*Vampire Academy* #	2007	12				
Douglas Rees	*Vampire High*	2003	12				
Serena Robar	*Braced2Bite*	2006	15				
Ellen Schreiber	*Vampire Kisses*	2008	12				
Cynthia Leitich Smith	*Tantalize*	2008	15				
R. L. Stine	*Dangerous Girls*	2005	12				
Bram Stoker	*Dracula*	1897					
Vivian Vande Velde	*Companions of the Night* ¶¶¶	2002	12				
Scott Westerfeld	*Peeps* #	2005	15				
Chris Wooding	*The Haunting of Alaizabel Cray*	2004	12				
Patricia C. Wrede	*Sorcery and Cecelia or the Enchanted Chocolate Pot*	2003	12				

▢ Juvenile Nonfiction   ▢ Juvenile Fiction   ■ Fiction   ■ Nonfiction

Harry Potter Read-Alikes

Now that the enchanting Harry Potter series by J. K. Rowling is finished, do you find yourself missing the spells and magic of Harry, Ron, and Hermoine? Are you craving a visit to another mystifying world? This list of Harry Potter read-alikes from Mesa Library (AZ) offers thirty-two books to curb your *Harry Potter* fever. Become a magician's apprentice, plunder with trolls, capture a fairy, or ride on a dragon in some of the amazing books featured on the list. For a synopsis of each title, visit www.mesalibrary.org/Kids/books/harrypotter.aspx.

Author	Title	Year	Age	Own	Recommend	To Read	Want
P. B. Kerr	Akhenaten Adventure	2004	9				
Jonathan Stroud	Amulet of Samarkand	2003	9				
Dia Calhoun	Aria of the Sea ᵛᵛᵛ	2003	12				
Eoin Colfer	Artemis Fowl ##,ii	2002	12				
Robin McKinley	Blue Sword	1950	12				
Lloyd Alexander	Book of Three	1979	12				
C. S. Lewis	Chronicles of Narnia	1950	12				
Patricia C. Wrede	Dealing with Dragons	1990	12				
Cornelia Funke	Dragon Rider	2005	9				
Edith Pattou	East (East of the Sun, West of the Moon)	2003	12				
Christopher Paolini	Eragon #,##,♦♦♦,♫♫,Ω,‡,¶,33,•••,∩,¿¿¿,○,¿, ∩∩,oo,3,••	2007	12				
Gail Carson Levine	Ella Enchanted ♦♦♦,♪,‡‡	1997	9				
Tony DiTerlizzi	Field Guide	2003	9				
M. T. Anderson	Game of Sunken Places	2004	9				
Philip Pullman	Golden Compass	2001	15				
Suzanne Collins	Gregor the Overlander	2005	9				
J. R. R. Tolkien	Hobbit	1937					
Jenny Nimmo	Midnight for Charlie Bone	2007	9				
Garth Nix	Mister Monday	2003	9				
Eloise McGraw	Moorchild	1996	12				
Charlotte Haptie	Otto and the Flying Twins	2004	12				

Author	Title	Year	Age	Own	Recommend	To Read	Want
Susan Cooper	*Over Sea Under Stone*	2000	12				
Dian Curtis Regan	*Princess Nevermore*	2006	9				
Tamora Pierce	*Sandry's Book*	1999	9				
Nancy Farmer	*Sea of Trolls*	2004	12				
Eva Ibbotson	*Secret of Platform 13*	1995	9				
Diane Duane	*So You Want to be a Wizard*	2003	9				
William Nicholson	*Wind Singer: An Adventure*	2000	9				
Vivian Vande Velde	*Wizard at Work*	2004	9				
Jane Yolen	*Wizard's Hall*	1999	9				
Ursula K. Le Guin	*Wizard of Earthsea*	1999	12				
Madeleine L'Engle	*Wrinkle in Time*	1962	12				

A Child Called It Read-Alikes

Springfield City Library (MA) offers this great list for anyone who has enjoyed *A Child Called It* by Dave Pelzer. The Springfield Library's website has a multitude of lists for teens, including subjects such as forensic science, science fiction in space, classic horror novels, and great summer reading lists. Check them out at www.springfieldlibrary.org/reading/teenbooks.html.

Author	Title	Year	Age	Own	Recommend	To Read	Want
E. R. Frank	*America*	2004	15				
Thalia Chaltas	*Because I am Furniture*	2009	12				
Han Nolan	*Born Blue*	2003	15				
Gigi Amateau	*Claiming Georgia Tate*	2007	15				
Margaret Peterson Haddix	*Don't You Dare Read This, Mrs. Dunphrey* ~~~.¶¶	2004	12				
Antwone Fisher	*Finding Fish: A Memoir*	2001					

☐ Juvenile Nonfiction   ☐ Juvenile Fiction   ▨ Fiction   ■ Nonfiction

A Child Called It Read-Alikes			Age	Own	Recommend	To Read	Want
Author	Title	Year					
Sharon M. Draper	*Forged by Fire*	2006	12				
Torey L. Hayden	*Ghost Girl: The True Story of a Child in Peril and the Teacher Who Saved Her*	1994					
Irene Hunt	*The Lottery Rose*	2002	12				
Ben Mikaelson	*Petey* ˣˣˣ	2000	9				
Patricia McCord	*Pictures in the Dark*	2004	12				
Julie Gregory	*Sickened: The Memoir of a Munchausen by Proxy Childhood*	2004					
Sharon M. Draper	*Tears of a Tiger* ³ʼ··	1994	15				
James M. Deem	*The Three NBs of Julian Drew*	2004	15				
M. Sindy Felin	*Touching Snow*	2007	12				
Carolyn Coman	*What Jamie Saw*	1995	12				
Catherine Atkins	*When Jeff Comes Home*	2001	15				
Truddi Chase	*When Rabbit Howls*	2002					
Norma Fox Mazer	*When She Was Good*	2000	12				

Agatha Award for Best Children's and Young Adult Novel &&

Malice Domestic® is a convention held annually since 1989 in metropolitan Washington, D.C., for fans of the traditional mystery. Traditional mystery books usually revolve around the activities of an amateur detective among characters very familiar with each other. The books typically also avoid explicit sex and violence, and unfold in a household or other confined setting. The books of Agatha Christie exemplify this genre. Mysteries first published in the United States by a living author during the preceding calendar year in hardcover, as paperback originals, or electronically by an e-publishing firm are eligible to receive an Agatha Award in one of five categories. The best children's/young adult mystery winners (aimed at audiences 18 and younger) are listed here. Awards are announced at the annual convention banquet. For more information, see http://www.malicedomestic.org/agathaawards.html.

Year	Author	Title	Age	Own	Recommend	To Read	Want
2010							
2009							
2008	Chris Grabenstein	The Crossroads	9				
2007	Sarah Masters Buckey	A Light in the Cellar	9				
2006	Nancy Means Wright	Pea Soup Poisonings	9				
2005	Peter Abrahams	Down the Rabbit Hole: An Echo Falls Mystery	9				
2004	Blue Balliett	Chasing Vermeer	9				
2003	Kathleen Karr	The 7Th Knot	9				
2002	Daniel J. Hale and Matthew Labrot	Red Card: A Zeke Armstrong Mystery	12				
2001	Penny Warner	Mystery of the Haunted Caves: A Troop 13 Mystery	9				

Arthur Ellis Crime Award—Best Juvenile Book &&&

Established in 1983, the Arthur Ellis Crime Award, commonly called the "Arthurs," is presented annually by the Crime Writers of Canada. Invoking the nom de travail of Canada's official hangman, these awards honor the best crime writing published in the preceding year by Canadian authors or resident Canadians, regardless of setting or publisher. Arthurs are awarded for best novel, best first novel, best true crime, best genre criticism, best short story, best juvenile book, and best play. For more information about the Arthurs, or the Crime Writers of Canada, visit www.crimewriterscanada.com/cwc/index.html.

Year	Author	Title	Age	Own	Recommend	To Read	Want
2011							
2010							
2009	Vicki Grant	*Res Judicata*	12				
2008	Shane Peacock	*Eye of the Crow*	9				
2007	Sean Cullen	*Hamish X and the Cheese Pirates*	12				
2006	Vicki Grant	*Quid Pro Quo*	15				
2005	Carrie Mac	*The Beckoners*	12				
2004	Graham McNamee	*Acceleration* ▼,ΩΩ	12				
2003	Norah McClintock	*Break and Enter*	12				
2002	Norah McClintock	*Scared to Death*	15				
2001	Tim Wynne-Jones	*The Boy in the Burning House* ▼	12				
2000	Linda Bailey	*How Can a Brilliant Detective Shine in the Dark?*	12				
1999	Norah McClintock	*Sins of the Father*	15				
1998	Norah McClintock	*The Body in the Basement*	12				
1997	Linda Bailey	*How Can a Frozen Detective Stay Hot on the Trail*	12				
1996	Norah McClintock	*Mistaken Identity*	12				
1995	James Heneghan	*Torn Away*	12				
1994	John Dowd	*Abalone Summer*	12				

Edgar Allan Poe Award—Best Young Adult ▼

The Mystery Writers of America award ceramic statuettes of Edgar Allan Poe, known as "Edgars," annually for outstanding contributions to mystery, crime, and suspense writing. They honor the best in mystery fiction, nonfiction, television, film, and theater. See www.theedgars.com for all categories and winners.

Year	Author	Title	Age	Own	Recommend	To Read	Want
2011							
2010							
2009	John Green	*Paper Towns* #	15				
2008	John Hart	*Down River*					
2007	Robin Merrow MacCready	*Buried*	15				
2006	John Feinstein	*Last Shot: A Final Four Mystery*	10				
2005	Dorothy and Thomas Hoobler	*In Darkness Death*	10				
2004	Graham McNamee	*Acceleration* [&&&,ΩΩ]	12				
2003	Daniel Parker	*The Wessex Papers Vols. 1-3*					
2002	Tim Wynne-Jones	*The Boy in the Burning House* [&&&]	12				
2001	Elaine Marie Alphin	*Counterfeit Son*	12				
2000	Vivian Vande Velde	*Never Trust a Dead Man*	10				
1999	Nancy Werlin	*The Killer's Cousin* [Σ,ii]	15				
1998	Will Hobbs	*Ghost Canoe* ¡¡¡	12				
1997	Willo Davis Roberts	*Twisted Summer*	12				
1996	Rob MacGregor	*Prophecy Rock*	10				
1995	Nancy Springer	*Toughing It*	15				
1994	Joan Lowery Nixon	*The Name of the Game Was Murder* ♦♦♦	12				
1993	Chap Reaver	*A Little Bit Dead*	12				
1992	Theodore Taylor	*The Weirdo*	12				
1991	Chap Reaver	*Mote*	10				
1990	Alane Ferguson	*Show Me the Evidence*	15				
1989	Sonia Levitin	*Incident at Loring Groves*	10				

Juvenile Nonfiction   Juvenile Fiction   Fiction   Nonfiction

Paranormal Fiction

Molly Lundquist of LitLovers.com defines the paranormal genre as "stories involving supernatural beings and occurrences—phenomena outside the realm of scientific explanation. Tales of werewolves, vampires, ghosts, and apparitions are good examples of this genre." The 24/7 Teen site of the Tulsa City-County Library (OK) provides a sampling of books in this very popular genre. For more great lists, visit www.teens.tulsalibrary.org/booksandreading/read_next.htm.

Author	Title	Year	Age	Own	Recommend	To Read	Want
Jennifer Lynn Barnes	Tattoo	2007	12				
Meg Cabot	Missing You	2007	12				
Kate Cary	Bloodline	2006	12				
Thomas Fahy	The Unspoken	2008	12				
Anthony Horowitz	More Horowitz Horror	2007	9				
A. M. Jenkins	Repossessed	2007	12				
Derek Landy	Skulduggery Pleasant	2008	9				
Amanda Marrone	Uninvited	2007	12				
Andrew Nance	Daemon Hall	2008	15				
Wendy Corsi Staub	Lily Dale: Awakening	2009	12				
Cora Taylor	Adventure in Istanbul	2005	9				
Adrienne Maria Vrettos	Sight	2007	12				

Mysteries and Thrillers

The Seattle Public Library (WA) describes its mysteries and thriller list as "quick action and dark mysteries, sometimes in the same book." From murder in a friary to an encounter with a Chinese mummy, this list has a title to entice any thrill seeker. For more great lists from the Seattle Public Library's Teen site, go to www.spl.org/default.asp?pageID=audience_teens_bmm_categorybrowser.

Author	Title	Year	Age	Own	Recommend	To Read	Want
Peter Abrahams	*Behind the Curtain*	2006	12				
Tedd Arnold	*Rat Life*	2009	12				
Paul Bajoria	*God of Mischief*	2007					
Edward Bloor	*Taken*	2007					
Kate Brian	*Confessions*	2009	15				
Kevin Brooks	*The Road of the Dead*	2007	12				
Kevin Brooks	*Being*	2007	15				
Melissa de la Cruz	*Angels on Sunset Boulevard*	2007	15				
Gail Giles	*What Happened to Cass McBride?*	2006	15				
Lauren Henderson	*Kiss Me Kill Me*	2009	15				
Mary Hoffman	*The Falconer's Knot*	2007	12				
Graham Marks	*Missing in Tokyo*	2006	12				
Alex McAulay	*Oblivion Road*	2007					
Rune Michaels	*Genesis Alpha*	2007	12				
Kirsten Miller	*The Empress's Tomb*	2007	9				
Jacqueline Mitchard	*Now You See Her*	2008	15				
Mal Peet	*Tamar* **	2007	15				
Carol Plum-Ucci	*The Night My Sister Went Missing*	2008	15				
Malcolm Rose	*Blood Brother*	2008	12				
Adrienne Maria Vrettos	*Sight*	2007	12				

☐ Juvenile Nonfiction   ▨ Juvenile Fiction   ■ Fiction   ■ Nonfiction

Locus Fantasy Award for Young Adults ᵛᵛ

Locus Magazine established an annual reader's poll in the early 1970s to provide recommendations to Hugo Award voters. (The Hugo Award is a prestigious science fiction and fantasy award—it does not currently have a young adult category). Since its inception, the *Locus* Award has often had more voters than the Hugo and Nebula awards (given by the Science Fiction and Fantasy Writers of America) combined. The award is given in several categories: novel (split into science fiction, fantasy/horror, and first novel), short fiction, anthology, collection, nonfiction, art book, publisher, magazine, and artist. In February of each year, *Locus* Magazine publishes a recommended reading list. The nominations usually come from but are not limited to this list. The winners in the young adult fantasy category are listed here. For more information, visit www.locusmag .com/SFAwards/Db/*Locus*.html.

Year	Author	Title	Age	Own	Recommend	To Read	Want
2011							
2010							
2009	Neil Gaiman	*The Graveyard Book* #	9				
2008	China Miéville	*Un Lun Dun*	9				
2007	Terry Pratchett	*Wintersmith*	12				
2006	Jane Yolen	*Pay the Piper (Pied Piper)*	9				
2005	Terry Pratchett	*A Hat Full of Sky* ᵛᵛᵛ	12				
2004	Terry Pratchett	*The Wee Free Men*	12				
2003	Neil Gaiman	*Coraline* †††	9				

Mythopoeic Fantasy Award ᵛᵛᵛ

The Mythopoeic Fantasy Award for Adult Literature is given to the novel, multivolume novel, or single-author story collection published during the previous year that best exemplifies "the spirit of the Inklings." The Mythopoeic Fantasy Award for Children's Literature honors books—from young adult novels to picture books—for younger readers in the tradition of the *Hobbit* or the *Chronicles of Narnia*. These awards are chosen from books nominated by individual members of the Mythopoeic Society, and selected by a committee of members. For more information about the Mythopoeic Society and its award, visit www.mythsoc.org/awards/.

Year	Author	Title	Age	Own	Recommend	To Read	Want
2011							
2010							
2009	Kristin Cashore	*Graceling* #	15				
2008	J. K. Rowling	The Harry Potter Series	9				
2007	Catherine Fisher	*Corbenic*	12				
2006	Jonathan Stroud	*The Bartimaeus Trilogy Consisting of the Amulet of Samarkand the Golem's Eye and Ptolemy's Gate*	9				
2005	Terry Pratchett	*A Hat Full of Sky* ᵛᵛ	12				
2004	Clare B. Dunkle	*The Hollow Kingdom*	12				
2003	Michael Chabon	*Summerland*	9				
2002	Peter Dickinson	*The Ropemaker*	12				
2001	Dia Calhoun	*Aria of the Sea*	12				
2000	Franny Billingsley	*The Folk Keeper* ***	15				
1999	Diana Wynne Jones	*Dark Lord of Derkholm*	9				
1998	Jane Yolen	*Young Merlin Trilogy (Consisting of Passager Hobby and Merlin)*	9				
1997	Combined with adult literature award						
1996	Diana Wynne Jones	*The Crown of Dalemark*	10				
1995	Patrice Kindle	*Owl in Love*	12				

☐ Juvenile Nonfiction   ▨ Juvenile Fiction   ▧ Fiction   ■ Nonfiction

Mythopoeic Fantasy Award ᵛᵛᵛ

Year	Author	Title	Age	Own	Recommend	To Read	Want
1994	Suzy McKee Charnas	The Kingdom of Kevin Malone	15				
1993	Debra Doyle And James D. Macdonald	Knight's Wyrd	12				
1992	Salman Rushdie	Haroun and the Sea of Stories					

Golden Duck—Clement Award ˣ

Super-Con-Duck-Tivity, Inc., a charitable corporation, funds the Golden Duck Awards for Excellence in Children's Science Fiction. Anyone may suggest a title for Golden Duck consideration. The Hal Clement Young Adult Award honors the pen name of Harry Stubbs, a well-known science fiction writer and science teacher. The award is for science fiction books with a young adult protagonist, appropriate for grades 6–12. The science in the book should be as correct as possible, without sacrificing story. To see other Golden Duck categories and winners, go to www.goldenduck.org.

Year	Author	Title	Age	Own	Recommend	To Read	Want
2011							
2010							
2009 (tie)	Cory Doctorow	Little Brother $$	12				
2009 (tie)	Suzanne Collins	The Hunger Games ###,#	15				
2008	David Brin	Sky Horizon	0				
2007	Pete Hautman	Rash £	12				
2006	Scott Westerfeld	Uglies Ω,ΩΩΩ,‡,¶¶¶,ii,••	12				
2005	Sharon Lee and Steve Miller	Balance of Trade					
2004	Harry Turtledove	Gunpowder Empire					
2003	M. T. Anderson	Feed ¹	12				
2002	Steven Layne	This Side of Paradise					

Year	Author	Title	Age	Own	Recommend	To Read	Want
2001	David Gerrold	*Jumping Off the Planet*					
2000	Roger MacBride Allen	*The Game of Worlds: Out of Time*					
1999	Larry Segriff	*Alien Dreams*					
1998	Garth Nix	*Shade's Children*	12				
1997	Steven Gould	*Wildside*					
1996 (tie)	H. M. Hoover	*The Winds of Mars*					
1996 (tie)	E. M. Goldman	*Night Room*					
1995	Nancy Farmer	*The Ear, the Eye, and the Arm* **	12				
1994	Lois Lowry	*The Giver* ♦♦♦.‡.¶¶.¶¶¶.ii.¿¿¿¿.**	12				
1993	Caroline Stevermer	*River Rats*	12				
1992	Monica Hughes	*Invitiation to the Game*	12				

Andre Norton Award for Young Adult Fiction ˣˣ

In 200, the Science Fiction and Fantasy Writers of America (SFWA) created the Andre Norton Award to recognize outstanding science fiction and fantasy novels written for the young adult market. Ms. Norton, an SFWA Grand Master, has written more than one hundred influential novels, including the Witch World series, many of them for young adult readers. For more information about the SWFA, see www.sfwa.org.

Year	Author	Title	Age	Own	Recommend	To Read	Want
2010							
2009							
2008	Ysabeau S. Wilce	*Flora's Dare*	14				
2007	J. K. Rowling	*Harry Potter and the Deathly Hallows*	9				

▢ Juvenile Nonfiction   ▢ Juvenile Fiction   ■ Fiction   ■ Nonfiction

Andre Norton Award for Young Adult Fiction ^xx			Age	Own	Recommend	To Read	Want
Year	Author	Title					
2006	Holly Black	*Valiant*	15				
2005	Justine Larbalestier	*Magic or Madness*	12				

First Fantasies

First Fantasies is an ingenious list found on the Boulder Teens portion of the Boulder Public Library (CO) website. First Fantasies provides a list of the first book in notable fantasy series. If a reader enjoys the first book, he or she can continue on in the series with the promise of more fairies, wizards, dragons, and knights. For a variety of teen book lists, see www.boulderteens.org.

Author	Title	Year	Age	Own	Recommend	To Read	Want
Tamora Pierce	*Alanna: The First Adventure*	2002	9				
Pamela F. Service	*Being of Two Minds*						
Meredith Ann Pierce	*Birth of the Firebringer*	2003	12				
Tanith Lee	*Black Unicorn*	2005					
Lloyd Alexander	*Book of Three*	1979	12				
Diana Wynne Jones	*Dark Lord of Derkholm* vvv	2001	9				
Patricia C. Wrede	*Dealing with Dragons*	1990	12				
E. Nesbit	*Five Children and It*	2008	9				
Patricia A. McKillip	*Forgotten Beasts of Eld*	1974	12				
Philip Pullman	*Golden Compass*	2001	15				
J. K. Rowling	*Harry Potter and the Sorcerer's Stone* ♦♦♦,♫♪,‡,∩,oo	2008	9				
Robin McKinley	*Hero and the Crown*	1984	12				
Diana Wynne Jones	*Howl's Moving Castle* $	2001	12				
T. A. Barron	*Lost Years of Merlin*	2002	15				
Patricia A. McKillip	*Riddle-Master of Hed*	1976	12				
Garth Nix	*Sabriel*	1997	15				

Author	Title	Year	Age	Own	Recommend	To Read	Want
Tamora Pierce	*Sandry's Book*	1999	9				
Victoria Hanley	*Seer and the Sword*	2000	12				
Gerald Morris	*Squire's Tale*	1998	15				
Kate Thompson	*Switchers*	1998	9				
Pamela F. Service	*Winter of Magic's Return*	1985	12				
Ursula K. Le Guin	*Wizard of Earthsea*	1999	12				
Madeleine L'Engle	*Wrinkle in Time*	1962	12				

Science Fiction

This science fiction list is another remarkable list from Connected Youth (Austin Public Library, TX). It offers a current mix of some of the best science fiction authors writing for young adults today. To see a list of titles, visit www.connectedyouth.org/books/index.cfm?booklist=scifi.

Author	Title	Year	Age	Own	Recommend	To Read	Want
Mary Pearson	*The Adoration of Jenna Fox*	2007	15				
Philip Reeve	*Mortal Engines*	2004	12				
Michael Carroll	*Quantum Prophecy: The Awakening*	2006	12				
Pete Hautman	*Rash* ^{x,£}	2007	12				
Charlotte Agel	*Shift*	2008	12				
Ann Halam	*Siberia*	2006	12				
Clare B. Dunkle	*The Sky Inside*	2008	12				
Chris Wooding	*Storm Thief*	2006	12				
Brian Falkner	*The Tomorrow Code*	2008	9				
Scott Westerfeld	*Uglies* ^{x,Ω,ΩΩΩ,‡,¶¶¶,ii,••}	2009	12				
Susan Beth Pfeffer	*Life As We Knew It* ^{#,Σ,ii,•••}	2006	12				

Science Fiction

Author	Title	Year	Age	Own	Recommend	To Read	Want
William Sleator	*The Last Universe*	2006	12				
Rodman Philbrick	*The Last Book in the Universe*	2002	12				
Kevin Brooks	*Being*	2007	15				
Dom Testa	*The Comet's Curse*	2009	15				
L. J. Adlington	*The Diary of Pelly D*	2008	12				
Conor Kostick	*Epic*	2007	12				
M. T. Anderson	*Feed* [1,x]	2004	12				
Nancy Farmer	*The House of the Scorpion* ##,♦♦♦,¶¶¶,o,¿,oo,3	2004	12				
Suzanne Collins	*The Hunger Games* ###,x,#	2009	15				
Patrick Ness	*The Knife of Never Letting Go*	2008	15				
Chris Roberson	*Iron Jaw and Hummingbird*	2008	12				
Neil Shusterman	*Unwind*	2009	12				

Paranormal Romance

Molly Lundquist of LitLovers.com defines paranormal romance as "paranormal stories that focus on romantic relationships and tortured lovers, often werewolves or vampires." The Twilight series by Stephenie Meyer is perhaps the most famous of these types of novels, but this list from Connected Youth (Austin Public Library, TX) proves the genre is full of other wonderful writers exploring the possibility of love with beings not quite of this world. For an abstract of each novel, see www.connectedyouth.org/books/index.cfm?booklist=paranormalrom.

Author	Title	Year	Age	Own	Recommend	To Read	Want
Alex Flinn	*Beastly*	2007	12				
Annette Curtis Klause	*Blood and Chocolate* [ii,oo]	2007	15				
Melissa de la Cruz	*Blue Bloods*	2009	12				
Cassandra Clare	*City of Bones* [#]	2008	15				

Author	Title	Year	Age	Own	Recommend	To Read	Want
Alyson Noel	*Evermore*	2009	15				
Claudia Gray	*Evernight*	2008	12				
Libba Bray	*A Great and Terrible Beauty* #,‡‡	2005	12				
P. C. Cast	*Marked: A House of Night Novel*	2007	12				
Suzanne Weyn	*Reincarnation*	2008	12				
Kelley Armstrong	*The Summoning*	2008	12				
Cynthia Leitich Smith	*Tantalize*	2008	15				
Holly Black	*Tithe*	2002	15				
Stephenie Meyer	*Twilight* #,♦♦♦,♫♫♫,Ω,ΩΩ,ΩΩΩ,‡,‡‡‡,¶,¶¶,¶¶¶, ii,•••,¿¿¿,◊,∩∩,3,¡,Σ	2005	15				
Ellen Schreiber	*Vampire Kisses*	2008	12				
Lisa McMann	*Wake* #	2008	15				
Melissa Marr	*Wicked Lovely (Faerie Queen)*	2007	12				

Romance

Looking for love? The Seattle Public Library (WA) has created a list filled with smitten teens, new boys, new friends, first kisses, crushes, matchmaking, and even true love—enough romance to satisfy even the most hopeless romantic. For a complete abstract of each title, visit www.spl.org/default.asp?pageID=audience_teens_bmm_readinglistAcid=1236960411248.

Author	Title	Year	Age	Own	Recommend	To Read	Want
Catherine Clark	*So Inn Love*	2007	15				
Dana Davidson	*Jason and Kyra*	2004	12				
Cameron Dokey	*The Storyteller's Daughter*	2007	12				
Jo Edwards	*Go Figure*	2007	12				
Debra Garfinkle	*Storky: How I Lost My Nickname and Won the Girl*	2005	14				

⬜ Juvenile Nonfiction   ⬜ Juvenile Fiction   ⬛ Fiction   ⬛ Nonfiction

Romance				Age	Own	Recommend	To Read	Want
Author	Title	Year						
Judy Goldschmidt	Raisin Rodriguez and the Big-Time Smooch	2007	9					
Shannon Hale	Book of a Thousand Days (Maid Maleen) ###	2007	12					
Eva Ibbotson	The Morning Gift	2007	15					
Steve Kluger	My Most Excellent Year	2009	12					
D. Anne Love	Defying the Diva	2008	12					
Jaclyn Moriarty	The Year of Secret Assignments **	2004	12					
Tyne O'Connell	True Love, the Sphinx, and Other Unsolvable Riddles	2007	12					
Julie Anne Peters	Far from Xanadu	2007	15					
Laura Peyton Roberts	The Queen of Second Place	2005	11					
Elizabeth Scott	Perfect You	2008	12					
Tucker Shaw	The Hookup Artist	2005	15					
Polly Shulman	Enthusiasm	2006	12					
Tanya Lee Stone	A Bad Boy Can be Good for a Girl	2007	12					
Rachel Vail	If We Kiss	2006	12					
Sara Zarr	Sweethearts	2009	12					

Love Stories for 13- to 15-Year-Olds

Common Sense Media "is dedicated to improving the media and entertainment lives of kids and families. [It exists] because media and entertainment profoundly impact the social, emotional, and physical development of our nation's children. As a non-partisan, not-for-profit organization, [it provides] trustworthy information and tools, as well as an independent forum, so that families can have a choice and a voice about the media they consume." Each listing has ratings and reviews from both parents and kids. More book lists and reviews can be found on the Common Sense Media website: www .commonsensemedia.org.

Author	Title	Year	Age	Own	Recommend	To Read	Want
Katherine Sturtevant	A True and Faithful Narrative	2006	12				
Stephenie Meyer	Twilight #,♦♦♦,♫♫♫,Ω,ΩΩ,ΩΩΩ,‡,‡‡‡,¶,¶¶,¶¶¶, ii,•••,¿¿¿,○,∩∩,∃,¡,Σ	2005	15				
John Green	An Abundance of Katherines	2008	15				
Norma Howe	The Adventures of Blue Avenger	2000	12				
Sonya Hartnett	The Ghost's Child	2008	15				
Kristin Cashore	Graceling ᵛᵛᵛ,#	2009	15				
Neil Gaiman	Stardust ˜	1999					
Meg Rosoff	Just in Case **	2008					
Walter Dean Myers	What They Found: Love on 145th Street	2007	15				

☐ Juvenile Nonfiction   ☐ Juvenile Fiction   ▉ Fiction   ▉ Nonfiction

Spur Storyteller Award—Best Juvenile Fiction and Nonfiction xxx

Since 1953, the Spur Award has been given annually by the Western Writers of America for distinguished writing about the American West. Reprinted with permission from the Western Writers of America, Inc. www .westernwriters.org.

Year	Author	Title	Age	Own	Recommend	To Read	Want
2011							
2010							
2009	Tanya Landman	I Am Apache	12				
2009	Frank Keating	The Trial of Standing Bear					
2008	Nancy Plain	Sagebrush and Paintbrush: The Story of Charlie Russell, the Cowboy Artist					
2008	Johnny D. Boggs	Doubtful Canon					
2007	Jeff C. Young	Bleeding Kansas and the Violent Clash Over Slavery in the Heartland	12				
2007	Joseph Bruchac	Geronimo	12				
2006	Diane Lee Wilson	Black Storm Comin'	12				
2006	Anthony Aveni	The First Americans: The Story of Where They Came From and Who They Became	12				
2005	Mary Cronk Farrell	Fire in the Hole!	9				
2005	Ednah New Rider Weber	Rattlesnake Mesa: Stories From A Native American Childhood	10				
2004	Ginger Wadsworth	Words West: Voices of Young Pioneers					
2004	E. Cody Kimmel	In the Eye of the Storm: The Adventures of Young Buffalo Bill	9				
2003	Mark G. Mitchell	Raising La Belle	12				
2003	Jeanette Ingold	The Big Burn	12				
2002	Gloria Skurzynski	Rockbuster	12				
2002	Russell Freedman	In the Days of the Vaqueros: America's First True Cowboys	12				

Year	Author	Title	Age	Own	Recommend	To Read	Want
2001	Violet T. Kimball	*Stories of Young Pioneers in Their Own Words*	10				
2001	Erika Tamar	*The Midnight Train Home*	12				
2000	Richard Maurer	*The Wild Colorado*	12				
2000	Brian Burks	*Wrango*					
1999	Ben Mikaelson	*Petey*	9				
1999	Erwin E. Smith	*Cowboy with a Camera*	12				
1998	Jennifer Owings Dewey	*Rattlesnake Dance*	10				
1998	Patricia Willis	*Danger Along the Ohio*	9				
1997	No award given						
1996	Will Hobbs	*Far North*	12				
1996	Russell Freedman	*The Life And Death Crazy Horse*	12				
1995	Sherry Garland	*Indio*	12				
1995	Diane Yancey	*Camels for Uncle Sam*	12				
1994	David Fremon	*A Trail of Tears*	12				
1993	Joann Mazzio	*Leaving Eldorado*	12				
1993	Albert Marrin	*Cowboys, Indians and Gunfighters* [†]	12				
1992	Gary Paulsen	*The Haymeadow*	12				
1992	Jerry Stanley	*Children of the Dust Bowl: The True Story of the School at Weedpatch* %%%	12				
1991	Ben Mikaelson	*Rescue Josh McGuire* ~~~,♪	12				
1990	Madge Harrah	*Honey Girl*					
1990	Gary Paulsen	*Woodsong*	12				
1989	Pam Conrad	*My Daniel*	12				
1988	Joan Lowery Nixon	*In the Face of Danger*	9				
1987	Joan Lowery Nixon	*The Orphan Train*	12				
1986	Jean Fritz	*Make Way for Sam Houston*	9				
1985	Pam Conrad	*Prairie Songs* ~~~,†	12				

☐ Juvenile Nonfiction ☐ Juvenile Fiction ■ Fiction ■ Nonfiction

Spur Storyteller Award—Best Juvenile Fiction and Nonfiction ˣˣˣ

Year	Author	Title	Age	Own	Recommend	To Read	Want
1984	Gloria Skurzynski	*Trapped in Slickrock Canyon*					
1983	Gary Clifton Wisler	*Thunder on the Tennessee*	12				
1982	Irene Bennett Brown	*Before the Lark*	12				
1981	Mark Jonathan Harris	*The Last Run*	12				

Western Heritage Award for Best Juvenile Book †

The National Cowboy and Western Heritage Museum in Oklahoma City presents the Western Heritage Award. By recognizing works of literature, music, television, and film, these awards help to preserve the legends and spirits of the West. Each honoree receives a Wrangler, an impressive bronze sculpture of a cowboy on horseback. More information is available at www .nationalcowboymuseum.org.

Year	Author	Title	Age	Own	Recommend	To Read	Want
2011							
2010							
2009	Melodie A. Cuate	*Journey to Gonzales*	9				
2008	Melodie A. Cuate	*Journey to San Jacinto*	8				
2007	James M. McPherson	*Into the West: From Reconstruction to the Final Days of the American Frontier*	10				
2006	Charlotte Foltz Jones	*Westward Ho! Eleven Explorers of the American West*	9				
2005	Simon J. Ortiz	*The Good Rainbow Road*	8				
2004	Hershell H. Nixon	*The Long Way West*					
2003	Lisa Waller Rogers	*The Great Storm: The Hurricane Diary of J.T. King*	12				
2002	Jo Harper	*Delfino's Journey*	12				
2001	Sharon E. Heisel	*Precious Gold Precious Jade*	12				
2000	Louise Erdrich	*The Birchbark House* ▼▼▼	9				

Year	Author	Title	Age	Own	Recommend	To Read	Want
1999	Kathryn Lasky	*Alice Rose & Sam*	10				
1998	Diane Johnston Hamm	*Daughter of Suqua*	8				
1997	Dayton Duncan	*The West*	12				
1996	Linda Theresa Raczek	*The Night the Grandfathers Danced*	7				
1995	Robert Crum	*Eagle Drum*	15				
1994	Albert Marrin	*Cowboys, Indians and Gunfighters* ˣˣˣ	12				
1993	Russell Freedman	*An Indian Winter*	9				
1992	Vee Brown	*Monster Slayer: A Navajo Folktale*	10				
1991	Diane Johnston Hamm	*Bunkhouse Journal*					
1990	Marj Gurasich	*Letters to Oma*					
1989	Francis G. Tunbo	*Stay Put Robbie Mcamis*					
1988	Lynn H. Scott	*The Covered Wagon and Other Adventures*	9				
1987	Arlene B. Hirshfelder	*Happily May I Walk* ♦♦♦	10				
1986	Pam Conrad	*Prairie Songs* ~~~,ˣˣˣ	12				
1984	Russell Freedman	*Children of the Wild West*	12				

Aesop Award ††

Since 1992, the Children's Folklore Section of the American Folklore Society has awarded the Aesop Prize and Aesop Accolades annually. Eligible books must be in the English language in fiction or nonfiction. Eligible nominees must be written in English and published during the previous two years. Folklore must be central to the book's content, and accurate to the beliefs and world-view of the represented culture. For more information, see www.ysu.edu/maag/service/research/subject_guides/Aesop.html.

Year	Author	Title	Age	Own	Recommend	To Read	Want
2010							

☐ Juvenile Nonfiction ◻ Juvenile Fiction ■ Fiction ■ Nonfiction

Aesop Award ††			Age	Own	Recommend	To Read	Want
Year	Author	Title					
2009							
2008	Scott Reynolds Nelson with Marc Aronson	Ain't Nothing But a Man: My Quest to Find the Real John Henry	8				
2007	Kathy Henderson	Lugalbanda: The Boy Who Got Caught Up in a War Kathy Henderson	8				
2007	Anne Sibley O'Brien	The Legend of Hong Kil Dong: The Robin Hood of Korea	9				
2006	Marge Bruchac	Malian's Song	7				
2006	Kathleen Ragan	Outfoxing Fear: Folktales from Around the World					
2005	Elvia Perez	From the Winds of Manguito: Cuban Folktales in English and Spanish					
2005	Mary E. Lyons	Roy Makes a Car	6				
2004	Baba Wague Diakite	The Magic Gourd					
2004	Sarah Conover and Freda Crane	Ayat Jamilah	15				
2003	Neil Philip	Horse Hooves and Chicken Feet	12				
2003	Jane Yolen	Mightier Than the Sword	12				
2002	Irma Molnar	One-time Dog Market at Buda and Other Hungarian Folktales	9				
2002	Judy Sierra	Can You Guess My Name?	15				
2001	Mary-Joan Gerson	Fiesta Feminina	12				
2000	Howard Schwartz	The Day the Rabbi Disappeared: Jewish Holiday Tales of Magic	12				
1999	Elie Wiesel	King Solomon and His Magic Ring	10				
1999	Howard Norman	Trickster and the Fainting Birds					
1998	Chief Lelooska	Echoes of the Elders	9				
1997	Robert San Souci	The Hired Hand: An African-American Folktale	9				
1997	Michael Caduto	Earth Tales from Around the World					
1996	Judy Sierra	Nursery Tales Around the World	7				

Year	Author	Title	Age	Own	Recommend	To Read	Want
1996	Howard Schwartz	*Next Year in Jerusalem*	9				
1995	Sharon Creeden	*Fair is Fair: World Folktales of Justice*					
1994	Julius Lester	*John Henry*	10				
1993	Paul Goble	*Love Flute*	10				
1993	Robert San Souci	*Cut from the Same Cloth*	12				
1992	Eric Kimmel	*Days of Awe*	12				
1992	Barbara Bader	*Aesop and Company with Scenes from His Legendary Life*	12				

Retellings: Fractured Fairy Tales and Folklore

Remember the first time you heard the story of Rapunzel, Hansel and Gretel, or Sleeping Beauty? Do you miss the enchantment these stories offered? The Cedar Mill Community Library (OR) and the Allen County Public Library (IN) offer some great suggestions that revive beloved fairy tales and folklore in this combined list. If you are missing the tales you loved as a kid or would like to explore some fairy tales and folklore you are unfamiliar with, this list offers some fun options. Be sure to check out both libraries' websites for other great lists: www.cedarmill.plinkit.org/kids-teens and www.booksforteens.pbworks.com.

Author	Title	Year	Age	Own	Recommend	To Read	Want
Elizabeth C. Bunce	*A Curse Dark as Gold (Rumpelstiltskin)*	2008	12				
Janet McNaughton	*An Earthly Knight (Tam Lin)*	2005	12				
Tiffany Grace	*Ariel (The Tempest)*	2005	12				
Donna Jo Napoli	*Beast (Beauty and the Beast)*	2004	12				
Alex Flinn	*Beastly (Beauty and the Beast)*	2007	12				
Robin McKinley	*Beauty (Beauty and the Beast)*	1993	12				
Cameron Dokey	*Beauty Sleep (Sleeping Beauty)*	2006	12				

☐ Juvenile Nonfiction   ☐ Juvenile Fiction   ■ Fiction   ■ Nonfiction

Retellings: Fractured Fairy Tales and Folklore							
Author	Title	Year	Age	Own	Recommend	To Read	Want
Shannon Hale	Book of a Thousand Days (Maid Maleen) ###	2007	12				
Donna Jo Napoli	Bound (Cinderella)	2004	12				
Donna Jo Napoli	Breath (The Pied Piper of Hamelin)	2005	12				
Jane Yolen	Briar Rose (Sleeping Beauty)	1993					
Donna Jo Napoli	Crazy Jack (Jack and the Beanstalk)	2001	12				
Lisa Feidler	Dating Hamlet: Ophelia's Story (Hamlet)	2002	15				
Juliet Marillier	Daughter of the Forest (The Wild Swans) ~	2001					
Jessica George	Day Sun and Moon, Ice and Snow (East of the Sun, West of the Moon)	2008	12				
Robin McKinley	Deerskin (Donkeyskin)	1994					
Edith Pattou	East (East of the Sun, West of the Moon)	2003	12				
Orson Scott Card	Enchantment (Sleeping Beauty)	2000					
Caroline B. Cooney	Enter Three Witches (Macbeth)	2007	12				
Cameron Dokey	Golden (Rapunzel)	2007	12				
Shannon Hale	Goose Girl (Goose Girl)	2005	12				
Donna Jo Napoli	Great God Pan (Pan)	1995	9				
Patrice Kindle	Lost in the Labyrinth (Minotaur)	2002	12				
Donna Jo Napoli	Magic Circle (Hansel & Gretel)	1995	12				
Elizabeth Marie Pope	The Perilous Gard (Tamlin)	2001	12				
Debbie Viguie	Midnight Pearls (The Little Mermaid)	2006	12				
Mette Ivie Harrison	Mira, Mirror (Snow White)	2006	12				
Jane Yolen	Pay the Piper (Pied Piper) vv	2005	9				
Dave Barry	Peter and the Starcatchers (Peter Pan)	2004	9				
Dia Calhoun	Phoenix Dance (12 Dancing Princesses)	2005	11				

Author	Title	Year	Age	Own	Recommend	To Read	Want
Stephanie Spinner	*Quiver (Atlanta)*	2002	9				
Robin McKinley	*Rose Daughter (Beauty and the Beast)*	1997	12				
Debbie Viguie	*Scarlet Moon (Little Red Riding Hood)*	2004	12				
Frank Beddor	*Seeing Redd: Looking Glass Wars (Alice in Wonderland)*	2007	12				
Susan Fletcher	*Shadow Spinner (Arabian Nights)*	1999	12				
L. G. Bass	*Sign of the Qin (Chinese Myths)*	2004	9				
Donna Jo Napoli	*Sirena (The Little Mermaid)*	2000	12				
Tracy Lynn	*Snow (Snow White)*	2006	12				
Robin McKinley	*Spindle's End (Sleeping Beauty)*	2001	12				
Donna Jo Napoli	*Spinners (Rumpelstiltskin)*	1999	12				
Cameron Dokey	*Storyteller's Daughter (Scherazade)*	2007	12				
Cameron Dokey	*Sunlight and Shadow (The Magic Flute)*	2004	12				
Margo Lanagan	*Tender Morsels (Snow White & Rose Redd)*	2008	15				
Mercedes Lackey	*The Firebird (The Firebird)*	1996					
Rick Riordan	*The Lightning Thief (Greek Myth)* ##,♦♦♦,‡‡,£££,¶¶,33,¿¿¿¿,3,••	2005	9				
Donna Jo Napoli	*The Magic Circle (Hansel and Gretel)*	1995	12				
Suzanne Weyn	*The Night Dance (The Twelve Dancing Princesses)*	2008	12				
Suzanne Weyn	*Water Song (The Frog Prince)*	2006	12				
Gregory Maguire	*Wicked (Wizard of Oz)*	1995					
Melissa Marr	*Wicked Lovely (Faerie Queen)*	2007	12				
Patricia A. McKillip	*Winter Rose (Tamlin)*	2002					
Diana Jones	*Wynne Fire and Hemlock (Tamlin)*	1985					
Donna Jo Napoli	*Zel (Rapunzel)*	1998	12				

Juvenile Nonfiction   Juvenile Fiction   ■ Fiction   ■ Nonfiction

Will Eisner Comic Industry Award—Best Title for a Younger Audience †††

Each year at Comic-Con International, the largest and oldest comics convention in the United States, the Will Eisner Comic Industry Award is handed out in a gala ceremony. The awards, named for cartoonist Eisner, creator of the *Spirit* and several award-winning graphic novels, encompass more than two dozen categories including best short story, best graphic album, best title for a younger audience, and more. A committee of famous and well-renowned members select finalists from thousands of entries submitted by publishers and creators. For more information, see http://www.comic-con.org/cci/cci_eisners_main.shtml.

Year	Author	Title	Age	Own	Recommend	To Read	Want
2011							
2010							
2009	Neil Gaiman	*Coraline* Ⱳ	9				
2008	Nick Abadzis	*Laika*					
2007	Bob Burden and Rick Geary	*Gumby*	12				
2006	Andy Runton	*Owly: Flying Lessons*	12				
2005	Kyle Baker and Scott Morse	*Plastic Man*	12				
2004	Various	*Walt Disney's Uncle Scrooge*					
2003	Mike Kunkel	*Herobear and the Kid*	10				
2002	Mike Kunkel	*Herobear and the Kid*	10				
2001	Jill Thompson	*Scary Godmother: The Boo Flu*	8				
2000	Various	*Simpsons Comics*					
1999	Ty Templeton, Rick Burchett and Terry Beatty	*Batman: The Gotham Adventures*					
1998	Ty Templeton, Brandon Kruse, Rick Burchett and Others	*Batman & Robin Adventures*					
1997	James Robinson and Paul Smith	*Leave It to Chance*					
1996	Paul Dini, Ty Templeton and Rick Burchett	*The Batman and Robin Adventures*					

YALSA Top Ten Graphic Novels

The Young Adult Library Services Association (YALSA) published its first annual list Great Graphic Novels for Teens in January 2007. In doing so, YALSA, the fastest growing division of the American Library Association (ALA), acknowledged the burgeoning popularity of this genre among young adults. To qualify for consideration, books must be written and illustrated in a sequential, comic-book-style format, suitable for readers aged 12–18, and published between September 1 of the previous year and December 31 of the award year. Each year's selection committee tries to include high-quality graphic novels from the whole spectrum of nominated works–from serious nonfiction to rich fantasy and from romantic manga to parodies of classic superhero comics. In addition, each of the Great Graphic Novels for Teens committees creates a top-ten list exemplifying the quality, range, and appeal of graphic novels appropriate for teen audiences. To see all the graphic novel picks since 2007, got to www.ala .org/yalsa/ggnt.

Year	Author	Title	Age	Own	Recommend	To Read	Want
2009	Jessica Abel, Gabriel Soria and Warren Pleece	*Life Sucks*	12				
2009	Hinako Ashihara	*Sand Chronicles, Vol. 1*	12				
2009	Hinako Ashihara	*Sand Chronicles, Vol. 2*	12				
2009	Hinako Ashihara	*Sand Chronicles, Vol. 3*	12				
2009	Brian Clevinger and Steve Wegener	*Atomic Robo: Atomic Robo and the Fightin' Scientists of Tesladyne*					
2009	Takehiko Inoue	*Real Vol. 1*					
2009	Takehiko Inoue	*Real Vol. 2*					
2009	Junki Ito	*Uzumaki Vol. 1*	15				
2009	Youme Landowne and Anthony Horton	*Pitch Black*					
2009	Aimee Major Steinberger	*Japan Ai: A Tall Girl's Adventures in Japan*	12				
2009	Mariko Tamaki and Jilliam Tamaki	*Skim*	12				
2009	Gerard Way and Gabriel Ba	*Umbrella Academy: Apocalypse Suite*					

☐ Juvenile Nonfiction   ☐ Juvenile Fiction   ■ Fiction   ■ Nonfiction

YALSA Top Ten Graphic Novels			Age	Own	Recommend	To Read	Want
Year	Author	Title					
2009	G. Willow Wilson and M. K. Perker	Cairo					

Manga Mania

The Carnegie Public Library's (PA) Manga Mania list is perfect for anyone interested in Manga, but not sure where to start. Most of the titles on the Manga Mania list are a series, therefore the earliest publication year for the first in the series is listed. To see a synopsis of each series, visit www.carnegielibrary.org/teens/books/showbooklist2.cfm?catid=6&list=manga.

Author	Title	Year	Age	Own	Recommend	To Read	Want
Arakawa Hiromu	Fullmetal Alchemist	2005	12				
Hirano Kohta	Hellsing						
Kawai Chigusa	La Esperanca	2005					
Kishimoto Masashi	Naruto	2002					
Konomi Takeshi	The Prince of Tennis	2008					
Kubo Tite	Bleach	2008					
Maki Murakami	Gravitation	2004	8				
Hisaya Nakajo	Hana-Kimi: For You in Full Blossom	2004					
Nonaka Eiji	Cromartie High School	2005					
Oda Eiichiro	One Piece	2003	12				
Ohba Tsugumi	Death Note	2008					
Tsuda Masami	Kare Kano: His and Her Circumstances	2003	12				

Rainbow Project

"The Rainbow Project is proud to announce the 2009 Rainbow List, a joint undertaking of the American Library Association's Gay, Lesbian, Bisexual, and Transgendered Round Table and Social Responsibilities Round Table. Featuring well-written and/or well-illustrated titles with authentic and significant gay/lesbian/bisexual/transgendered/queer/questioning (GLBTQ) content for youth from birth through age 18, this year's bibliography presents 34 outstanding titles, published in the last eighteen months and representing a broad range of GLBTQ experience." For a summary of each title and more information about the Rainbow Project, see www.rainbowlist.wordpress.com/rl-2009.

Author	Title	Year	Age	Own	Recommend	To Read	Want
A. C. E. Bauer	No Castles Here	2007	9				
Jacqueline Woodson	After Tupac & D Foster	2008	12				
Tamara Bach	Girl from Mars	2008	12				
Meagan Brothers	Debbie Harry Sings in French	2008	12				
Rachel Cohn and David Levithan	Naomi and Ely's No Kiss List	2007	15				
Mayra Lazara Dole	Down to the Bone	2008	15				
Kristyn Dunnion	Big Big Sky	2008	15				
Michael Thomas Ford	Suicide Notes	2008	12				
Marjetta Geerling	Fancy White Trash	2008	12				
Steven Goldman	Two Parties, One Tux, and a Very Short Film about the Grapes of Wrath	2008	12				
Stephanie Grant	Map of Ireland	2008	13				
Mark Hardy	Nothing Pink	2008	15				
Michael Harmon	Last Exit to Normal	2008	15				
Tonya Cherie Hegamin	M+O 4EVR	2008	12				
Susan Juby	Another Kind of Cowboy	2007	12				
Steve Kluger	My Most Excellent Year: A Novel of Love, Mary Poppins, & Fenway Park	2008	12				
Bill Konigsberg	Out of the Pocket	2008	15				

☐ Juvenile Nonfiction   ☐ Juvenile Fiction   ■ Fiction   ■ Nonfiction

Rainbow Project

Author	Title	Year	Age	Own	Recommend	To Read	Want
David Levithan	*How They Met, and Other Stories*	2008	12				
Leanne Lieberman	*Gravity*	2008	12				
Jennifer McMahon	*My Tiki Girl*	2008	15				
Patricia G. Penny	*Belinda's Obsession*	2007	12				
Selina Rosen	*Sword Masters*	2008					
Jeff Rud	*Crossover*	2008	9				
Paul Ruditis	*Entrances and Exits*	2008	12				
Mariko Tamaki and Jil-liam Tamaki	*Skim*	2008	12				
Martin Wilson	*What They Always Tell Us*	2008	12				
Ellen Wittlinger	*Love & Lies: Marisol's Story*	2008	12				
Nonfiction							
Linas Alsenas	*Gay America: Struggle for Equality*	2008	15				
Robert Leleux	*The Memoirs of a Beautiful Boy*	2008					
Joanne Passet	*Sex Variant Woman: The Life of Jeannette Howard Foster*	2008					
Scott Turner Schofield	*Two Truths and a Lie: A Memoir*	2008					
Ariel Schrag	*Awkward and Definition*	2008					

Best GLBTQ Fiction and Nonfiction

The Hennepin County Library (MN) hosts an amazing website called Teen-Links, dedicated to everything teen related. Links on the website include Web comics, puzzles, quizzes, and book talks, as well as author websites and blogs. In addition, Teenlinks contains comprehensive reading resources by publishing over fifty book lists. Teenlinks' GLBTQ list aims to be the best in gay, lesbian, bisexual, transgender and questioning fiction and nonfiction for teens. See www.hclib.org/teens/read.cfm for all of these resources.

Author	Title	Year	Age	Own	Recommend	To Read	Want
Charlie Anders	*Choir Boy*	2005	12				

Author	Title	Year	Age	Own	Recommend	To Read	Want
Catherine Atkins	*Alt Ed*	2004	12				
Cris Beam	*Transparent: Love Family and Living the T with Transgender Teenagers*	2007					
Meagan Brothers	*Debbie Harry Sings in French*	2008	12				
Eddie De Oliveira	*Lucky*	2004	15				
Michael Thomas Ford	*Suicide Notes*	2008	12				
Garret Freymann-Weyr	*My Heartbeat*	2002	12				
Nancy Garden	*Annie on My Mind*	2007	15				
John Hall	*Is He or isn't He?*	2006	15				
Brent Hartinger	*Geography Club*	2003	12				
Kelly Huegel	*GLBTQ (Gay, Lesbian, Bisexual, Transgender, Questioning): The Survival Guide for Queer and Questioning Teen*	2003	12				
Catherine Ryan Hyde	*Becoming Chloe*	2006	15				
Maureen Johnson	*The Bermudez Triangle*	2005	15				
Susan Juby	*Another Kind of Cowboy*	2007	12				
Lisa Keen	*Out Law: What LGBT Youth Should Know About Their Legal Rights*	2007	15				
Ronald Koertge	*Boy Girl Boy*	2005	15				
Kathe Koja	*Talk*	2008	12				
Bill Konigsberg	*Out of the Pocket*	2008	15				
David LaRochelle	*Absolutely Positively Not*	2005	15				
James Lecesne	*Absolute Brightness*	2008	12				
David Levithan	*Boy Meets Boy*	2005	12				
David Levithan	*Wide Awake*	2006	15				
Leanne Lieberman	*Gravity*	2008	12				
Brian Malloy	*Twelve Long Months* ££	2008	15				
Sarra Manning	*Pretty Things*	2006	12				

☐ Juvenile Nonfiction   ☐ Juvenile Fiction   ■ Fiction   ■ Nonfiction

Best GLBTQ Fiction and Nonfiction

Author	Title	Year	Age	Own	Recommend	To Read	Want
Lauren Myracle	*Kissing Kate*	2007	15				
Julie Anne Peters	*Grl2grl: Short Fictions*	2007	15				
Julie Anne Peters	*Keeping You a Secret*	2005	15				
Julie Anne Peters	*Luna*	2006	15				
Sara Ryan	*Empress of the World* ⌊⌊	2001	9				
Alex Sanchez	*So Hard to Say*	2004	12				
Alex Sanchez	*The God Box*	2007	12				
Tucker Shaw	*The Hookup Artist*	2005					
Brian K. Vaughan	*Runaways, Vol. 1 Pride Joy*	2003	12				
Rich Wallace	*Dishes*	2008	15				
Martin Wilson	*What They Always Tell Us*	2008	12				
Ellen Wittlinger	*Hard Love* £	2001	12				
Ellen Wittlinger	*Parrotfish*	2007	12				
Sharon Dennis Wyeth	*Orphea Proud*	2006	12				

IRA Lee Bennett Hopkins Promising Poet Award *

The International Reading Association (IRA) Lee Bennett Hopkins Promising Poet Award is given every three years to the author of new children's poetry (birth to grade 12) who has published no more than two books. The award is for published works only. A book-length single poem may be submitted. Poetry in any language may be submitted; non-English poetry must be accompanied by an English translation. The next award will be for poetry copyrighted from 2007 to 2009.

Year	Author	Title	Age	Own	Recommend	To Read	Want
2013							
2010							
2007	Joyce Lee Wong	*Seeing Emily*	15				
2004	Lindsay Lee Johnson	*Soul Moon Soup*	12				

Year	Author	Title	Age	Own	Recommend	To Read	Want
2001	Craig Crist-Evans	Moon Over Tennessee: A Boy's Civil War Journal	8				
1998	Kristine O'Connell George	The Great Frog Race and Other Poems	7				
1995	Deborah Chandra	Rich Lizard and Other Poems	8				

Poetry for Teens

The Carnegie Library in Pittsburgh, Pennsylvania, publishes a beautiful website dedicated to teens (www.clpgh.org/teens/books). Included on the site are multiple book lists devoted to teens and their interests. Listed here is the library's recommended list of poetry for teens.

Author	Title	Year	Age	Own	Recommend	To Read	Want
Kathi Appelt	Poems from Homeroom: A Writer's Place to Start	2002	15				
Lori M. Carlson	Red Hot Salsa: Bilingual Poems on Being Young and Latino in the United States	2005	12				
Paul B. Janeczko	Blushing: Expressions of Love in Poems and Letters	2004	12				
Naomi Shihab Nye	A Maze Me: Poems for Girls	2005	12				
Liz Rosenberg	I Just Hope It's Lethal: Poems of Sadness, Madness, and Joy	2005	12				
Liz Rosenberg	Roots & Flowers: Poets and Poems on Family	2001	12				
Cynthia Rylant	Boris	2005	15				
Joyce Sidman	The World According to Dog: Poems and Teen Voices	2008	9				
Gary Soto	A Fire in My Hands: Poems	1991	9				
WritersCorps	Paint Me Like I Am: Teen Poems	2003	12				

☐ Juvenile Nonfiction ▨ Juvenile Fiction ■ Fiction ■ Nonfiction

Novels in Verse

The Connected Young Site of the Austin Public Library provides a varied, updated list of novels in verse, a style that is quickly becoming popular with teens. The novel in verse is a novel-length story told through free verse poetry instead of prose. There is no rhyming system or meter. For more information, see www.connectedyouth.org/books/index.cfm?booklist=verse.

Author	Title	Year	Age	Own	Recommend	To Read	Want
Karen Hesse	*Aleutian Sparrow*	2005	12				
Tanya Lee Stone	*A Bad Boy Can be Good for a Girl*	2007	12				
Steven Herrick	*By the River*	2006	12				
Judith Ortiz Cofer	*Call Me Maria*	2006	12				
Ellen Hopkins	*Crank* ΩΩΩ,¶,*,ΩΩ	2008	12				
Juan Felipe Herrera	*CrashBoomLove: A Novel in Verse* ♥♥	1999	15				
Kristen Smith	*The Geography of Girlhood*	2007	12				
Cynthia Rylant	*God Went to Beauty School*	2003	12				
Ann Warren Turner	*Hard Hit*	2006	12				
Susan Taylor Brown	*Hugging the Rock*	2006	12				
Margaret Wild	*Jinx*	2004	12				
Helen Frost	*Keesha's House*	2007	12				
Sonya Sones	*One of Those Hideous Books Where The Mother Dies* ‡‡,o,3	2005	15				
Margaret Wild	*One Night*	2004	15				
Karen Hesse	*Out of the Dust* ^	2006	12				
David Levithan	*The Realm of Possiblility*	2004	12				
Ellen Yeomans	*Rubber Houses*	2009	12				
Kelly Bingham	*Shark Girl*	2007	12				
Lisa Ann Sandell	*Song of the Sparrow*	2007	12				
Sonya Sones	*Stop Pretending: What Happened When My Big Sister Went Crazy*	2001	12				
Walter Dean Myers	*Street Love*	2007	12				

Author	Title	Year	Age	Own	Recommend	To Read	Want
Stephanie Hemphill	*Things Left Unsaid*	2005	12				
Mel Glenn	*Who Killed Mr. Chippendale?: A Mystery in Poems*	1999	12				

101 Great Books: Recommended for College-Bound Readers

The College Board, sponsors of the Scholastic Assessment Test (SAT) and the Advance Placement (AP) Program, has compiled the next two reading lists, 101 Great Books: Recommended for College-Bound Readers and Poetry and Cultural Classics, as part of its High School Steps for helping kids get to college. See www.collegeboard.com/parents/plan/hs-steps/index.html for more information.

Author	Title	Year	Age	Own	Recommend	To Read	Want
James Agee	*A Death in the Family*	1956					
Henrik Ibsen	*A Doll's House*	1879					
Ernest Hemingway	*A Farewell to Arms*	1929					
Flannery O'Connor	*A Good Man is Hard to Find*	1955					
William Shakespeare	*A Midsummer Night's Dream*	1623					
James Joyce	*A Portrait of the Artist as a Young Man*	1917					
Charles Dickens	*A Tale of Two Cities*	1859					
Erich Maria Remarque	*All Quiet on the Western Front*	1929					
Theodore Dreiser	*An American Tragedy*	1925					
George Orwell	*Animal Farm*	1945					
Sophocles	*Antigone*	442 BC					
William Faulkner	*As I Lay Dying*	1930					
Sinclair Lewis	*Babbitt*	1922					
Herman Melville	*Bartleby the Scrivener*	1853					

▢ Juvenile Nonfiction   ▢ Juvenile Fiction   ▪ Fiction   ▪ Nonfiction

101 Great Books: Recommended for College-Bound Readers			Age	Own	Recommend	To Read	Want
Author	Title	Year					
Toni Morrison	Beloved	1987					
--	Beowolf	est 1010					
Aldous Huxley	Brave New World	1932					
Henry Roth	Call It Sleep	1934					
Voltaire	Candide	1759					
Joseph Heller	Catch-22	1961					
Leslie Marmon Silko	Ceremony	1977					
Eudora Welty	Collected Stories	1980					
Fyodor Dostoyevsky	Crime and Punishment	1866					
Edmond Rostand	Cyrano De Bergerac	1897					
Willa Cather	Death Comes for the Archbishop	1927					
Boris Pasternak	Doctor Zhivago	1957					
Miguel De Cervantes	Don Quixote	1605					
Ivan Turgenev	Fathers and Sons	1862					
Johann Wolfgang Von Goethe	Faust	1806					
Mary Wollstonecraft Shelley	Frankenstein or the Modern Prometheus	1818					
James Baldwin	Go Tell It on the Mountain	1953					
Jonathan Swift	Gulliver's Travels	1726					
William Shakespeare	Hamlet	1599					
Joseph Conrad	Heart of Darkness	1899					
Dante	Inferno	est 1300					
Ralph Ellison	Invisible Man	1952					
Charlotte Bronte	Jane Eyre	1847					
Walt Whitman	Leaves of Grass	1855					
Eugene O'Neill	Long Day's Journey Into Night	1956					
William Golding	Lord of the Flies	1955					
William Shakespeare	Macbeth	1606					

Author	Title	Year	Age	Own	Recommend	To Read	Want
Gustave Flaubert	Madame Bovary	1857					
Herman Melville	Moby Dick	1851					
Frederick Douglass	Narrative of the Life of Frederick Douglass	1845					
Richard Wright	Native Son	1940					
Sophocles	Oedipus Rex	429 BC					
Alexander Solzhenitsyn	One Day in the Life of Ivan Denisovich	1963					
Gabriel García Márquez	One Hundred Years of Solitude	1970					
Jane Austen	Pride and Prejudice	1813					
George Bernard Shaw	Pygmalion	1967					
Daniel Defoe	Robinson Crusoe	1719					
William Shakespeare	Romeo and Juliet	1595					
Ralph Waldo Emerson	Selected Essays	1860					
Edgar Allan Poe	Selected Tales	1850					
Kurt Vonnegut Jr.	Slaughterhouse-Five	1969					
Marcel Proust	Swann's Way	1927					
Thomas Hardy	Tess of the D'Urbervilles	1891					
Saul Bellow	The Adventures of Augie March	1953					
Mark Twain	The Adventures of Huckleberry Finn	1884					
Kate Chopin	The Awakening	1899					
Sylvia Plath	The Bell Jar	1963					
Jack London	The Call of the Wild	1903	12				
Geoffrey Chaucer	The Canterbury Tales	est 1400					
J. D. Salinger	The Catcher in the Rye	1951					
Anton Chekhov	The Cherry Orchard	1904					
Alice Walker	The Color Purple	1982					
Arthur Miller	The Crucible	1953					

☐ Juvenile Nonfiction ☐ Juvenile Fiction ■ Fiction ■ Nonfiction

101 Great Books: Recommended for College-Bound Readers			Age	Own	Recommend	To Read	Want
Author	**Title**	**Year**					
Thomas Pynchon	The Crying of Lot 49	1966					
Tennessee Williams	The Glass Menagerie	1944					
Ford Madox Ford	The Good Soldier	1915					
John Steinbeck	The Grapes of Wrath	1939					
F. Scott Fitzgerald	The Great Gatsby	1925					
Edith Wharton	The House of Mirth	1905					
Victor Hugo	The Hunchback of Notre Dame	1831					
Homer	The Iliad	800 BC					
James Fenimore Cooper	The Last of the Mohicans	1826					
Thomas Mann	The Magic Mountain	1924					
Franz Kafka	The Metamorphosis	1915					
George Eliot	The Mill on the Floss	1860					
Homer	The Odyssey	800 BC					
Oscar Wilde	The Picture of Dorian Gray	1890					
Henry James	The Portrait of a Lady	1881					
Stephen Crane	The Red Badge of Courage	1895	12				
Nathaniel Hawthorne	The Scarlet Letter	1850					
William Faulkner	The Sound and the Fury	1929					
Albert Camus	The Stranger	1943					
Alexandre Dumas	The Three Musketeers	1844					
Henry James	The Turn of the Screw	1898					
Maxine Hong Kingston	The Woman Warrior	1975					
Zora Neale Hurston	Their Eyes Were Watching God	1937					
Chinua Achebe	Things Fall Apart	1958					
Harper Lee	To Kill a Mockingbird	1960					
Virginia Woolf	To the Lighthouse	1927					
Henry Fielding	Tom Jones	1749					
Robert Louis Stevenson	Treasure Island	1883					
Harriet Beecher Stowe	Uncle Tom's Cabin	1852					

Author	Title	Year	Age	Own	Recommend	To Read	Want
William Thackeray	*Vanity Fair*	1848					
Samuel Beckett	*Waiting for Godot*	1953					
Henry David Thoreau	*Walden*	1854					
Leo Tolstoy	*War and Peace*	1869					
Emily Bronte	*Wuthering Heights*	1847					

Poetry and Cultural Classics—College Board

Author	Title	Year	Age	Own	Recommend	To Read	Want
Classic Cultural and Historical Texts							
---	*The Arabian Nights*	1706					
John F. Kennedy	*Profiles in Courage*	1955					
---	*The Bible*						
Martin Luther Jr. King	*A Testament of Hope: The Essential Writings and Speeches of Martin Luther King, Jr.*	1986					
Henry Adams	*The Education of Henry Adams*	1918					
Sir Thomas Malory	*Le Morte D'Arthur*	1485					
Aesop	*Aesop's Fables*	560 BC	8				
Niccolo Machiavelli	*The Prince*	1535					
Hans Christian Andersen	*Andersen's Fairy Tales*	1836	8				
Karl Marx	*The Communist Manifesto*	1848					
Aristotle	*Nicomachean Ethics*	350 BC					
Thomas Paine	*Common Sense*	1776					
W. E. B. DuBois	*The Souls of Black Folk*	1903					
Plato	*The Republic*	380 BC					

☐ Juvenile Nonfiction   ☐ Juvenile Fiction   ■ Fiction   ■ Nonfiction

Poetry and Cultural Classics—College Board			Age	Own	Recommend	To Read	Want
Author	Title	Year					
Benjamin Franklin	Autobiography	1793					
Alexis de Tocqueville	Democracy in America	1835					
Edith Hamilton	Mythology	1942					
Malcolm X	The Autobiography of Malcolm X	1965					
John Hamilton	The Federalist Papers	1788					
Poetry							
William Blake	London and the Tyger	1794					
John Keats	Ode on a Grecian Urn, La Belle Dame Sans Merci, and the Eve of St. Agnes	1819					
Gwendolyn Brooks	We Real Cool, the Mother, and the Bean Eaters	2003					
Marianne Moore	Marriage, Poetry, and the Fish	1940					
Samuel Taylor Coleridge	The Rime of the Ancient Mariner, Kubla Khan, and Frost at Midnight	1798					
Frank O'Hara	Why I Am Not a Painter, the Day Lady Died, and Poem (Lana Turner Has Collapsed)	1966					
Emily Dickinson	There's a Certain Slant of Light (258), I Felt a Funeral, in My Brain (280), and Because I Could Not Stop for Death (712)	1862					
William Shakespeare	Sonnets	1609					
John Donne	A Valediction: Forbidding Mourning, Death, Be Not Proud (Holy Sonnet 10), and the Flea	1633					
Gertrude Stein	Tender Buttons and Stanzas in Meditation	1914					
T. S. Eliot	The Waste Land and the Love Song of J. Alfred Prufrock	1922					
William Carlos Williams	The Red Wheelbarrow, This is Just to Say, and Spring and All	1923					
Gerard Manley Hopkins	God's Grandeur, Windhover, and Carrion Comfort	1889					

Author	Title	Year	Age	Own	Recommend	To Read	Want
William Wordsworth	*Tintern Abbey, Prelude, and Lyrical Ballads (with S.T. Coleridge)*	1850					
Langston Hughes	*Theme for English B and the Negro Speaks of Rivers*	1922					

Outstanding Books for the College Bound— Arts and Humanities

The Young Adult Library Services Association, part of the America Library Association, has created five suggestion lists for teens bound for college. The association's website provides a description of the lists and their intentions: "The books on this list offer opportunities to discover new ideas, and provide an introduction to the fascinating variety of subjects within an academic discipline. Readers will gain an understanding of our diverse world and build a foundation to deepen their response to that world. A YALSA Committee of public, secondary school, and academic librarians selects the list. Revised every five years as a tool for several audiences (students preparing for college, educators, librarians, and parents) it offers opportunities for independent reading and lifelong learning. Use it to round out your reading as you prepare for college entrance exams and courses, to strengthen your knowledge in a variety of subject areas and enhance appreciation for different cultures and times." For more information, visit www.ala.org/yalsa/booklists/obcb.

Author	Title	Year	Age	Own	Recommend	To Read	Want
Carmen Bernier-Grand	*Frida: Viva la Vida! Long Live Life!*	2007	12				
Karen Blumenthal	*Let Me Play: The Story of Title IX: The Law That Changed the Future of Girls in America*	2005	9				
John Bowker	*World Religions: The Great Faiths Explored and Explained*	2006					
Bill Bryson	*Shakespeare: The World as Stage*	2007					

☐ Juvenile Nonfiction　☐ Juvenile Fiction　■ Fiction　■ Nonfiction

Outstanding Books for the College Bound—Arts and Humanities							
Author	Title	Year	Age	Own	Recommend	To Read	Want
Joseph Campbell and Bill Moyers	The Power of Myth	1991					
Anita Diamant	The Red Tent	1997					
Michael D'Orso	Eagle Blue: A Team, a Tribe, and a High School Basketball Season in Arctic Alaska ~	2006					
Margarita Engle	The Poet Slave of Cuba: A Biography of Juan Francisco Manzano ~~~,♥♥	2006	12				
Ken Follett	Pillars of the Earth	1989					
Russell Freedman	The Voice That Challenged A Nation: Marian Anderson and the Struggle for Equal Rights ♦♦,♦♦♦	2004	9				
Jan Greenberg	Heart to Heart: New Poems Inspired by Twentieth-Century American Art	2001	12				
Sara Gruen	Water for Elephants ~	2006					
Stephanie Hemphill	Your Own, Sylvia: A Verse Portrait of Sylvia Plath	2007	12				
Peter Howe	Shooting Under Fire: The World of the War Photographer	2002					
A. J. Jacobs	The Year of Living Biblically: One Man's Humble Quest to Follow the Bible as Literally as Possible	2007					
Melissa King	She's Got Next: A Story of Getting In, Staying Open, and Taking a Shot	2005					
Deborah Nadoolman Landis	Dressed: A Century of Hollywood Costume Design	2007					
Steve Martin	Born Standing Up: A Comic's Life	2008					
Tom McGreevey and Joanne L . Yeck	Our Movie Heritage	1997					
Elizabeth Partridge	John Lennon: All I Want is the Truth	2005	12				
Elizabeth Partridge	This Land Was Made For You and Me: The Life and Songs of Woody Guthrie ***	2002	12				

Author	Title	Year	Age	Own	Recommend	To Read	Want
Matthew Polly	American Shaolin: Flying Kicks, Buddhist Monks, and the Legend of Iron Crotch: An Odyssey in the New China ˜	2007					
Martin Sandler	Photography: An Illustrated History	2002	15				
Carol Strickland	The Annotated Mona Lisa: A Crash Course in Art History from Prehistoric to Post-Modern	2007					
Sheila Weller	Girls Like Us: Carole King, Joni Mitchell, Carly Simon, and the Journey of a Generation	2008					

Outstanding Books for the College Bound— History and Cultures

Author	Title	Year	Age	Own	Recommend	To Read	Want
Dohra Ahmad	Rotten English: A Literary Anthology	2007					
Sherman Alexie	The Absolutely True Diary of a Part-Time Indian ˙˙˙˙˙♥♥♥♪♪♪	2007	12				
Adam Bagdasarian	Forgotten Fire: A Novel	2002	12				
Rajiv Chandrasekaran	Imperial Life in the Emerald City: Inside Iraq's Green Zone	2007					
Iris Chang	The Rape of Nanking: The Forgotten Holocaust of World War II	1998					
David Chotjewitz	Daniel Half-Human and the Good Nazi	2004	12				
Guy Delisle	Pyongyang: A Journey in North Korea	2007					
Jared Diamond	Collapse: How Societies Choose to Fail or Succeed	2005					
Junot Diaz	The Brief Wondrous Life of Oscar Wao	2007					

☐ Juvenile Nonfiction   ☐ Juvenile Fiction   ■ Fiction   ■ Nonfiction

Outstanding Books for the College Bound— History and Cultures			Age	Own	Recommend	To Read	Want
Author	**Title**	**Year**					
Timothy Egan	The Worst Hard Time: The Untold Story of Those Who Survived the Great American Dust Bowl	2005					
Dave Eggers	What is the What: The Autobiography of Valentino Achak Deng	2007					
Anne Fadiman	The Spirit Catches You and You Fall Down: A Hmong Child, Her American Doctors, and the Collision of Two Cultures	1998					
Anne Marie Fleming	The Magical Life of Long Tack Sam	2007					
Edward P. Jones	The Known World	2003					
Tony Horwitz	A Voyage Long and Strange: Rediscovering the New World	2008					
Erik Larson	The Devil in the White City: Murder, Magic and Madness at the Fair that Changed America	2004					
Thomas Maltman	The Night Birds ~	2008					
Gene Roberts and Hank Klibanoff	The Race Beat: The Press, the Civil Rights Struggle, and the Awakening of a Nation	2007					
Benjamin Alire Sáenz	Sammy and Juliana in Hollywood ▾▾	2006					
Marjane Satrapi	The Complete Persepolis	2007					
Art Spiegelman	The Complete Maus: A Survivor's Tale	1996					
Loung Ung	First They Killed My Father: A Daughter of Cambodia Remembers	2006					
Tim Weiner	Legacy of Ashes: The History of the CIA	2008					
David Williams	Bitterly Divided: The South's Inner Civil War	2008					
Allan Wolf	New Found Land: Lewis and Clark's Voyage of Discovery	2007	12				

Outstanding Books for the College Bound— Literature and Language Arts

Author	Title	Year	Age	Own	Recommend	To Read	Want
Dorothy Allison	*Bastard Out of Carolina*	1993					
M. T. Anderson	*The Astonishing Life of Octavian Nothing: Traitor to the Nation, Vol. 1: The Pox Party* *.***	2006	15				
Jenny Bond and Chris Sheedy	*Who the Hell is Pansy O'Hara?: The Fascinating Stories Behind 50 of the World's Best-Loved Books*	2008					
Peter Cameron	*Someday This Pain Will be Useful to You*	2007	12				
Sandra Cisneros	*Caramelo*	2003					
Mark Dunn	*Ella Minnow Pea: A Novel in Letters*	2002					
Jonathan Safran Foer	*Extremely Loud and Incredibly Close*	2006					
Ernest Gaines	*A Lesson Before Dying*	1997					
John Green	*Looking for Alaska* !!,#,‡‡‡,·	2005	15				
Mark Haddon	*The Curious Incident of the Dog in the Night-Time* ~	2003					
Khaled Hosseini	*The Kite Runner* ~	2003					
Kazuo Ishiguro	*Never Let Me Go* ~	2005					
Lloyd Jones	*Mister Pip* ~	2008					
Garrison Keillor	*Good Poems*	2002					
Sue Monk Kidd	*Secret Life of Bees*	2003					
Aryn Kyle	*The God of Animals* ~	2008					
Gregory Maguire	*Wicked: The Life and Times of the Wicked Witch of the West*						
Cormac McCarthy	*The Road*	2006					
Haruki Murakami	*Kafka on the Shore*	2006					
Walter Dean Myers	*Sunrise Over Fallujah*	2009	15				
Philip Roth	*The Plot Against America*	2004					

☐ Juvenile Nonfiction ☐ Juvenile Fiction ■ Fiction ■ Nonfiction

Outstanding Books for the College Bound— Literature and Language Arts

Author	Title	Year	Age	Own	Recommend	To Read	Want
Alice Sebold	*Lucky: A Memoir*	2002					
Tom Stoppard	*Rosencrantz & Guildenstern are Dead*	1994					
Craig Thompson	*Blankets*	2003					
Markus Zusak	*The Book Thief*	2006	12				

Outstanding Books for the College Bound— Science and Technology

Author	Title	Year	Age	Own	Recommend	To Read	Want
Scott Adams	*God's Debris: A Thought Experiment*	2004					
M. T. Anderson	*Feed* [1,x]	2004	12				
Ian Ayres	*Super Crunchers: Why Thinking-By-Numbers is the New Way to Be Smart*	2008					
Joel Best	*Damned Lies and Statistics: Untangling Numbers from the Media, Politicians, and Activists*	2001					
Bill Bryson	*A Short History of Nearly Everything*	2003					
Susan Casey	*The Devil's Teeth: A True Story of Obsession and Survival Among America's Great White Sharks*	2006					
Joanne Chen	*The Taste of Sweet: Our Complicated Love Affair with Our Favorite Treats*	2008					
Cory Doctorow	*Little Brother* [$$,x]	2008	12				
Katrina Firlik	*Another Day in the Frontal Lobe: A Brain Surgeon Exposes Life on the Inside*	2007					
Tim Flannery	*The Weather Makers: How Man is Changing the Climate and What It Means for Life on Earth*	2006	15				

Author	Title	Year	Age	Own	Recommend	To Read	Want
Rose George	*The Big Necessity: The Unmentionable World of Human Waste and Why It Matters*	2008					
Phillip M. Hoose	*The Race to Save the Lord God Bird* •••	2004	12				
Chris Jones	*Out of Orbit: The Incredible True Story of Three Astronauts Who Were Hundreds of Miles Above Earth When They Lost Their Ride Home*	2008					
Aldo Leopold	*A Sand County Almanac*	1949					
David Macaulay	*Mosque*	2008					
David Macaulay	*The Way We Work: Getting to Know the Amazing Human Body*	2008					
Bill McKibben	*American Earth: Environmental Writing Since Thoreau*	2008					
Greg Melville	*Greasy Rider: Two Dudes, One Fry-Oil-Powered Car, and a Cross-Country Search for a Greener Future*	2008					
Michael Pollan	*The Botany of Desire: A Plant's Eye View of the World*	2001					
Richard Preston	*The Wild Trees: A Story of Passion and Daring*	2008					
Mary Roach	*Stiff: The Curious Lives of Human Cadavers* ˜	2003					
Gerald Schroeder	*Hidden Face of God: How Science Reveals the Ultimate Truth*	2002					
Ken Silverstein	*The Radioactive Boy Scout: The True Story of a Boy and His Backyard Nuclear Reactor*	2005					
Gina Smith	*The Genomics Age: How DNA Technology is Transforming the Way We Live and Who We Are*	2004					
Dick Teresi	*Lost Discoveries: The Ancient Roots of Modern Science--From the Babylonians to the Maya*	2003					

▢ Juvenile Nonfiction   ▢ Juvenile Fiction   ◼ Fiction   ◼ Nonfiction

Outstanding Books for the College Bound—Social Sciences

Author	Title	Year	Age	Own	Recommend	To Read	Want
Mitch Albom	*Tuesdays with Morrie: An Old Man, a Young Man, and Life's Greatest Lesson*	2002					
Ishmael Beah	*A Long Way Gone: Memoirs of a Boy Soldier ~*	2008					
Richard Nelson Bolles	*What Color is Your Parachute? 2009: A Practical Manual for Job-Hunters and Career-Changers*	2008					
Ben Casnocha	*My Start-Up Life: What a (Very) Young CEO Learned on His Journey through Silicon Valley*	2007					
Mary W. George	*The Elements of Library Research: What Every Student Needs to Know*	2008					
Malcolm Gladwell	*The Tipping Point: How Little Things Can Make a Big Difference*	2002					
Melvin Juette and Ronald J. Berger	*Wheelchair Warrior: Gangs, Disability, and Basketball*	2008					
Lisa Keen	*Out Law: What LGBT Youth Should Know About Their Legal Rights*	2007	15				
Jana Kohl	*A Rare Breed of Love: The True Story of Baby and the Mission She Inspired to Help Dogs Everywhere*	2008					
Patricia McCormick	*Sold ♪,♪♪♪*	2008	12				
Faith D'Aluisio and Peter Menzel	*Hungry Planet: What the World Eats*	2007					
Greg Mortenson and David Oliver Relin	*Three Cups of Tea: One Man's Mission to Promote Peace One School at a Time*	2007					
Jodi Picoult	*Nineteen Minutes [i]*	2007					
Mary Pipher	*The Middle of Everywhere: Helping Refugees Enter the American Community*	2003					
Loren Pope	*Colleges That Change Lives: 40 Schools That Will Change the Way You Think About Colleges*	2006					

Author	Title	Year	Age	Own	Recommend	To Read	Want
Thomas M. Kostigen and Elizabeth Rogers	*The Green Book: The Everyday Guide to Saving the Planet One Simple Step at a Time*	2007					
David Sheff	*Beautiful Boy: A Father's Journey Through His Son's Addiction*	2008					
Nic Sheff	*Tweak: Growing Up on Methamphetamines*	2009	15				
Jodi R. R. Smith	*From Clueless to Class Act: Manners for the Modern Man*	2006					
Jessica Stern	*Terror in the Name of God: Why Religious Militants Kill*	2004					
Luis Alberto Urrea	*The Devil's Highway: A True Story*	2005					
David Wallis	*Killed Cartoons: Casualties from the War on Free Expression*	2007					
Jeannette Walls	*The Glass Castle ˜·'' *	2005					
Charles Wheelan	*Naked Economics: Undressing the Dismal Science*	2002					

Autobiographies for Teens

The teen section of the Santa Clara County Library (CA) contains sections for homework help, reading, video, and audio recommendations; information on events; teens issues; and guidance regarding college and career choices. The autobiographies for teens list contains books by (and about) famous authors, Holocaust survivors, doctors, people with troubled childhoods, and more. See www.santaclaracountylib.org/teen/lists/index.html for a variety of lists.

Author	Title	Year	Age	Own	Recommend	To Read	Want
Lori Arviso Alvord	*The Scalpel and the Silver Bear*	2000					
Mawi Asgedom	*Of Beetles and Angels*	2001	12				
Livia Bitton-Jackson	*I Have Lived a Thousand Years: Growing up in the Holocaust*	1999	12				

☐ Juvenile Nonfiction   ☐ Juvenile Fiction   ■ Fiction   ■ Nonfiction

Autobiographies for Teens

Author	Title	Year	Age	Own	Recommend	To Read	Want
Chris Crutcher	*King of the Mild Frontier*	2003	12				
Firoozeh Dumas	*Funny in Farsi: A Memoir of Growing up Iranian in America*	2004					
June Jordan	*Soldier: A Poet's Childhood*						
Haven Kimmel	*A Girl Named Zippy: Growing Up Small in Mooreland, Indiana*	2002					
Stephen King	*On Writing: A Memoir of the Craft*	2001					
Adeline Yen Mah	*Chinese Cinderella*	2001	12				
Paul Monette	*Becoming a Man*	2004					
Gary Paulsen	*Guts: The True Story Behind Hatchet and the Brian Books*	2002	12				

Biographies for Teens

The combined biography lists from Austin Public Library's site Connected Youth (TX) and Hennepin Country Library (MN) contains a collection of titles that will suit any interest and biography homework assignment. From 50 Cent to Charles Darwin, Frida Kahlo to a female Israeli soldier, teenagers on death row to John Lennon, these amazing stories will stay with you long after you finish your term paper. Make sure to check out both sites: www.connectedyouth.org and www.hclib.org/teens/read.cfm.

Author	Title	Year	Age	Own	Recommend	To Read	Want
50 Cent	*50 x 50: 50 Cent in His Own Words*	2007					
Scott Reynolds Nelson with Marc Aronson	*Ain't Nothing But a Man: My Quest to Find the Real John Henry* [tt]	2007	8				
Tanya Lee Stone	*Almost Astronauts: 13 Women Who Dared to Dream*	2009	9				
Jan Greenberg	*Andy Warhol: Prince of Pop*	2004	12				
Carole Boston Weatherford	*Becoming Billie Holiday*	2008	15				

Author	Title	Year	Age	Own	Recommend	To Read	Want
Daniel Tammet	Born on a Blue Day: Inside the Extraordinary Mind of an Autistic Savant: A Memoir	2007					
Marilyn Nelson	Carver: A Life in Poems	2001	12				
Deborah Heiligman	Charles and Emma: The Darwins' Leap of Faith	2008	12				
Susan Goldman Rubing	Delicious: The Life and Art of Wayne Thiebaud	2007	9				
Carmen Bernier-Grand	Frida: Viva la Vida! Long Live Life!	2007	12				
Ryan Smithson	Ghosts of War: The True Story of a 19-year-old GI	2009	15				
Lynne Cox	Grayson	2006					
Michael D'Antonio	Hershey: Milton S. Hershey's Extraordinary Life of Wealth Empire and Utopian Dreams	2007					
Jack Gantos	Hole in My Life	2002	15				
Jason Lutes	Houdini: The Handcuff King	2007	12				
Charles J. Shields	I Am Scout: A Biography of Harper Lee	2008	12				
Ted Lewin	I Was a Teenage Professional Wrestler	1994	9				
Aimee Major Steinberger	Japan Ai: A Tall Girl's Adventures in Japan	2007	12				
Elizabeth Partridge	John Lennon: All I Want is the Truth	2005	12				
Chris Crutcher	King of the Mild Frontier: An Ill-advised Autobiography	2003	12				
George Sullivan	Knockout!: Photobiography of Boxer Joe Louis	2008	9				
Peter Nelson	Left for Dead: A Young Man's Search for Justice for the USS Indianapolis	2003	12				
Russell Freedman	The Life and Death of Crazy Horse [xxx]	1996	12				
Cunxin Li	Mao's Last Dancer	2005	12				

Biographies for Teens				Own	Recommend	To Read	Want
Author	Title	Year	Age				
Cheryl Diamond	Model: A Memoir	2008	12				
Tracy Kidder	Mountains Beyond Mountains	2003					
Susan Kuklin	No Choirboy: Murder, Violence and Teenagers on Death Row	2008	15				
Tina Grimberg	Out of Line: Growing Up Soviet	2007	9				
Jim Murphy	Pick & Shovel Poet: The Journeys of Pascal D'Angelo	2000	12				
Youme Landowne and Anthony Horton	Pitch Black	2008					
Elizabeth Partridge	Restless Spirit: The Life and Work of Dorothea Lange	2001	9				
Michael Rosen	Shakespeare: His Work & His World	2006	11				
Laura Flynn	Swallow the Ocean: A Memoir	2008					
Ned Vizzini	Teen Angst? Naaah – A Quasi-Autobiography	2002	12				
Mariatu Kamara	The Bite of the Mango	2008	12				
Brent Runyon	The Burn Journals	2004	15				
Freedom Writers	The Freedom Writers Diary 292						
Candace Fleming	The Lincolns: A Scrapbook Look at Abraham and Mary	2008	9				
Ken Silverstein	The Radioactive Boy Scout: The True Story of a Boy and His Backyard Nuclear Reactor	2005					
Sid Fleischman	The Trouble Begins at 8: A Life of Mark Twain in the Wild, Wild West	2008	9				
Cylin Busby and John Busby	The Year We Disappeared: A Father-Daughter Memoir ###	2008	12				
Diane Ackerman	The Zookeeper's Wife	2007					
Ashley Rhodes-Courter	Three Little Words: A Memoir	2008	12				
Nic Sheff	Tweak	2008	15				
Valérie Zenatti	When I Was a Soldier: A Memoir	2005	15				
Stephanie Hemphill	Your Own, Sylvia: A Verse Portrait of Sylvia Plath	2007	12				

Robert F. Sibert Medal **

The Robert F. Sibert Informational Book Award is awarded annually to the author(s) and illustrator(s) of the most distinguished informational book published in English during the preceding year. Established in 2001 by the Association for Library Service to Children (ALSC), with support from Bound to Stay Bound Books, Inc., of Jacksonville, Illinois, the award honors Sibert, a long-serving president of Bound to Stay Bound Books. See www.ala.org/ala/mgrps/divs/alsc/awardsgrants/bookmedia/sibertmedal/index.cfm for more information about the award and the ALCS.

Year	Author	Title	Age	Own	Recommend	To Read	Want
2011							
2010							
2009	Kadir Nelson	We Are the Ship	7				
2008	Peter Sis	The Wall: Growing Up Behind the Iron Curtain ***	8				
2007	Catherine Thimmesh	Team Moon: How 400,000 People Landed Apollo 11 On the Moon	12				
2006	Sally M. Walker	Secrets of a Civil War Submarine: Solving the Mysteries of the H. L. Hunley	12				
2005	Russell Freedman	The Voice That Challenged A Nation: Marian Anderson and the Struggle for Equal Rights •••	12				
2004	Jim Murphy	An American Plague: The True and Terrifying Story of the Yellow Fever Epidemic of 1793 ***					
2003	James Giblin	The Life And Death of Adolf Hitler	12				
2002	Susan Campbell Bartoletti	Black Potatoes: The Story of the Great Irish Famine 1845-1850	14				
2001	Marc Aronson	Sir Walter Ralegh and the Quest for El Dorado ***	12				

Carter G. Woodson Book Award ***

The National Council for the Social Studies established the Carter G. Woodson Book Award for the most distinguished social science books appropriate for young readers. First presented in 1974, this award is intended to "encourage the writing, publishing, and dissemination of outstanding social studies books for young readers that treat topics related to ethnic minorities and race relations sensitively and accurately." The winners in the middle and secondary categories are listed here. For more information, see www.socialstudies.org/awards/woodson.

Year	Author	Title	Age	Own	Recommend	To Read	Want
Middle							
2011							
2010							
2009	James Haskins and Kathleen Benson with Virginia Schomp	*Drama of African-American History: The Rise of Jim Crow*	12				
2008	John Fleischman	*Black and White Airmen: Their True History*	9				
2007	Russell Freedman	*Freedom Walkers: The Story of the Montgomery Bus Boycott*	9				
2006	Barbara C. Cruz	*Cesar Chavez: A Voice for Farmworkers*	12				
2005	Russell Freedman	*The Voice That Challenged a Nation: Marian Anderson and the Struggle for Equal Rights* **	12				
2004	Kimberly Komatsu and Kaleigh Komatsu	*In America's Shadow*	12				
2003	Michael L. Cooper	*Remembering Manzanar: Life in a Japanese Relocation Camp*	15				
2002	Alice Hinkel	*Prince Estabrook: Slave and Soldier*	12				
2001	Andrea Davis Pinkney	*Let It Shine: Stories of Black Women Freedom Fighters*	9				
Secondary							
2011							
2010							
2009	Francisco Jiménez	*Reaching Out*	12				

Year	Author	Title	Age	Own	Recommend	To Read	Want
2008	Vincent Collin Beach with Anni Beach	*Don't Throw Away Your Stick Till You Cross the River: The Journey of an Ordinary Man*					
2007	Joanne Oppenheim	*Dear Miss Breed: True Stories of the Japanese-American Incarceration During World War II and a Librarian Who Made a Difference*	12				
2006	Calvin Craig Miller	*No Easy Answers: Bayard Rustin and the Civil Rights Movement*	15				
2005	Robert H. Mayer, ed.	*The Civil Rights Act of 1964*	15				
2004	James Tackach	*Early Black Reformers*	12				
2003	Harvey Fireside	*The Mississippi Burning Civil Rights Murder Conspiracy Trial: A Headline Court Case*	12				
2002	Barbara C. Cruz	*Multiethnic Teens and Cultural Identity*	9				
2001	Albert Marrin	*Tatan'Ka Iyota'Ke: Sitting Bull and His World*	12				
2000	Sharon Linnea	*Princess Ka'Iulani: Hope of a Nation Heart of a People*	12				
1999	Rinna Evelyn Wolfe	*Edmonia Lewis: Wildfire in Marble*	12				
1998	Milton Meltzer	*Langston Hughes*	12				
1997	Jim Haskins	*The Harlem Renaissance*	10				
1996	Ellen Levine	*A Fence Away from Freedom: Japanese Americans and World War II*	10				
1995	Zak Mettger	*Till Victory is Won: Black Soldiers in the Civil War*	12				
1994	James Haskins	*The March on Washington*	12				
1993	Mildred Pitts Walter	*Mississippi Challenge*	12				
1992	Jeri Ferris	*Native American Doctor: The Story of Susan Laflesche Picotte*	10				
1991	Mary E. Lyons	*Sorrow's Kitchen: The Life and Folklore of Zora Neal Hurston*	12				

☐ Juvenile Nonfiction ☐ Juvenile Fiction ■ Fiction ■ Nonfiction

Carter G. Woodson Book Award •••			Age	Own	Recommend	To Read	Want
Year	Author	Title					
1990	Rebecca Larsen	*Paul Robeson*	12				
1989	Charles Patterson	*Marian Anderson*	12				
1988	James Haskins	*Black Music in America: A History Through Its People*	12				
1987	Arlene B. Hirshfelder	*Happily May I Walk* †	12				
1986	Brent Ashabranner	*Dark Harvest: Migrant Farmworkers in America*	12				
1985	Brent Ashabranner	*To Live in Two Worlds: American Indian Youth Today*	12				
1984	Ernest Barksdale Fincher	*Mexico and the United States*	12				
1983	Brent Ashabranner	*Morning Star Black Sun*	8				
1982	Susan Carver and Paula McGuire	*Coming to North America from Mexico Cuba and Puerto Rico*					
1981	Milton Meltzer	*The Chinese Americans*	12				
1980	Nancy Wood	*War Cry on a Prayer Feather: Prose and Poetry of the Ute*					
1979	Peter Nabokov	*Native American Testimony: An Anthology of Indian and White Relations Edited*	12				
1978	Jan Goodsell	*The Biography of Daniel Inouye*	12				
1977	Dorothy Sterling	*The Trouble They Seen*	10				
1976	Laurence Yep	*Dragonwings* ~~~,$	12				
1975	Jesse Jackson	*Make a Joyful Noise Unto the Lord: The Life of Mahalia Jackson Queen of the Gospel Singers*					
1974	Eloise Greenfield	*Rosa Parks*	10				

Green Earth Book Award '

The Green Earth Book Award, overseen by the Newton Marasco Foundation and in partnership with Salisbury University, was created to promote "books that inspire a child to grow a deeper appreciation, respect and responsibility for his or her environment." The categories of young adult fiction and nonfiction are listed here. See www.newtonmarascofoundation.org/programs/a_ge.cfm for forthcoming winners.

Year	Author	Title	Age	Own	Recommend	To Read	Want
2011							
2010							
2009 tie	Pamela Todd	*Blind Faith Hotel*	13				
2009 tie	Peter Gould	*Write Naked*	12				
2008	O. R. Melling	*The Light-Bearer's Daughter*	9				
2007	Sneed B. Collard III	*Flash Point*					
2006	Carl Hiaasen	*Flush*	9				

Nonfiction

This varied nonfiction list for teens from the Seattle Public Library (WA) entitled "Get Real" will enlighten any reader on subjects ranging from the mysteries of the Twinkie, codes and ciphers, the history of jeans, and the Berlin Wall. To view a summary of each title see www.spl.org/default.asp?pageID=audience_teens_bmm_readinglist&cid=1130886948572.

Author	Title	Year	Age	Own	Recommend	To Read	Want
Michael Benabib and Bill Adler	*In Ya Grill: The Faces of Hip-hop*						
Jamie Brisick	*Have Board, Will Travel: The Definitive History of Surf, Skate & Snow*	2009					

☐ Juvenile Nonfiction ☐ Juvenile Fiction ■ Fiction ■ Nonfiction

Nonfiction			Age	Own	Recommend	To Read	Want
Author	**Title**	**Year**					
Bill Bryson	A Short History of Nearly Everything	2003					
Megan Carle and Jill Carle	Teens Cook: How to Cook What You Want to Eat	2005	12				
Steve Ettlinger	Twinkie, Deconstructed	2008					
Albert Gore	An Inconvenient Truth: The Crisis of Global Warming	2006					
Laban Carrick Hill	Harlem Stomp!: A Cultural History of the Harlem Renaissance	2004	12				
Sid Jacobsen and Ernie Colon	The 9/11 Report: A Graphic Adaptation	2004					
Robert T. Kiyosaki	Rich Dad/Poor Dad for Teens	2004	15				
Patrick Neate	Where You're At: Notes from the Frontline of a Hip-hop Planet						
Megan Nicolay	Generation T: 108 Ways to Transform a T-shirt	2006					
Stephen Pincock	Codebreaker: The History of Codes and Ciphers, from the Ancient Pharaohs to Quantuam Cryptography	2006					
Paul B. Raushenbush	Teen Spirit: One World, Many Faiths	2004	12				
Deborah Reber	In their Shoes: Extraordinary Women Describe their Amazing Careers	2007	15				
Ina Saltz	Body Type: Intimate Messages Etched in Flesh	2006					
Ellie Schiedermayer	Got Tape?						
Serge Schmemann	When the Wall Came Down	2007	9				
Edward T. Sullivan	The Ultimate Weapon: The Race to Develop the Atomic Bomb	2007	12				
James Sullivan	Jeans: A Cultural History of an American Icon						
Frank Warren	PostSecret: Extraordinary Confessions from Ordinary Lives	2005					
Daniel H. Wilson	How to Survive a Robot Uprising	2005					

National Science Teachers Association— Outstanding Science Trade Books for Students

Since 1996, the National Science Teachers Association (NSTA) has compiled a list each year of outstanding science books for kids of all ages. "Today's classrooms have no real walls! Students explore the world on field trips, during virtual journeys on the World Wide Web, and through the books they read. These pathways help them fly to the ends of the universe to satisfy their scientific curiosity. [T]he professionals of the NSTA/CBC Review Panel for Outstanding Science Trade Books for Students K–12 [are] pleased to serve as travel guides, identifying the best in trade books for student explorations. Their recommendations encourage young readers to fly *Over the Rivers*, brave the Antarctic with *Emperors of the Ice*, come *Face to Face With Elephants*, or help a family of mountain gorillas *Looking for Miza*. There are journeys to micro-worlds as well, inviting students into Dr. Frankenstein's lab to investigate the human body, to search nests for eggs, or work with a National Geographic scientist to explore genetics." To view lists from previous years and to learn more about the NSTA, visit www.nsta.org/publications/ostb.

Year	Author	Title	Age	Own	Recommend	To Read	Want
2009	James M. Deem	*Bodies from the Ice: Melting Glaciers and the Recovery of the Past*	9				
2008	Thomas R. Holtz Jr.	*Dinosaurs: The Most Complete, Up-to-Date Encyclopedia for Dinosaur Lovers of All Ages*	12				
2008	Lowell Dingus, Luis M. Chiappe, and Rodolfo Coria	*Dinosaur Eggs Discovered! Unscrambling the Clues*	9				
2008	Judith Williams	*The Discovery and Mystery of a Dinosaur Named Jane*	8				
2008	Caroline Arnold	*Giant Sea Reptiles of the Dinosaur Age*	9				
Science Biography							
2009	Pamela S. Turner	*A Life in the Wild: George Schaller's Struggle to Save the Last Great Beasts*	9				
2009	Richard Farr	*Emperors of the Ice: A True Story of Disaster and Survival in the Antarctic, 1910–13*	12				

☐ Juvenile Nonfiction   ☐ Juvenile Fiction   ■ Fiction   ■ Nonfiction

National Science Teachers Association—Outstanding Science Trade Books for Students			Age	Own	Recommend	To Read	Want
Year	Author	Title					
2008	Philip Steele	*Isaac Newton: The Scientist Who Changed Everything*	9				
2008	Kathleen Krull	*Giants of Science: Marie Curie*					
2008	Don Nardo	*Tycho Brahe: Pioneer of Astronomy*	9				
Earth and Space Science							
2009	Pamela S. Turner	*Life on Earth—And Beyond*	9				
2009	Richard Platt	*Moon Landing*	8				
2009	Michael Collier	*Over the Rivers: An Aerial View of Geology*					
2008	Joy Hakim	*The Story of Science: Einstein Adds a New Dimension*	12				
2008	DK Publishing	*Map: Satellite*	0				
Environment and Ecology							
2009	Jinny Johnson	*Animal Tracks and Signs: Track Over 400 Animals: From Big Cats to Backyard Birds*	12				
2009	Sandra Pobst	*Animals on the Edge: Science Races to Save Species Threatened With Extinction*	9				
2009	Dorothy Hinshaw Patent	*When the Wolves Returned: Restoring Nature's Balance in Yellowstone*	6				
2008	Michael Collier	*Over the Mountains: An Aerial View of Geology*					
Health Science							
2009	Laine Scott	*All About Sleep from A to Zzzz*	8				
2009	Richard Walker	*Dr. Frankenstein's Human Body Book*	9				
2009	Lesli J. Favor	*Food as Foe: Nutrition and Eating Disorders*	15				
2009	Charles Piddock	*Outbreak: Science Seeks Safeguards for Global Health*	9				
2008	Thomasine E. Lewis Tilden and Franklin Watts	*Belly-Busting Worm Invasions! Parasites That Love Your Insides!*	12				

Year	Author	Title	Age	Own	Recommend	To Read	Want
2008	Alvin Silverstein, Virginia Silverstein, and Laura Silverstein Nunn	*The Breast Cancer Update*	9				
2008	Cherie Winner	*Circulating Life: Blood Transfusion from Ancient Superstition to Modern Medicine*	9				
Life Science							
2009	Kathleen Simpson	*Genetics: From DNA to Designer Dogs*	9				
2009	Sandra Markle	*Praying Mantises: Hungry Insect Heroes*	9				
2008	Alvin Silverstein, Virginia Silverstein, and Laura Silverstein Nunn	*Adaptation*	12				
2008	Lynn M. Stone	*Box Turtles*	9				
2008	Nic Bishop	*Spiders*	7				
2008	Sandra Markle	*Octopuses*	9				
2008	Connie Goldsmith	*Superbugs Strike Back: When Antibiotics Fail*	9				
Physical Science							
2009	Richard Hammond	*Car Science*	8				
2008	Ron Miller	*Rockets*	9				
Technology and Engineering							
2009	Chris Woodford	*Cool Stuff Exploded*	9				
2008	Rebecca Stefoff	*Great Inventions: Microscopes and Telescopes*	15				
2008	Edward T. Sullivan	*The Ultimate Weapon: The Race to Develop the Atomic Bomb*	12				

▢ Juvenile Nonfiction   ▣ Juvenile Fiction   ■ Fiction   ■ Nonfiction

Green Reads

The West Milford Township Library (NJ) publishes a list of selected books concerning the environment. From Rachel Carson's classic *Silent Spring*, widely credited with launching the environmental movement, to the contemporary award-winning *An Inconvenient Truth* by Al Gore, the list will start any reader down a green path of earth understanding. For more great lists see www.wmtl .org/reading/TeenReading.htm.

Author	Title	Year	Age	Own	Recommend	To Read	Want
Environmental Classics							
Annie Dillard	*Pilgrim at Tinker Creek*	1974					
Rachel Carson	*Silent Spring*	1962					
Albert Gore	*An Inconvenient Truth: The Crisis of Global Warming*	2006					
Henry David Thoreau	*Walden*	1854					
Living with Nature							
Julie Fisher-McGarry	*Be the Change You Want to See in the World*	2006					
Bill McKibben	*Deep Economy*	2007					
Newt Gingrich	*A Contract with the Earth*	2007					
Wendy Williams	*Cape Wind*	2007					
Chad Pregracke	*From the Bottom Up*	2007					
Barbara Kingsolver	*Animal, Vegetable, Miracle*	2007					
Shay Salomon	*Little House on a Small Planet*	2006					
Ann Thorpe	*The Designer's Atlas of Sustainability*	2007					
Human Impact on Nature							
Alan Weisman	*The World Without Us*	2007					
Fred Pearce	*When the Rivers Run Dry*	2006					
Charles Clover	*The End of the Line*	2006					
Tim Flannery	*The Weather Makers: How Man is Changing the Climate and What It Means for Life on Earth*	2006					

Américas Book Award for Children's and Young Adult Literature **

The Américas Award is given in recognition of U.S. works of fiction, poetry, folklore, or selected nonfiction from picture books. Published in the preceding year, the titles must be written for young adults in English or Spanish. The titles authentically and engagingly portray Latin America, Caribbean, or Latino culture in the United States. Sponsored by the national Consortium of Latin American Studies Programs (CLASP), the award reaches beyond borders and boundaries, focusing on cultural heritages within the hemisphere. Award winners and commended titles are selected for their distinctive literary quality; cultural contextualization; exceptional integration of text, illustration, and design; and potential for classroom use. Eligible nominees must be written in English and published during the previous two years. Folklore must be central to the book's content and accurate to the beliefs and worldview of the represented culture, and sources must be appropriately cited. www4.uwm.edu/clacs/aa/index.cfm.

Year	Author	Title	Age	Own	Recommend	To Read	Want
2011							
2010							
2009	Margarita Engle	The Surrender Tree: Poems of Cuba's Struggle for Freedom **	12				
2008	Laura Resau	Red Glass ~~~	12				
2008	Pat Mora	YUM! ¡MMMM! ¡QUE RICO!: America's Sproutings	7				
2007	Jennifer Elvgren	Josias, Hold the Book					
2007	Margarita Engle	The Poet Slave of Cuba: A Biography of Juan Francisco Manzano ~~~	9				
2006	Juan Felipe Herrera	Cinnamon Girl: Letters Found Inside a Cereal Box	9				
2005	Monica Brown	My Name is Celia					
2005	Benjamin Alire Sáenz	Sammy and Juliana in Hollywood	15				
2004	Judith Ortiz Cofer	The Meaning of Consuelo					
2004	Yuyi Morales	Just a Minute	7				
2003	Julia Alvarez	Before We Were Free **	12				

☐ Juvenile Nonfiction   ▨ Juvenile Fiction   ■ Fiction   ■ Nonfiction

Américas Book Award for Children's and Young Adult Literature ˇˇ							
Year	Author	Title	Age	Own	Recommend	To Read	Want
2002	Jorge Argueta	A Movie in My Pillow	7				
2002	Francisco Jiménez	Breaking Through	12				
2001	Antonio Skármeta	The Composition	9				
2001	Lynn Joseph	The Color of My Words	9				
2000	Juan Felipe Herrera	CrashBoomLove: A Novel in Verse	15				
1999	Amelia Lau Carling	Mama and Papa Have a Store	7				
1999	George Ancona	Barrio: José's Neighborhood	9				
1998	Francisco Jiménez	The Circuit: Stories from the Life of a Migrant Child ˇˇˇ	12				
1998	Regina Hanson	The Face at the Window	8				
1997	Victor Martínez	Parrot in the Oven ˇˑˇˇ	12				
1997	Carmen Lomas Garza	In My Family	7				
1996	Frances Temple	Tonight, by Sea	9				
1995	Lynn Joseph	The Mermaid's Twin Sister	8				
1994	Lulu Delacre	Vejigante Masquerader					

APALA Award—Children's and Young Adult Literature ˑ

The Asian/Pacific American Librarians Association (APALA) awards a top title and honor other books in each of three categories for the Asian/Pacific American Awards for Literature (APAAL). Books in these categories-adult fiction, illustration in children's literature, and text in children's and young adult literature-must promote Asian/Pacific Americans' culture and heritage, based on literary and artistic merit. www.apalaweb.org/awards/awards.htm.

Year	Author	Title	Age	Own	Recommend	To Read	Want
2011							
2010							
2009	Many Ly	Roots and Wings	12				
2008	Kelly Easton	Hiroshima Dreams	9				

Year	Author	Title	Age	Own	Recommend	To Read	Want
2007	Justina Chen Headley	*Nothing But the Truth*	9				
2004–2005	Cynthia Kadohata	*Kira-Kira*	9				
2001–2003	An Na	*A Step from Heaven* ~~~.‼	12				

American Indian Youth Services Literature Award ⁓

The American Indian Youth Services Literature award, sponsored by the American Library Association, honors the best titles authored by and about American Indians. The award is given every two years in three categories: picture book, middle school, and young adult. The middle school and young adult winners are listed. Visit www.ailanet.org/activities/youthlitaward.htm for more information and future winners.

Year	Author	Title	Age	Own	Recommend	To Read	Want
Middle School							
2012							
2010							
2008	Joseph Medicine Crow	*Counting Coup: Becoming a Crow Chief on the Reservation and Beyond*	6				
2006	Louise Erdrich	*The Birchbark House* †	8				
Young Adult							
2012							
2010							
2008	Sherman Alexie	*The Absolutely True Diary of a Part-Time Indian* ·.***·♫♫	12				
2006	Joseph Bruchac	*Hidden Roots*	9				

☐ Juvenile Nonfiction ☐ Juvenile Fiction ■ Fiction ■ Nonfiction

Pura Belpré Award **

Established in 1996, the Pura Belpré Award is presented to a Latino/Latina writer and illustrator whose outstanding work of literature for children and youth best portrays, affirms, and celebrates Latino culture. The award is co-sponsored by the Association for Library Service to Children (ALSC), a division of the American Library Association (ALA), and the National Association to Promote Library and Information Services to Latinos and the Spanish-Speaking (REFORMA), an ALA affiliate. Pura Belpré, the first Latina librarian at the New York Public Library, was a storyteller and author who enriched the lives of children by preserving and disseminating Puerto Rican folklore.

Year	Author	Title	Age	Own	Recommend	To Read	Want
2011							
2010							
2009	Margarita Engle	The Surrender Tree: Poems of Cuba's Struggle for Freedom ▼▼	12				
2008	Pam Muñoz Ryan	The Poet Slave of Cuba: A Biography of Juan Francisco Manzano					
2006	Viola Canales	The Tequila Worm	12				
2004	Julia Alvarez	Before We Were Free ▼▼	12				
2002	Pam Muñoz Ryan	Esperanza Rising	9				
2000	Alma Flor Ada	Under the Royal Palms: A Childhood in Cuba					
1998	Victor Martínez	Parrot in the Oven	12				
1996	Judith Ortiz Cofer	An Island Like You: Stories of the Barrio	12				

30 Multicultural Books Every Teen Should Know

The Cooperative Children's Book Center (CCBC), defines multicultural literature as books by and about people of color: African and African Americans, American Indians, Asian/Pacific and Asian Pacific Americans, and Latinos. This listing introduces thirty essential books and a range of authors for teens. For more great lists from the CCBC, go to www.education.wisc.edu/ccbc/default.asp.

Author	Title	Year	Age	Own	Recommend	To Read	Want
Arnold Adoff	I Am the Darker Brother: An Anthology of Modern Poems by African Americans	1997	12				
Sherman Alexie	The Absolutely True Diary of a Part-Time Indian *,***,♥♥♥,♫♫♫	2007	12				
Julia Alvarez	Before We Were Free ♦♦,♥♥	2002	12				
Joseph Bruchac	The Heart of a Chief	2001	10				
Joseph Bruchac	Bowman's Store: A Journey to Myself	1997	14				
Lori M. Carlson	Cool Salsa: Bilingual Poems on Growing Up Latino in the United States	1995	9				
Judith Ortiz Cofer	An Island Like You: Stories of the Barrio ♦♦	1999	15				
Tom Feelings	The Middle Passage: White Ships/ Black Cargo	1995					
Sharon G. Flake	The Skin I'm In	1998	12				
Pearl Fuyo Gaskins	What Are You? Voices of Mixed-Race Young People	1999	9				
Virginia Hamilton	Sweet Whispers, Brother Rush ***	1982	12				
Juan Felipe Herrera	CrashBoomLove: A Novel in Verse ♥♥	1999	15				
Tanuja Desai Hidier	Born Confused	2002	15				
Ann Jaramillo	La Línea	2006	12				
Ji-Li Jiang	Red Scarf Girl: A Memoir of the Cultural Revolution	1997	12				

☐ Juvenile Nonfiction   ☐ Juvenile Fiction   ■ Fiction   ■ Nonfiction

30 Multicultural Books Every Teen Should Know			Age	Own	Recommend	To Read	Want
Author	Title	Year					
Francisco Jiménez	The Circuit: Stories from the Life of a Migrant Child ˙˙˙,♥♥	2001	12				
Angela Johnson	The First Part Last ‖,#,ΩΩ,˙	2003	12				
Cynthia Kadohata	Kira-Kira ♦	2006	9				
Walter Dean Myers	Monster ‖,‡‡‡	1999	12				
Walter Dean Myers	Now is Your Time! The African-American Struggle for Freedom	1991	12				
An Na	A Step from Heaven ~~~,‖,♦	2001	12				
Marilyn Nelson	A Wreath for Emmett Till	2009	12				
Nancy Osa	Cuba 15	2005	12				
Linda Sue Park	When My Name Was Keoko: A Novel of Korea in World War II	2002	12				
Doreen Rappaport	The Flight of Red Bird: The Life of Zitkala-Sa	1999	11				
Kashmira Sheth	Blue Jasmine	2004	9				
Gary Soto	Baseball in April and Other Stories	2000	8				
Jacqueline Woodson	I Hadn't Meant to Tell You This	2006	15				
Jacqueline Woodson	If You Come Softly Σ,˙˙	1998	9				
Gene Luen Yang and Lark Pien	American Born Chinese ‖,###	2007	12				

Grand Canyon Reader Award—Arizona ***

The Grand Canyon Reader Award (formerly the Arizona Young Reader Award) is an award program for students in Arizona. Originally given to a single title, the award is now granted annually in the following categories: picture book, nonfiction, intermediate, and teen. Beginning with the 2008 award, the categories will be picture book, nonfiction, intermediate, and teen (tween). The teen (tween) award winners are listed here. Look for more information at www .grandcanyonreaderaward.org.

Year	Author	Title	Age	Own	Recommend	To Read	Want
Teen/Tween							
2011							
2010							
2009	Jordan Sonnenblick	*Drums, Girls and Dangerous Pie*	12				
2008	Stephenie Meyer	*Twilight* #,♪♪♪,Ω,ΩΩ,ΩΩΩ,‡,‡‡‡,¶,¶¶,¶¶¶,ii,•• •,¿¿¿,○,∩∩,3,¡,Σ	15				
2008	Rick Riordan	*The Lightning Thief* ##,‡‡,£££,¶¶,33,¿¿¿,¿,3,••	9				
2007	Gordon Korman	*Son of the Mob* ~~,##,‡‡‡	12				
2006	Christopher Paolini	*Eragon* #,##,♪♪,Ω,‡,¶,33,•••,∩,¿¿¿,○,¿,∩∩, ○○,3,••	12				
2005	Nancy Farmer	*The House of the Scorpion* •,##,¶¶¶,○,¿,○○,3	12				
2004	Cornelia Funke	*The Thief Lord* #,ii	12				
2003	Jerry Spinelli	*Stargirl* ‡‡,ii	12				
2002	Christopher Paul Curtis	*Bud, Not Buddy* ~~~,iii	12				
2001	Louis Sachar	*Holes* •,•••,##,♪♪,iii,•••,∩,¿¿¿,¿,∩∩	9				
2000	J. K. Rowling	*Harry Potter and the Sorcerer's Stone* ♪♪,‡,∩,○○	9				
1999	Gail Carson Levine	*Ella Enchanted* ♪,‡‡	9				
1998	Karen Hesse	*Phoenix Rising* ~~,○○	12				
1997	Joan Lowery Nixon	*The Name of the Game Was Murder* ▼	12				

Grand Canyon Reader Award—Arizona ***			Age	Own	Recommend	To Read	Want
Year	Author	Title					
1996	W. R. Philbrick	*Freak the Mighty* ♪,¶¶.∩∩	9				
1995	Lois Lowry	*The Giver* ×.‡.¶¶.¶¶¶.ii.¿¿¿.¿.**	12				
1994	Avi	*Nothing But the Truth: A Documentary Novel* ii	12				

California Young Reader Award ♪

The California Young Reader Medal (CYRM) program encourages young Californians to read popular literature for recreation. Since 1974, millions of children have nominated, read, and voted for the winners of the medal. Four statewide organizations committed to books and reading sponsor the CYRM program: California Association of Teachers of English (CATE), California Library Association (CLA), California Reading Association (CRA), and California School Library Association (CSLA). Young people suggest the names of favorite books for nomination, and teachers and librarians nominate repeatedly read or requested titles. Members of the medal committee read the suggested books, discuss their merits and appeal, and then construct a well-balanced list of nominees. To be considered for nomination, a book must be an original work of fiction published within the last five years by a living author. Books are nominated for the medal in four categories: primary (K–2), intermediate (3–6), middle school/junior high (6–9), and young adult (9–12) (the later two categories are listed here). Students may read and vote for books in any and all categories, but they must read all the books nominated in a category to be eligible to vote. See www.cla-net.org/awards/cyrm.php.

Year	Author	Title	Age	Own	Recommend	To Read	Want
Middle School							
2011							
2010							
2009	Mike Lupica	*Heat*	9				
2008	Neal Shusterman	*The Schwa was Here* ***,♪	12				
2007	Gennifer Choldenko	*Al Capone Does My Shirts* ii	9				

Year	Author	Title	Age	Own	Recommend	To Read	Want
2006	Sue Corbett	*12 Again*	9				
2005	Andrew Clements	*Things Not Seen* [!!!,£££]	12				
2004	Wendelin Van Draanen	*Flipped* [oo,••]	9				
2003	Ben Mikaelson	*Touching Spirit Bear* [£££,¶¶,¶¶¶,33,∩,∩∩]	9				
2002	Jack Gantos	*Joey Pigza Swallowed the Key* [••]	9				
2001	Margaret Peterson Haddix	*Among the Hidden* [£££,¿¿¿]	9				
2000	Gail Carson Levine	*Ella Enchanted* [•••,‡‡]	9				
1999	Graham Salisbury	*Under the Blood-Red Sun* [^]	9				
1998	Christopher Paul Curtis	*The Watsons Go to Birmingham* [iii]	12				
1997	Ben Mikaelson	*Sparrow Hawk Red*	9				
1996	W. R. Philbrick	*Freak the Mighty* [•••,¶¶,∩∩]	9				
1995	Ben Mikaelson	*Rescue Josh McGuire* [~~~,xxx]	8				
1994	Jerry Spinelli	*There's a Girl in My Hammerlock*	9				
1993	Avi	*Something Upstairs*	12				
1992	Theodore Taylor	*Sniper 33*	12				
1991	Mary Downing Hahn	*December Stillness*	15				
1990	Joan Lowery Nixon	*The Other Side of Dark*	12				
1989	Joan Lowery Nixon	*The Stalker*					
1988	Janet Lunn	*The Root Cellar*	12				
1987	Patricia Hermes	*You Shouldn't Have to Say Goodbye* [‡‡]	9				
1986	Willo Davis Roberts	*Girl with the Silver Eyes*	9				
1985	Norma Fox Mazer	*Taking Terri Mueller*	9				
1984	Paula Danziger	*There's a Bat in Bunk Five*	12				
1983	Judy Blume	*Tiger Eyes*	12				
1982	Ellen Conford	*Hail Hail Camp Timberwood*	9				
1981	No Award Given						
1980	Betsy Byars	*The Pinballs*	9				

▭ Juvenile Nonfiction ▬ Juvenile Fiction ▮ Fiction ■ Nonfiction

California Young Reader Award ♪							
Year	Author	Title	Age	Own	Recommend	To Read	Want
Young Adult							
2011							
2010							
2009	Patricia McCormick	*Sold* ♪♪♪	12				
2008	Michael Morpugo	*Private Peaceful*	12				
2007	Gail Giles	*Shattering Glass*	15				
2006	Francine Prose	*After* [#]	12				
2005	Anthony Horowitz	*Stormbreaker* [‡‡,∩,oo]	9				
2004	Lensey Namioka	*Ties That Bind Ties That Break*	12				
2002	Jean Ferris	*Bad*	15				
2001	Jane Yolen and Bruce Coville	*Armageddon Summer*	12				
2000	A. M. Jenkins	*Breaking Boxes*					
1999	Kristen Randle	*The Only Alien on the Planet* [£]	12				
1998	Chris Crutcher	*Ironman*	12				
1997	Chris Crutcher	*Staying Fat for Sarah Byrnes*	12				
1996	Sherry Garland	*Shadow of the Dragon*	12				
1995	Will Hobbs	*Downriver* ♪♪	12				
1994	Robert Cormier	*We All Fall Down*	15				
1993	Annette Curtis Klause	*The Silver Kiss* [¿]	12				
1992	Eve Bunting	*A Sudden Silence* [¿,3]	15				
1991	M. E. Kerr	*Night Kites*	12				
1990	Cynthia Voigt	*Izzy Willy Nilly* [••]	12				
1989	Eve Bunting	*Face at the Edge of the World* [••,oo]	12				
1988	William Sleator	*Interstellar Pig*	12				
1987	Michael French	*Pursuit*					
1986	Meredith Ann Pierce	*The Darkangel* [~~~]	12				
1985	Frances Miller	*The Truth Trap*					
1984	Lois Duncan	*Stranger with My Face* [oo]	12				

Year	Author	Title	Age	Own	Recommend	To Read	Want
1983	Lois Duncan	*Summer of Fear*	12				
1982	No Award Given						
1981	Lois Lowry	*A Summer to Die* ~~~	9				
1979	Sandra Scoppettone	*The Late Great Me*	15				
1978	No Award Given						
1977	Richard Adams	*Watership Down* **					

Colorado Blue Spruce Award ♪♪

The Colorado Blue Spruce Young Adult Book Award, organized and administered by the Blue Spruce Book Award Committee, recognizes the most popular books among middle and high school students in Colorado. Teens nominate their favorite titles and select the winner—adults may not vote. All materials needed to participate in the Blue Spruce Award can be found on this website: www.cal-webs.org/bluespruce.

Year	Author	Title	Age	Own	Recommend	To Read	Want
2011							
2010							
2009	Stephenie Meyer	*Eclipse* #,±,±±	12				
2008	J. K. Rowling	*Harry Potter and the Half Blood Prince* #,∩	9				
2007	Christopher Paolini	*Eldest* #,∩∩,±±	12				
2006	J. K. Rowling	*Harry Potter and the Order of the Phoenix* #	9				
2005	Christopher Paolini	*Eragon* #,##,♦♦♦,Ω,‡,¶,33,•••,∩,¿¿¿,o,¿,∩∩ oo,3,••	12				
2004	J. K. Rowling	*Harry Potter and the Prisoner of Azkaban* ∩∩	9				

Colorado Blue Spruce Award ♪♪			Age	Own	Recommend	To Read	Want
Year	Author	Title					
2003	Nicholas Sparks	A Walk to Remember ‡‡					
2002	David J. Pelzer	The Lost Boy					
2001	J. K. Rowling	Harry Potter and the Sorcerer's Stone ♦♦♦,‡,∩,oo	9				
2000	Louis Sachar	Holes *,***,##,♦♦♦,¡¡¡,•••,∩,¿¿¿,¿,∩∩	9				
1999	Jack Canfield	Chicken Soup for the Teenage Soul •••,∩∩,••	15				
1997-1998	Will Hobbs	Downriver ♪	12				
1996	Caroline B. Cooney	The Face on the Milk Carton ³,♪♪	12				
1995	John Grisham	The Client •••					
1994	Stephen King	It					
1993	Michael Crichton	Jurassic Park ‡‡,¶¶¶,∩∩,oo					
1992	Will Hobbs	Changes in Latitude	12				
1991	Stephen King	Pet Sematary					
1990	Mary Higgins Clark	The Cradle Will Fall					
1989	Stephen King	Eyes of the Dragon					
1988	Joan Lowery Nixon	The Other Side of Dark ♪,‡‡,33,¿,••	12				
1987	Lois Duncan	The Third Eye	12				
1986	Katherine Paterson	The Bridge to Terabithia	9				
1985	Judy Blume	Tiger Eyes ♪,‡‡	12				

Delaware Diamonds ♪♪♪

Since 1990, the Delaware Diamond Book Award, administered by the Diamond State Reading Association, has engaged the children of Delaware in a reader's choice award. The purpose of the award as explained by the award administrator's website is "to encourage young readers in Delaware to become better acquainted with quality literature, to expose students to recent books, to honor favorite books and authors, and to broaden students' awareness of literature as a lifelong pleasure." For more information, visit www.doe.k12.de.us/dsra/deldiamonds.htm.

Year	Author	Title	Age	Own	Recommend	To Read	Want
Middle School							
2011							
2010							
2009	Stephenie Meyer	*Twilight* #,♦♦♦,Ω,ΩΩ,ΩΩΩ,‡,‡‡‡,¶,¶¶,¶¶¶,ii,•• •,¿¿¿,o,∩∩,3,¡,Σ	15				
High School							
2011							
2010							
2009	Sherman Alexie	*The Absolutely True Diary of a Part-Time Indian* •,•••,♥♥♥	12				
2009	Sharon M. Draper	*November Blues*	12				
2009	Patricia McCormick	*Sold* ♪	12				

Florida Teens Read Award $^\Omega$

The mission of the Floria Teens Read Award program is "to encourage Florida teens to read enjoyable, quality literature that will stimulate imagination, awaken curiosity, expand horizons, enhance verbal fluency, and foster critical thinking and a lifelong love for reading and learning." The award, which is administered by the Florida Association for Media in Education, is given each year to a fiction or nonfiction title with a copyright within the last three years. High school students in 9th through 12th grade vote for their favorite books. To find out more, including upcoming winners, visit www.floridamedia.org/displaycommon.cfm?an=12.

Year	Author	Title	Age	Own	Recommend	To Read	Want
2011							
2010							
2009	Jay Asher	Thirteen Reasons Why ~~,‡‡‡	12				
2008	Scott Westerfeld	Uglies ×,ΩΩΩ,‡,¶¶¶,ii,••	12				
2007	Stephenie Meyer	Twilight #,♦♦♦,♫♫♫,ΩΩ,ΩΩΩ,‡,‡‡‡,¶,¶¶,¶¶¶,ii,•••,¿¿¿,○,∩∩,3,¡,Σ	15				
2006	Christopher Paolini	Eragon #,##,♦♦♦,♫♫,‡,¶,33,•••,∩,¿¿¿,○,¿,∩∩○○,3,••	12				

Georgia Peach Teen Award $^{\Omega\Omega}$

The purpose of the Georgia Peach Award, first given in 2006, is to highlight and promote the best current young adult literature for Georgia high-school-age students, to encourage young adults to read, and to promote the development of cooperative school and public library services for young adults. Teens may vote for their favorite books from a list of the year's top twenty nominees at their high schools and local public libraries. Find more information at www.glma-inc .org/peachaward.htm.

Year	Author	Title	Age	Own	Recommend	To Read	Want
2011							
2010							

Year	Author	Title	Age	Own	Recommend	To Read	Want
2009	Ellen Hopkins	*Impulse* ‡‡‡	15				
2008	Stephenie Meyer	*Twilight* #,♦♦♦,♫♫♫,Ω,ΩΩΩ,‡,‡‡‡,¶,¶¶,¶¶¶,ii, •••,¿¿¿,०,∩∩,३,¡,Σ	15				
2006	Graham McNamee	*Acceleration* &&&,▼	12				
2005	L. A. Meyer	*Bloody Jack*	12				
2004	Angela Johnson	*The First Part Last* ‼,#,•	12				

Abraham Lincoln Award: Illinois' High School Readers' Choice Award ΩΩΩ

"The Abraham Lincoln Award is awarded annually to the author of the book voted as most outstanding by participating students in grades nine through twelve in Illinois. The award is named for Abraham Lincoln, one of Illinois' most famous residents and himself an avid reader and noted author. The award is sponsored by the Illinois School Library Media Association (ISLMA). The Abraham Lincoln Award is designed to encourage high school students to read for personal satisfaction and become familiar with authors of young adult and adult books." For more information, and to view the next winners, visit www .islma.org/lincoln.htm

Year	Author	Title	Age	Own	Recommend	To Read	Want
2011							
2010							
2009	Ellen Hopkins	*Crank* ¶,•,∩∩	12				
2008	Stephenie Meyer	*Twilight* #,♦♦♦,♫♫♫,Ω,ΩΩ,‡,‡‡‡,¶,¶¶,¶¶¶,ii,••• ,¿¿¿,०,∩∩,३,¡,Σ	15				
2007	Scott Westerfeld	*Uglies* x,Ω,‡,¶¶¶,ii,••	12				
2006	Jodi Picoult	*My Sister's Keeper* ~,~~,#,••,Σ					
2005	David J. Pelzer	*A Child Called It: One Child's Courage to Survive* ∩∩					

☐ Juvenile Nonfiction ☐ Juvenile Fiction ■ Fiction ■ Nonfiction

Indiana High School Book Award [‡]

The ingeniously titled Eliot Rosewater Award is named after the fictional character in books by the Indiana-born author, Kurt Vonnegut, including probably the best known, *God Bless You, Mr. Rosewater*. The award was established to honor Vonnegut and other Hoosier writers while at the same time encouraging Indiana high school students to read for fun and enjoyment. High school students (grades 9–12) throughout Indiana vote each year on approximately twenty nominated titles for the book they enjoyed the most. The winning title, announced annually in April, wins its author the "Rosie Award" at a special event that is sponsored by the Association of Media Educators and the Indiana Library Federation. For more information on the Rosie, visit www .schoolbookcenter.com./html/eliot_rosewater_awards.html.

Year	Author	Title	Age	Own	Recommend	To Read	Want
2010							
2009							
2008	Laurie Halse Anderson	*Twisted* #	15				
2007	Stephenie Meyer	*Twilight* #,♦♦♦,♪♪,Ω,ΩΩ,ΩΩΩ,‡‡‡,¶,¶¶,¶¶¶,ii, •••,ὲὲὲ,o,∩∩,3,¡,Σ	15				
2006	Scott Westerfeld	*Uglies* x,Ω,ΩΩΩ,¶¶¶,ii,••	12				
2005	Christopher Paolini	*Eragon* #,##,♦♦♦,♪♪,Ω,¶,33,•••,∩,ὲὲὲ,o,ὲ,∩ ∩,oo,3,••	12				
2004	Alice Sebold	*The Lovely Bones* ‡‡,‡‡‡,¶,oo					
2003	Ann Brashares	*The Sisterhood of the Traveling Pants* ~~,‡‡,Σ,¶,ii,•••,3	15				
2002	Sarah Dressen	*Dreamland*	12				
2001	Connie Rose Porter	*Imani All Mine*					
2000	J. K. Rowling	*Harry Potter and the Sorcerer's Stone* ♦♦♦,♪♪,∩,oo	9				
1999	Billie Letts	*Where the Heart Is*	0				
1998	Caroline B. Cooney	*Driver's Ed* ii,•••,3	12				
1997	Beatrice Sparks	*It Happened to Nancy*					
1996	Lois Lowry	*The Giver* x,♦♦♦,¶¶,¶¶¶,ii,ὲὲὲ,••	12				
1995	Jennings Michael Burch	*They Cage Animals at Night*					

Iowa Teen Book Award ‡‡

Administered by the Iowa Association of School Librarians, the Iowa Teen Book Award (grades 6–9) and the Iowa High School Book Award (grades 9–12) provides Iowa students with a diversified, quality reading list and promotes leisure reading among Iowa students. For more information and the Iowa's pre-teen lists, see awards.iasl.iowapages.org/id3.html

Year	Author	Title	Age	Own	Recommend	To Read	Want
Iowa Teen Award (grades 6–9)							
2010							
2009							
2008	Rick Riordan	*The Lightning Thief* ‡‡,♦♦♦,£££,¶¶,33,¿¿¿,¿,3,••	9				
2007	Sonya Sones	*One of Those Hideous Books Where The Mother Dies* o,3	15				
2006	Sonya Sones	*What My Mother Doesn't Know*	12				
2005	Anthony Horowitz	*Stormbreaker* ♪,∩,oo	9				
2004	Ann Brashares	*The Sisterhood of the Traveling Pants* ~~,‡,Σ,¶,ii,•••,3	15				
2003	Jerry Spinelli	*Stargirl* ♦♦♦,i¡	12				
2002	Gary Paulsen	*The Transall Saga* ¶¶	15				
2001	Beatrice Sparks	*Annie's Baby*	15				
2000	Gail Carson Levine	*Ella Enchanted* ♦♦♦,♪	9				
1999	Jerry Spinelli	*Crash* £££,¿¿¿,oo,••	9				
1998	Gary Paulsen	*Brian's Winter* ii,∩,3	12				
1997	Gary Paulsen	*Harris and Me* ∩,oo	12				
1996	Caroline B. Cooney	*Whatever Happened to Janie*	12				
1995	Michael Crichton	*Jurassic Park* ♪♪,¶¶¶,∩∩,oo					
1994	Ryan White	*Ryan White: My Own Story*					
1993	Caroline B. Cooney	*The Face on the Milk Carton* ♪♪,3	12				
1992	Lois Duncan	*Don't Look Behind You* 33,3	12				
1991	Norma Fox Mazer	*Silver*	12				

▢ Juvenile Nonfiction   ▢ Juvenile Fiction   ▮ Fiction   ▮ Nonfiction

Iowa Teen Book Award ‡‡

Year	Author	Title	Age	Own	Recommend	To Read	Want
1990	Gary Paulsen	Hatchet ££,£££,¿,∩∩,••	9				
1989	Joan Lowery Nixon	The Other Side of Dark ♪,♪♪,33,¿,••	12				
1988	Hadley Irwin	Abby My Love ¿	12				
1987	Patricia Hermes	You Shouldn't Have to Say Goodbye ♪	9				
1986	Norma Fox Mazer	When We First Met	12				
1985	Judy Blume	Tiger Eyes ♪,♪♪	12				

Iowa High School Book Award (grades 9–12)

Year	Author	Title	Age	Own	Recommend	To Read	Want
2010							
2009							
2008	Sarah Dessen	Just Listen #,¶	15				
2007	Libba Bray	A Great and Terrible Beauty #	12				
2006	Dan Brown	The Da Vinci Code ‡‡,i					
2005	Alice Sebold	The Lovely Bones ‡,‡‡‡,¶,∞					
2004	Nicholas Sparks	A Walk to Remember ♪♪					

Kentucky Bluegrass Award ‡‡‡

The Kentucky Bluegrass Award (KBA) was created to encourage K–12 students in Kentucky to read quality children's literature. One of approximately forty-five state children's choice awards nationwide, KBA welcomes participants from all Kentucky public and private schools as well as public libraries. The books listed here are from the grades 9–12 and 6–8 categories. More information is available at www.kba.nku.edu/index.shtml.

Year	Author	Title	Age	Own	Recommend	To Read	Want
2011							
2010							
2009	Gretchen Olson	Call Me Hope	9				
2009	Jay Asher	Thirteen Reasons Why ~~,Ω	12				

Year	Author	Title	Age	Own	Recommend	To Read	Want
2008	Cynthia Lord	*Rules* !!!	9				
2008	Ellen Hopkins	*Impulse* ΩΩ	15				
2007	Meg Cabot	*Avalon High*	12				
2007	Stephenie Meyer	*Twilight* #,♦♦♦,♪♪♪,Ω,ΩΩ,ΩΩΩ,‡,¶,¶¶,¶¶¶,ii, •••,¿¿¿,o,∩∩,3,¡	15				
2006	Sarah Weeks	*So B. It* iii,oo	9				
2006	John Green	*Looking for Alaska* !!,#,•	15				
2005	Gordon Korman	*Son of the Mob* ~~,##,♦♦♦	12				
2005	Stephanie S. Tolan	*Surviving the Applewhites*	9				
2004	Ann M. Martin	*A Corner of the Universe*	9				
2004	Alice Sebold	*The Lovely Bones* ‡,‡‡,¶,oo					
2003	Ronald Koertge	*The Brimstone Journals*	12				
2003	Louise Rennison	*Knocked Out by Nunga-Nungas: Further Confessions of Georgia Nicolson*	12				
2002	Terry Trueman	*Stuck in Neutral*	12				
2002	Walter Dean Myers	*Monster* !!	12				
2001	Shelley Tankaka	*Secrets of the Mummies*	10				
2001	Laurie Halse Anderson	*Speak* ~~,ii,•••,¿,oo,3	15				

Juvenile Nonfiction   Juvenile Fiction   Fiction   Nonfiction

Lupine Award—Maine °

"The Lupine Award is presented annually by the Youth Services Section Interest Group of the Maine Library Association, to recognize an outstanding contribution to children's literature of Maine. This award is granted to encourage the reading, writing and appreciation of children's books, and to foster pride in the state of Maine." The winners in the young adult category are listed here. To view young adult honor books and winners in other categories, visit www.mainelibraries.org/aw_lupine.php?mi=7&page_mi=4.

Year	Author	Title	Age	Own	Recommend	To Read	Want
2010							
2009							
2008	Les Becquets	*Season of Ice*	12				
2007	Sarah Thomson	*Dragon's Egg*	9				
2006	Garrett Conover	*Kristin's Wilderness: A Braided Trail*	9				
2005	Jennifer Jacobson	*Stained*	12				

Black-Eyed Susan Book Award—Maryland ᶻ

The Maryland Black-Eyed Susan Book Award is administered by the Maryland Association of School Librarians and represents student choices. Each year since 1992, the award has been given to one book in each of several grade-level categories. Maryland school children choose the winners from a master list of contemporary works that have been positively reviewed. The goal of the awards program is to encourage lifelong reading of quality literature. The Web address is www.annapolishigh.org/~media/html/black.htm.

Year	Author	Title	Age	Own	Recommend	To Read	Want
2011							
2010							
2009	Susan Beth Pfeffer	*Life As We Knew It* [#,ii,•••]	12				
2008	Stephanie Meyer	*Twilight* [#,•••,♫♫♫,Ω,ΩΩ,ΩΩΩ,‡,‡‡‡,¶,¶¶,¶¶¶,ii,•••,¿¿¿,◊,∩∩,3,¡]	15				

Year	Author	Title	Age	Own	Recommend	To Read	Want
2007	Jodi Picoult	My Sister's Keeper ~,~~,#,ΩΩΩ,••					
2006	Neal Shusterman	Full Tilt ¶¶¶	12				
2005	Margaret Bechard	Hanging on to Max	15				
2004	Alex Flinn	Breathing Underwater	12				
2003	Ann Brashares	The Sisterhood of the Traveling Pants ~~,‡,‡‡,¶,ii,•••,3	15				
2002	Jacqueline Woodson	If You Come Softly ••	9				
2001	Sarah Dessen	Someone Like You ºº	12				
2000	Nancy Werlin	The Killer's Cousin ▼,ii	15				
1999	David Klass	Danger Zone ¶¶,¿	14				

Thumbs Up! Award—Michigan £

The Thumbs Up! Award was established in 1986 to recognize the excellence in and celebrate the uniqueness of teen and young adult literature. A committee, consisting of librarians who work with young readers, meets several times during the year to identify a winner. Since 2001, the Thumbs Up! Committee has included a teenaged voter. For more information, see www .mla.lib.mi.us/tsdthumbsup. Reprinted with permission from the Michigan Library Association.

Year	Author	Title	Age	Own	Recommend	To Read	Want
2010							
2009							
2008	Robin Brande	Evolution, Me, and Other Freaks of Nature	12				
2007	Pete Hautman	Rash ˣ	12				
2006	David Lubar	Sleeping Freshmen Never Lie	12				
2005	Kenneth Oppel	Airborn 33,••	12				

▢ Juvenile Nonfiction   ▢ Juvenile Fiction   ■ Fiction   ▦ Nonfiction

Thumbs Up! Award—Michigan £			Age	Own	Recommend	To Read	Want
Year	Author	Title					
2004	Celia Rees	Pirates! The True and Remarkable Adventures of Minerva Sharpe and Nancy Kington Female Pirates. #	12				
2003	E. R. Frank	America: A Novel	15				
2002	David Klass	You Don't Know Me	12				
2001	Joan Bauer	Hope was Here ##	12				
2000	Ellen Wittlinger	Hard Love	12				
1999	Heather Quarles	A Door Near Here **	12				
1998	Rob Thomas	Doing Time: Notes from an Undergrad					
1997	Pete Hautman	Mr. Was	12				
1996	Kristen Randle	The Only Alien on the Planet ♪	12				
1995	Frances Temple	The Ramsay Scallop	12				
1994	Virginia Euwer Wolff	Make Lemonade	12				
1993	Walter Dean Myers	Somewhere in the Darkness	12				
1992	Chris Crutcher	Athletic Shorts	12				
1991	Mildred D. Taylor	Road to Memphis	12				
1990	Cynthia Grant	Phoenix Rising: Or How to Survive Your Life					
1989	Jenny Davis	Sex Education	12				
1988	Phyllis Reynolds Naylor	Year of the Gopher	12				
1987	John Lavert	Flight of the Cassowary					

Minnesota Book Award ££

The Minnesota Book Award annually recognizes books that reflect a clear Minnesota influence or are written by Minnesota writers. Begun in 1988, they are now sponsored by the Friends of the St. Paul Public Library. Award category names have varied greatly over the years, and not all categories are included in the honors every year. The award for young adult literature may be given to a work of fiction, nonfiction, graphic novel, or poetry for teens or young adults. For more information, see www.thefriends.org/mnbookawards.html.

Year	Author	Title	Age	Own	Recommend	To Read	Want
2011							
2010							
2009	Brian Malloy	*Twelve Long Months*	15				
2008	Will Weaver	*Defect*	12				
2007	Julie Schumacher	*The Book of One Hundred Truths*	9				
2006	Alison McGhee	*All Rivers Flow to the Sea*	15				
2005	Pete Hautman	*Godless* *	12				
2004	Dave Kenney	*Northern Lights: The Stories of Minnesota's Past*	8				
2004	Pete Hautman	*Sweetblood*	15				
2003	Jan Neubert Schultz	*Firestorm*	9				
2003	Thomas M. Peacock and Marlene Wisuri	*The Good Path*	8				
2002	Richard Mosher	*Zazoo*	12				
2001	Mary Casanova	*Curse of a Winter Moon*					
2000	Kristine L. Franklin	*Dove Song*	12				
1999	Gary Paulsen	*Soldier's Heart: A Novel of the Civil War*	15				
1998	William Durbin	*The Broken Blade*	12				
1997	Michael Dorris	*Sees Behind Trees*	8				
1996	Marsha Qualey	*Hometown*	12				
1995	Marion Dane Bauer	*Am I Blue?: Coming Out from the Silence*	10				

☐ Juvenile Nonfiction   ☐ Juvenile Fiction   ■ Fiction   ■ Nonfiction

Minnesota Book Award ££			Age	Own	Recommend	To Read	Want
Year	Author	Title					
1994	Jim Brandenburg	To the Top of the World: Adventures with Arctic Wolves	10				
1994	Marsha Qualey	Revolutions of the Heart					
1993	Marion Dane Bauer	What's Your Story? A Young Person's Guide to Writing Fiction	10				
1992	Marion Dane Bauer	Face to Face	10				
1991	Gary Paulsen and Ruth Wright Paulsen Illustrator	Woodsong	12				
1988	Gary Paulsen	Hatchet ‡‡,£££,¿,∩∩,••	9				

Maud Hart Lovelace Award—Minnesota £££

The Minnesota Youth Reading Award sponsors an award dedicated to the memory of Maud Hart Lovelace, a famous Minnesota author. The winners are announced on Maud's birthday, April 25th. The award is given in two divisions; one for grades 3–5 and another for grades 6–8. The second division winners are listed here. More information about Maud and the book award can be found at www.maudhartlovelace.org.

Year	Author	Title	Age	Own	Recommend	To Read	Want
2011							
2010							
2009	Rick Riordan	The Lightning Thief ##,♦♦♦,‡‡,¶¶,33,¿¿¿,¿,3,••	9				
2008	Jordan Sonnenblick	Drums, Girls and Dangerous Pie #,¿¿¿	12				
2007	Andrew Clements	Things Not Seen !!!,♪	12				
2006	Carl Hiaasen	Hoot ∩,¿¿¿	9				
2005	Roland Smith	Zach's Lie	12				
2004	Ben Mikaelson	Touching Spirit Bear ♪,¶¶,¶¶¶,33,∩,∩∩	9				
2003	Frances O'Roark Dowell	Dovey Coe	9				

Year	Author	Title	Age	Own	Recommend	To Read	Want
2002	Arvella Whitmore	Trapped Between the Lash and the Gun	9				
2001	Margaret Peterson Haddix	Among the Hidden ♪,ὶὶὶ	9				
2000	Edward Bloor	Tangerine ¶¶¶,ii,oo	9				
1999	Jerry Spinelli	Crash ‡‡,ὶὶὶ,oo,••	9				
1998	Barbara Park	Mick Harte Was Here oo	9				
1997	Jane Yolen	The Devil's Arithmetic	9				
1996	Peg Kehret	Cages	8				
1995	Peg Kehret	Nightmare Mountain	9				
1994	Mona Kerby	38 Weeks Til Summer Vacation	12				
1993	Mary Downing Hahn	Dead Man in Indian Creek oo,••	9				
1992	Gery Greer and Bob Ruddick	This Island Isn't Big Enough for the Four of Us	9				
1991	Gary Paulsen	Hatchet ‡‡,££,¿,nn,••	9				
1990	Mary Downing Hahn	Wait Til Helen Comes	9				
1989	Phyllis Green	Eating Ice Cream with a Werewolf	9				
1988	Ivy Ruckman	Night of the Twisters	8				
1987	John Gardiner	Stone Fox	9				
1986	Barbara Dana	Zucchini	9				
1985	Barbara Park	Skinnybones	9				
1984	Barthe DeClements	Nothing's Fair in Fifth Grade	9				
1983	Marilyn Singer	It Can't Hurt Forever	9				
1982	Barbara Robinson	The Best Christmas Pageant Ever	9				
1981	Betsy Byars	Pinballs	9				
1980	Wilson Rawls	The Summer of the Monkeys	9				

☐ Juvenile Nonfiction ☐ Juvenile Fiction ■ Fiction ■ Nonfiction

Gateway Readers Award—Missouri ¶

The Gateway Readers Award is given to authors of books chosen by high school students in the state of Missouri. The award received its name based on the philosophy that reading is the gateway to knowledge and lifelong learning, because the teen years are the gateway to adulthood, and because Missouri was the gateway to the Old West. Librarians serving young adults in school and public libraries were responsible for the naming of the program. The awards website is www.maslonline.org/awards/books/Gateway. The Missouri Association of School Libraries does not endorse or recommend any discussions relating to books that are on the reading lists for the Gateway, Mark Twain, Show Me, or Truman Reading Incentive Program. Visit http://www.maslonline .org/?page=gateway_readers for more information.

Year	Author	Title	Age	Own	Recommend	To Read	Want
2011							
2010							
2009	Sarah Dessen	*Just Listen* ‡‡,#	12				
2008	Stephenie Meyer	*Twilight* #,♦♦♦,♪♪♪,Ω,ΩΩ,ΩΩΩ,‡,‡‡‡,¶¶,¶¶¶,ii, •••,¿¿¿,◊,∩∩,3,¡,Σ	15				
2007	Ellen Hopkins	*Crank* ΩΩΩ,•,∩∩	12				
2006	Christopher Paolini	*Eragon* #,##,♦♦♦,♪♪,Ω,‡,33,•••,∩,¿¿¿,◊,¿, ∩∩ ,oo,3,••	12				
2005	Alice Sebold	*The Lovely Bones* ‡,‡‡,‡‡‡,oo					
2004	Ann Brashares	*The Sisterhood of the Traveling Pants* ~~,‡,‡‡,Σ,ii,•••,3	15				

Golden Sower Award—Nebraska ¶¶

"The Nebraska Library Association honors three books written for young people each year (Primary, Intermediate, and Young Adult) with the Golden Sower Award (website: www.goldensower.org). All nominations come from Nebraska students, teachers and library professionals, and the students themselves vote for their favorite books. The program's goals are to encourage independent reading, to stimulate children's thinking, to introduce different types of literature, and to foster an appreciation for excellence in writing and illustrating and a lifelong love of literature. The award is named for the 19,000-pound bronze statue that stands atop the Nebraska State Capitol in Lincoln. The statue of a man sowing seeds by hand symbolizes Nebraska's status as a major agricultural state and also the state's interest in sowing the seeds of life, hope and prosperity." The winning titles in the Young Adult category are listed here and can also be found at www.goldensower.org/winners/winners3.htm.

Year	Author	Title	Age	Own	Recommend	To Read	Want
2011							
2010							
2009	Stephenie Meyer	*Twilight* #,♦♦♦,♪♪♪,Ω,ΩΩ,ΩΩΩ,‡,‡‡‡,¶,¶¶¶,ii, •••,¿¿¿,○,∩∩,3,¡,Σ	15				
2008	Rick Riordan	*The Lightning Thief* ##,♦♦♦,‡‡,£££,33,¿¿¿,¿,3,••	9				
2007	Natasha Friend	*Perfect*	12				
2006	Carl Deuker	*High Heat*	12				
2005	Chris Crowe	*Mississippi Trial 1955* ~~~,%%%	12				
2004	Ben Mikaelson	*Touching Spirit Bear* ♪,£££,¶¶¶,33,∩,∩∩	9				
2003	Carl Deuker	*Night Hoops*	12				
2002	Gary Paulsen	*The Transall Saga* ‡‡	15				
2001	Joan Lowery Nixon	*The Haunting*	15				
2000	Margaret Peterson Haddix	*Don't You Dare Read This, Mrs. Dunphrey* ~~~	12				
1999	Carol Lynch Williams	*The True Colors of Caitlynne Jackson*	10				
1998	David Klass	*Danger Zone* Σ,¿	15				

☐ Juvenile Nonfiction   ☐ Juvenile Fiction   ■ Fiction   ■ Nonfiction

Golden Sower Award— Nebraska ¶¶			Age	Own	Recommend	To Read	Want
Year	Author	Title					
1997	W. R. Philbrick	*Freak the Mighty* ♦♦♦,♪,∩∩	9				
1996	Carl Deuker	*Heart of a Champion* ¿¿¿,3	12				
1995	Lois Lowry	*The Giver* x,♦♦♦,‡,¶¶,ii,¿¿¿,¿,••	12				
1994	Caroline B. Cooney	*Flight #116 is Down* ¿,••	12				
1993	Joan Lowery Nixon	*Whispers from the Dead* ¶¶,∩∩	12				

Nevada Young Reader's Award ¶¶

The Nevada Young Reader's Award was established in 1987 by the Nevada Department of Education to encourage improvement of Nevada students' reading skills through engagement with the best of modern children's literature. Winning books in each of several categories are nominated, read, and voted on by Nevada's young readers. The annual event is now co-sponsored by the Nevada Library Association, which presents the awards based on the previous school year's activities at its fall conference. Consult the library association's website for more information: www.nevadalibraries.org/Divisions/NYRA.

Year	Author	Title	Age	Own	Recommend	To Read	Want
2011							
2010							
2009	Roland Smith	*Peak*	12				
2008	Scott Westerfeld	*Uglies* x,Ω,ΩΩΩ,‡,ii,••	12				
2007	Stephenie Meyer	*Twilight* #,♦♦♦,♪♪♪,Ω,ΩΩ,ΩΩΩ,‡,‡‡‡,¶,¶¶,ii, ••,¿¿¿,◊,∩∩,3,¡,Σ	15				
2006	Neal Shusterman	*Full Tilt* Σ	12				
2005	Nancy Farmer	*The House of the Scorpion* •,##,♦♦♦,◊,¿,∞,3	12				
2004	Donna Jo Napoli	*Daughter of Venice*	12				
2003	Ben Mikaelson	*Touching Spirit Bear* ♪,£££,¶¶,33,∩,∩∩	9				
2002	Caroline B. Cooney	*Burning Up*	12				

Year	Author	Title	Age	Own	Recommend	To Read	Want
2001	S. L. Rottman	*Hero* ‡‡‡	12				
2000	Lois Duncan	*Gallows Hill* ³	12				
1999	Edward Bloor	*Tangerine* £££,ii,oo	9				
1998	Vivian Vande Velde	*Companions of the Night*	12				
1997	Joyce Sweeney	*Shadow*	12				
1996	Stephen Hoffius	*Winners and Losers*	12				
1995	Lois Lowry	*The Giver* x,♦♦♦,‡,¶¶,ii,ﺀﺀﺀ,ﺀ,ˮ	12				
1994	Stephanie S. Tolan	*Plague Year* ˮ	12				
1993	Michael Crichton	*Jurassic Park* ♫♫,‡‡,∩∩,oo	12				
1992	Joan Lowery Nixon	*Whispers from the Dead* ¶¶,∩∩	12				
1991	Richard Peck	*Princess Ashley* ∩∩	12				
1990	Bernal C. Payne Jr.	*Experiment in Terror*	12				
1989	Lois Duncan	*Locked in Time* oo	12				

The Flume: New Hampshire Teen Reader's Choice Award ¡

"The Flume: NH Teen Reader's Choice Award was created in 2005 in response to a New Hampshire teens' request to have a book award geared towards high school students. This award is a state-wide venture led by a collaborative effort from school and public librarians. Each year teens nominate titles, published within the last two years, they think deserve to be recognized. Librarians then narrow the group of titles to a list of 13. Teens then vote for the winning title from the list of 13." The award is named after a natural granite gorge at the base of Mount Liberty in Franconia Notch State Park. More information about the award, including current nominees, can be found at www.nashua.lib.nh.us/ YALS/Flume.htm.

Year	Author	Title	Age	Own	Recommend	To Read	Want
2011							

☐ Juvenile Nonfiction ☐ Juvenile Fiction ■ Fiction ■ Nonfiction

The Flume: New Hampshire Teen Reader's Choice Award [i]			Age	Own	Recommend	To Read	Want
Year	Author	Title					
2010							
2009	Jodi Picoult	*Nineteen Minutes*					
2008	Stephenie Meyer	*New Moon* [#,##,oo]	15				
2007	Stephenie Meyer	*Twilight* [#,♦♦♦,♪♪♪,Ω,ΩΩ,ΩΩΩ,‡,‡‡‡,¶,¶¶,¶¶¶,] [ii,•••,¿¿¿,o,ΩΩ,3,Σ]	15				
2006	Dan Brown	*The Da Vinci Code* [‡‡,±±]					

Garden State Teen Book Award—New Jersey [ii]

The New Jersey Library Association has sponsored the Garden State Teen Book Award since 1995. Each year, a committee of librarians nominates titles published in the three years prior to the award year, based on teen appeal and quality of writing. Ballots are then distributed to New Jersey schools and librarians, for teens to read and nominate their favorite books. Further information is located on the website: www.njla.org/honorsawards/book/teen.html.

Year	Author	Title	Age	Own	Recommend	To Read	Want
Grades —8							
2011							
2010							
2009	Susan Beth Pfeffer	*Life As We Knew It* [#,Σ,•••]	12				
2008	Scott Westerfeld	*Uglies* [x,Ω,ΩΩΩ,‡,¶¶¶,••]	12				
2007	Gennifer Choldenko	*Al Capone Does My Shirts* [♪]	9				
2006	Jeanne Duprau	*The City of Ember* [iii]	9				
2005	Cornelia Funke	*The Thief Lord* [#,♦♦♦]	12				
2004	Eoin Colfer	*Artemis Fowl* [##]	12				
2003	Jerry Spinelli	*Stargirl* [♦♦♦,‡‡]	12				
2002	David Almond	*Skellig* [**]	9				
2001	Cherie Bennett	*Life in the Fat Lane*	12				
2000	Edward Bloor	*Tangerine* [£££,¶¶¶,oo]	9				

Year	Author	Title	Age	Own	Recommend	To Read	Want
1999	Gary Paulsen	Brian's Winter ‡‡,∩,3	12				
1998	Chris Lynch	Slot Machine	12				
1997	Paul Zindel	Loch	12				
1996	Lois Lowry	The Giver X,♦♦♦,‡,¶¶,¶¶¶,¿¿¿,¿,··	12				
1995	Avi	Nothing But the Truth: A Documentary Novel ♦♦♦	12				
Grades 9–12							
2011							
2010							
2009	Markus Zusak	The Book Thief	12				
2008	Stephenie Meyer	Twilight #,♦♦♦,♫♫,∩,∩∩,∩∩∩,‡,‡‡‡,¶,¶¶,¶¶¶,···,¿¿¿,∘,∩∩,3,¡,Σ	15				
2007	Eireann Corrigan	Splintering	15				
2006	Mark Haddon	The Circuit: Stories from the Life of a Migrant Child	12				
2005	Meg Cabot	All-American Girl ···	12				
2004	Ann Brashares	The Sisterhood of the Traveling Pants ~~,‡,‡‡,Σ,¶,···,3	15				
2003	Louise Rennison	Angus, Thongs and Full-Frontal Snogging ··	12				
2002	Laurie Halse Anderson	Speak ~~,‡‡‡,···,¿,∘∘,3	15				
2001	Nancy Werlin	The Killer's Cousin ▼,Σ	15				
2000	Annette Curtis Klause	Blood and Chocolate	15				
1999	Douglas Preston and Lincoln Child	Mount Dragon	12				
1998	Douglas Preston and Lincoln Child	Relic					
1997	Caroline B. Cooney	Driver's Ed ‡,···,3	12				
1996	Wayne Smith	Thor					
1995	Dan Simmons	Children of the Night	13				

☐ Juvenile Nonfiction ☐ Juvenile Fiction ■ Fiction ■ Nonfiction

Land of Enchantment Book Award—New Mexico [iii]

The Land of Enchantment Book Award is New Mexico's annual state book award. Instituted in 1981, the program's goal is to introduce young people from New Mexico to outstanding examples of age-appropriate, high-quality literature. A committee selects two lists of books: children's and young adult. New Mexico's young people are encouraged read and vote for the winners from the list. For more information, see www.loebookaward.com.

Year	Author	Title	Age	Own	Recommend	To Read	Want
2011							
2010							
2009	Sarah Weeks	*So B. It* [‡‡‡,oo]	9				
2008	Ann M. Martin	*A Dog's Life: The Autobiography of a Stray*	9				
2007	Jeanne Duprau	*The City Of Ember* [ii]	9				
2006	Kate Dicamillo	*The Tale of Despereaux*	9				
2005	Sharon Creech	*Ruby Holler* [**]	9				
2004	Sharon Creech	*Love That Dog*	8				
2003	Christopher Paul Curtis	*Bud, Not Buddy* [~~~,♦♦♦]	12				
2002	Will Hobbs	*Ghost Canoe* [▼,z]	12				
2001	Louis Sachar	*Holes* [*,***,##,♦♦♦,♪♪,•••,∩,¿¿¿,¿,∩∩]	9				
2000	Christopher Paul Curtis	*The Watsons Go to Birmingham* [♪]	12				

North Carolina School Library Media Association Young Adult Book Award [±]

The North Carolina School Library Media Association Young Adult Book Award is a newly formed award program with categories focused in subjects for middle school and high school winners. To view the newest list of competing titles, visit www.ncslma.org/BookCompetitions/YAaward/NCSLMAYAaward.htm.

Year	Author	Title	Age	Own	Recommend	To Read	Want
High School							
2010							
2009							
2008	Stephenie Meyer	*Eclipse* [#,♪♪,±±]	12				
Middle School							
2010							
2009							
2008	Allan Wolf	*Zane's Trace*	12				

Teen Buckeye Book Award—Ohio [±±]

"The Teen Buckeye Book Award program is designed to encourage students in Ohio to read literature critically, to promote teacher and librarian involvement in young adult literature programs, and to commend authors of such literature. The Teen Buckeye Book Award category was added to the existing Buckeye Children's Book Award in 2005." More information and future winners can be found at www.bcbookaward.info/teens/index.html.

Year	Author	Title	Age	Own	Recommend	To Read	Want
2010							
2009							
2008	Stephenie Meyer	*Eclipse* [#,♪♪,±]	12				
2007	Christopher Paolini	*Eldest* [#,♪♪,∩∩]	12				
2005	Dan Brown	*The Da Vinci Code* [±±,i]					

☐ Juvenile Nonfiction ☐ Juvenile Fiction ■ Fiction ■ Nonfiction

Oklahoma Book Award ±±±

The Oklahoma Book Award was established in 1990 by the Oklahoma Center for the Book to recognize titles written with an Oklahoma-based theme and/or written by authors who live or have lived in Oklahoma. Any individual, organization, or company may nominate a book published in the previous calendar year in any appropriate category. Lists and more information are available on the web at www.odl.state.ok.us/ocb/08win.htm.

Year	Author	Title	Age	Own	Recommend	To Read	Want
2011							
2010							
2009	Anna Myers	*Spy*	9				
2008	P. C. Cast and Kristin Cast	*Marked: A House of Night Novel*	12				
2007	Tim Tharp	*Knights of the Hill Country*	12				
2006	Anna Myers	*Assassin*	12				
2005	Molly Levite Griffis	*Simon Says*	9				
2004	Sharon Darrow	*The Painters of Lexieville*	12				
2003	Darleen Bailey Beard	*The Babbs Switch Story*	9				
2002	Molly Levite Griffis	*The Rachel Resistance*	9				
2001	Joyce Carol Thomas	*Hush Songs*					
2000	Harold Keith	*Brief Garland: Ponytails Basketball and Nothing But Net*	9				
1999	Barbara Snow Gilbert	*Broken Chords*	12				
1998	S. L. Rottman	*Hero* ¶¶¶	12				
1997	Barbara Snow Gilbert	*Stone Water*	12				
1996	Anna Myers	*Graveyard Girl*	9				
1995	Russell G. Davis and Brent Ashabranner	*The Choctaw Code*	9				
1994	Diane Hoyt-Goldsmith	*Cherokee Summer*	10				
1993	Anna Myers	*Red Dirt Jessie*	10				
1992	Jess and Bonnie Speer	*Hillback to Boggy*	12				
1991	Stan Hoig	*A Capital for the Nation*					
1990	Helen Roney Sattler	*Tyrannosaurus Rex and Its Kin*	9				

Sequoyah Award—Oklahoma ¿

This award program, begun in 1959, honors the Native American leader Sequoyah who developed a Cherokee syllabary—eighty-five symbols that represent all spoken sounds in the language. An Oklahoma Library Association committee develops two lists featuring books published in the three years prior to the award year. Oklahoma students then vote for the winners. See the library association website at www.oklibs.org/sequoyah for more information.

Year	Author	Title	Age	Own	Recommend	To Read	Want
2011							
2010							
2009	Wendelin Van Draanen	*Runaway*	12				
2008	Rick Riordan	*The Lightning Thief* ##,♦♦♦,‡‡,£££,¶¶,33,¿¿¿,3,••	9				
2007	Priscilla Cummings	*Red Kayak*	9				
2006	Christopher Paolini	*Eragon* #,##,♦♦♦,♪♪,Ω,‡,¶,33,•••,∩,¿¿¿,o, ∩∩,oo,3,••	12				
2005	Nancy Farmer	*The House of the Scorpion* •,##,♦♦♦,¶¶,o,oo,3	12				
2004	Ann Brashares	*Sisterhood of the Traveling Pants* ##,o	15				
2002	Laurie Halse Anderson	*Speak* ~~,‡‡‡,ii,•••,oo,3	15				
2001	Louis Sachar	*Holes* •,•••,##,♦♦♦,♪♪,iii,•••,∩,¿¿¿,∩∩	9				
2000	Livia Bitton Jackson	*I Have Lived a Thousand Years: Growing up in the Holocaust*	12				
1999	David Klass	*Danger Zone* Σ,¶¶	15				
1998	Margaret Peterson Haddix	*Running Out of Time*	8				
1997	Sharon Creech	*Walk Two Moons* ~~,••	12				
1996	Lois Lowry	*The Giver* x,♦♦♦,‡,¶¶,¶¶¶,ii,¿¿¿,••	12				
1995	Caroline B. Cooney	*Flight #116 is Down* ¶¶,••	12				
1994	Neal Shusterman	*What Daddy Did*	12				
1993	Annette Curtis Klause	*The Silver Kiss* ⸮	12				

☐ Juvenile Nonfiction ☐ Juvenile Fiction ■ Fiction ■ Nonfiction

Sequoyah Award—Oklahoma ¿

Year	Author	Title	Age	Own	Recommend	To Read	Want
1992	Jean Thesman	*Appointment with a Stranger*	12				
1991	Eve Bunting	*A Sudden Silence* ♪,3	15				
1990	Gary Paulsen	*Hatchet* ‡‡,££,£££,∩∩,••	9				
1989	Joan Lowery Nixon	*The Other Side of Dark* ♪,♪♪,‡‡,33,••	12				
1988	Hadley Irwin	*Abby My Love* ‡‡	10				

Leslie Bradshaw Award—Oregon ¿¿

The Leslie Bradshaw for Young Adult Literature is part of the Oregon Book Award, a program of Literary Arts. Created in 1999 by friends and family to honor Leslie Bradshaw (1952–1998), this award spotlights the best young adult book of the year written by an Oregon-based writer. Bradshaw was well known for sharing her passion for reading and love of a good story, especially with children at Beaver Acres Elementary School in Beaverton. Prior to 2003, the young adult category was combined with the children's category. See www .literary-arts.org/awards/past_young_readers.php for more information.

Year	Author	Title	Age	Own	Recommend	To Read	Want
2009							
2008	Sara Ryan	*The Rules for Hearts*	15				
2007	Susan Fletcher	*Alphabet of Dreams*	12				
2006	Graham Salisbury	*Eyes of the Emperor*	12				
2005	Linda Crew	*A Heart for Any Fate*	12				
2004	Susanna Vance	*Deep*	12				
2003	Heather Vogel Frederick	*The Voyage of Patience Goodspeed*	12				
2002	Sara Ryan	*Empress of the World*	12				

Pennsylvania Young Readers' Choice Award ¿¿¿

"The purpose of the Pennsylvania Young Reader's Choice Award is to promote reading of quality books by young people in the Commonwealth of Pennsylvania, to promote teacher and librarian involvement in children's literature, and to honor authors whose work has been recognized by the children of Pennsylvania." For a list of upcoming winners and for more information, see www.psla.org/grantsandawards/pyrca.php4.

Year	Author	Title	Age	Own	Recommend	To Read	Want
Grades 6-8							
2011							
2010							
2009	Jordan Sonnenblick	*Drums, Girls and Dangerous Pie* #,£££	12				
2008	Rick Riordan	*The Lightning Thief* ##,♦♦♦,‡‡,£££,¶¶,33,¿,3,••	9				
2005	Christopher Paolini	*Eragon* #,##,♦♦♦,♪♪,Ω,‡,¶,33,•••,∩,o,¿,∩∩,oo,3,••	12				
2004	Carl Hiaasen	*Hoot* £££,∩	9				
2003	Gail Carson Levine	*Two Princesses of Bamarre*	9				
2002	Margaret Peterson Haddix	*Among the Hidden* ♪,£££	9				
2001	Christoher Paul Curtis	*Bud, Not Buddy*	12				
2000	Louis Sachar	*Holes* •,•••,##,♦♦♦,♪♪,iii,•••,∩,¿,∩∩	9				
1999	Jerry Spinelli	*Crash* ‡‡,£££,oo,••	9				
1998	Eve Bunting	*Spying on Miss Muller*	9				
1997	Carl Deuker	*Heart of a Champion* ¶¶,3	12				
1996	Chris Van Allsburg	*The Sweetest Fig*	6				
1995	Lois Lowry	*The Giver* x,♦♦♦,‡,¶¶,¶¶¶,ii,¿,••	12				
1994	Jon Sciescka and Lane Smith	*The Stinky Cheeseman & Other Fairly Stupid Tales*	7				
1993	Phyllis Reynolds Naylor	*Shiloh*	9				
1992	Jerry Spinelli	*Maniac Magee* •••,••	9				

Pennsylvania Young Readers' Choice Award ¿¿¿			Age	Own	Recommend	To Read	Want
Year	Author	Title					
Young Adult							
2011							
2010							
2009	Stephenie Meyer	*Twilight* #,♦♦♦,♫♫♫,Ω,ΩΩ,ΩΩΩ,‡,‡‡‡,¶,¶¶,¶¶¶, ii,•••,o,ΩΩ,3,¡,Σ	15				
2008	Catherine Gilbert Murdock	*Dairy Queen*	12				

Rhode Island Teen Book Award °

The Rhode Island Education Media Association (RIEMA) and the Rhode Island Library Association (RILA) sponsor the Rhode Island Teen Book Award. The goal of the program is to promote quality literature for teens by honoring well-written books of interest to readers between 12 and 18 years of age. Organizers hope to encourage teens to read more and also to discuss books with their friends and family. Teens can pick up ballots to vote for their choices at schools and local libraries all over Rhode Island. This list was produced by a group of librarians, school library media specialists, reading specialists, and teachers. For more information, visit www.yourlibrary.ws/ya_webpage/ritba/ritbaindex.htm.

Year	Author	Title	Age	Own	Recommend	To Read	Want
2011							
2010							
2009	Michael Scott	*The Alchemyst: The Secrets of the Immortal Nicholas Flamel*	12				
2008	Natasha Friend	*Lush*	12				
2007	Stephenie Meyer	*Twilight* #,♦♦♦,♫♫♫,Ω,ΩΩ,ΩΩΩ,‡,‡‡‡,¶,¶¶,¶¶¶, ii,•••,¿¿¿,ΩΩ,3,¡,Σ	15				
2006	Sonya Sones	*One of Those Hideous Books Where The Mother Dies* ‡‡,3	15				
2005	Christopher Paolini	*Eragon* #,##,♦♦♦,♫♫,Ω,‡,¶,33,•••,∩,¿¿¿,¿, ∩∩,oo,3,••	12				

Year	Author	Title	Age	Own	Recommend	To Read	Want
2004	Nancy Farmer	*The House of the Scorpion* ∗,##,♦♦♦,¶¶¶,¿,oo,3	12				
2003	No Award						
2002	Ann Brashares	*Sisterhood of the Traveling Pants* ##,¿	15				
2001	Todd Strasser	*Give a Boy a Gun*	12				

South Carolina Association of School Librarians Young Adult Book Award ᵒᵒ

The South Carolina Book Award was organized to encourage students to read high-quality contemporary literature and to honor the authors of books students identify as their favorites. Every South Carolina K–12 student is eligible to participate in the yearlong reading program, to nominate favorite books, and to cast a ballot. Medals are awarded to winning authors at the annual conference of the South Carolina Association of School Librarians (SCASL), the sponsoring organization. The SCASL website is www.scasl.net/bookawards/bkawguide.htm.

Year	Author	Title	Age	Own	Recommend	To Read	Want
Junior Book							
2010							
2009							
2008	Cynthia Kadohata	*Cracker!: The Best Dog in Vietnam*	12				
2007	Sarah Weeks	*So B. It* ‡‡,iii	9				
2006	Nancy Farmer	*The House of the Scorpion* ∗,##,♦♦♦,¶¶¶,o,¿,3	12				
2005	Anthony Horowitz	*Stormbreaker* ♪,‡‡,∩	9				
2004	Wendelin Van Draanen	*Flipped* ♪,··	9				
2003	Phyllis Reynolds Naylor	*Jade Green: A Ghost Story*	9				

☐ Juvenile Nonfiction ☐ Juvenile Fiction ■ Fiction ■ Nonfiction

South Carolina Association of School Librarians Young Adult Book Award [oo]			Age	Own	Recommend	To Read	Want
Year	Author	Title					
2002	Carol Gorman	*Dork in Disguise*	8				
2001	J. K. Rowling	*Harry Potter and the Sorcerer's Stone* ♦♦♦,♫♫,‡,∩	9				
2000	Edward Bloor	*Tangerine* £££,¶¶¶,ii	9				
1999	Jerry Spinelli	*Crash* ‡‡,£££,¿¿¿,••	9				
1998	Barbara Park	*Mick Harte Was Here* £££	9				
1997	Karen Hesse	*Phoenix Rising* ~~,•,♦♦♦	12				
1996	P. MacLachlan	*Baby*	9				
1995	B. Wright	*The Ghost in the House*	9				
1994	Mary Downing Hahn	*Stepping on the Cracks* ^	9				
1993	Mary Downing Hahn	*Dead Man in Indian Creek* £££,••	9				
Young Adult							
2010							
2009							
2008	Stephenie Meyer	*New Moon* #,##,i	15				
2007	Sarah Dessen	*The Truth About Forever* #	15				
2006	Christopher Paolini	*Eragon* #,##,♦♦♦,♫♫,Ω,‡,¶,33,•••,∩,¿¿¿,o,¿,∩∩,3,••	12				
2005	Alice Sebold	*The Lovely Bones* ‡,‡‡,‡‡‡,¶					
2004	Mary Pearson	*Scribbler of Dreams*	12				
2003	Carol Plum-Ucci	*Body of Christopher Creed*	12				
2002	Laurie Halse Anderson	*Speak* ~~,‡‡‡,ii,•••,¿,3	15				
2001	Sarah Dessen	*Someone Like You* Σ	12				
2000	Annette Curtis Klause	*Blood and Chocolate* ii	15				
1999	Walter Dean Myers	*Slam!*	12				
1998	Davida A. Hurwin	*Time for Dancing*	12				
1997	Gary Paulsen	*Harris and Me* ‡‡,∩	12				
1996	Marilyn Reynolds	*Detour for Emmy*	15				
1995	Fran Amick	*What You Don't Know Can Kill You*					
1994	Michael Crichton	*Jurassic Park* ♫♫,‡‡,¶¶¶,∩∩	12				

Year	Author	Title	Age	Own	Recommend	To Read	Want
1993	Annette Curtis Klause	*Silver Kiss*	12				
1992	Carl Deuker	*On the Devil's Court*	15				
1991	Walter Dean Myers	*Fallen Angels*	15				
1990	Susan Beth Pfeffer	*The Year Without Michael*	15				
1989	Eve Bunting	*Face at the Edge of the World* ♪, **	12				
1988	Lois Duncan	*Locked in Time* ♪♪♪	12				
1987	Ellen Conford	*If This is Love, I'll Take Spaghetti*	12				
1986	Phyllis Reynolds Naylor	*A String of Chances*	9				
1985	Paula Danziger	*The Divorce Express*	12				
1984	Lois Duncan	*Stranger with My Face* ♪	12				
1983	Susan Pfeffer	*About David*	12				
1982	Shep Greene	*The Boy Who Drank Too Much*	12				
1981	William Buchanan	*A Shining Season*	10				
1980	Jay Anson	*The Amityville Horror*					

Tennessee Volunteer Book Award [3]

A reader's choice award, the Tennessee Volunteer Book Award is voted on by Tennessee K–12 students who have read (or have had the titles read to them) at least three of the twenty titles placed on the annual master list compiled by the Volunteer State Book Award (VSBA) committee. The award seeks to promote literature that broadens understanding of the human experience and provides accurate, factual information. More information is located at www.discoveret .org/tasl/vsba.htm. Reprinted with permission of the VSBA.

Year	Author	Title	Age	Own	Recommend	To Read	Want
2011							
2010							

☐ Juvenile Nonfiction   ☐ Juvenile Fiction   ■ Fiction   ■ Nonfiction

Tennessee Volunteer Book Award [3]			Age	Own	Recommend	To Read	Want
Year	Author	Title					
2009	Rick Riordan	*The Lightning Thief* ##,♦♦♦,‡‡,£££,¶¶,33,¿¿¿,¿,••	9				
2008	Stephenie Meyer	*Twilight* #,♦♦♦,♫♫,Ω,ΩΩ,ΩΩΩ,‡,‡‡‡,¶,¶¶,¶¶¶, ii,•••,¿¿¿,o,∩∩,¡,Σ	15				
2007	Sonya Sones	*One of Those Hideous Books Where The Mother Dies* ‡‡,o	15				
2006	Christopher Paolini	*Eragon* #,##,♦♦♦,♫♫,Ω,‡,¶,33,•••,∩,¿¿¿,o,¿, ∩∩,oo,••	12				
2005	Nancy Farmer	*The House of the Scorpion* •,##,♦♦♦,¶¶¶,o,¿,oo	12				
2004	Ann Brashares	*The Sisterhood of the Traveling Pants* ~~,‡,‡‡,Σ,¶,ii,•••	15				
2003	Meg Cabot	*The Princess Diaries* •••	12				
2002	Vivian Vande Velde	*Smart Dog*	9				
2002	Laurie Halse Anderson	*Speak* ~~,‡‡‡,ii,•••,¿,oo	15				
2001	Lois Duncan	*Gallows Hill* ¶¶¶	12				
2000	Gary Paulsen	*Brian's Winter* ‡‡,ii,∩	12				
1999	Sharon M. Draper	*Tears of a Tiger* ••	15				
1998	Caroline B. Cooney	*Driver's Ed* ‡,ii,•••	12				
1997	Betsy Haynes	*Deadly Deception*	14				
1996	Carl Deuker	*Heart of a Champion* ¶¶,¿¿¿	12				
1995	Caroline B. Cooney	*The Face on the Milk Carton* ♫♫, ‡‡	12				
1993	Lynn Hall	*The Killing Freeze*	12				
1992	Lois Duncan	*Don't Look Behind You* ‡‡,33	12				
1992	Eve Bunting	*A Sudden Silence* ♫,¿	15				
1991	Julie Reece Deaver	*Say Goodnight Gracie* •••,••	15				
1991	Neal Shusterman	*The Shadow Club*	12				

Beehive Award—Utah [33]

Previously known as the Utah Children's Book Award, the Beehive Award was started in 1980 by the Children's Literature Association of Utah. This organization's purpose is to encourage the writing, reading, and discussion of children's literature. The association annually sponsors five book awards for children of all ages, voted on by the children of Utah. The winners of the young adult award are listed here. More information can be found at www.clau.org.

Year	Author	Title	Age	Own	Recommend	To Read	Want
2011							
2010							
2009	Juliet Marillier	*Wildwood Dancing*	12				
2008	Michele Jaffe	*Bad Kitty* #	12				
2006	Rick Riordan	*The Lightning Thief* ##,♦♦♦,‡‡,£££,¶¶,¿¿¿,¿,3,••	9				
2005	Kenneth Oppel	*Airborn* £,••	12				
2004	Christopher Paolini	*Eragon* #,##,♦♦♦,♫♫,Ω,‡,¶,•••,∩,¿¿¿,o,¿,∩∩ oo,3,••	12				
2003	Ben Mikaelson	*Touching Spirit Bear* ♪,£££,¶¶,¶¶¶,∩,∩∩	9				
2002	Neal Shusterman	*Downsiders*	12				
2001	Richard Peck	*Long Way from Chicago: A Novel in Stories*	12				
2000	Kara Dalkey	*Little Sister*					
1999	Eve Bunting	*Sos Titanic*	12				
1998	T. A. Barron	*Merlin Effect*	15				
1997	Ann Rinaldi	*In My Father's House*	12				
1996	Jackie French Koller	*Nothing to Fear*	9				
1995	A. E. Cannon	*Amazing Gracie*	12				
1994	Avi	*The True Confessions of Charlotte Doyle* •••,••••	12				
1993	Theodore Taylor	*Sniper* ♪	12				

□ Juvenile Nonfiction   □ Juvenile Fiction   ■ Fiction   ■ Nonfiction

Beehive Award—Utah [33]

Year	Author	Title	Age	Own	Recommend	To Read	Want
1992	Lois Duncan	*Don't Look Behind You* ‡‡,3	12				
1991	Joan Lowery Nixon	*The Other Side of Dark* ♪,♪♪,‡‡,¿,**	12				

Green Mountain Book Award—Vermont ·

The Vermont Department of Libraries has awarded the Green Mountain Book Award since 2004. The program was created to help high school students discover the pleasure of reading excellent books. The Green Mountain Book Award is a reader's choice award and can be awarded to either an adult or young adult title. See www.libraries.vermont.gov/libraries/gmba for more information.

Year	Author	Title	Age	Own	Recommend	To Read	Want
2011							
2010							
2009	Ellen Hopkins	*Crank* ΩΩΩ,¶,∩∩	12				
2008	John Green	*Looking for Alaska* ‖,#,‡‡‡	15				
2007	Jodi Picoult	*My Sister's Keeper*					
2006	Angela Johnson	*The First Part Last* ‖,#,ΩΩ	12				

Virgina Readers Choice Award ¨

The goal of this award program, established in 1982 by the Virginia State Reading Association, is to encourage Virginia students to become more familiar with high quality contemporary literature, foster a lifelong habit of reading for pleasure, promote reading aloud in classrooms, and honor favorite books and their authors. Since 1987, awards have been given to books for elementary, middle, and high school-aged readers. Any Virginian may suggest a title. A committee screens suggestions, determines eligibility, and may nominate additional books. Reading lists for the coming school year are announced each spring. Students read the nominated titles and then vote for winners. For lists of honored books and information about eligibility, please visit www.vsra.org/VRCindex.html.

Year	Author	Title	Age	Own	Recommend	To Read	Want
Middle School							
2011							
2010							
2009	Kenneth Oppel	*Airborn* £,33	12				
2008	Rick Riordan	*The Lightning Thief* ##,♦♦♦,‡‡,£££,¶¶,33,¿¿¿,¿,3	9				
2007	Nancy Farmer	*The Sea of Trolls*	12				
2006	Christopher Paolini	*Eragon* #,##,♦♦♦,♫♫,Ω,‡,¶,33,•••,∩,¿¿¿,o,¿, ∩∩,oo,3	12				
2005	Jerry Spinelli	*Loser*	8				
2004	Wendelin Van Draanen	*Flipped* ♪,oo	9				
2003	Gordon Korman	*No More Dead Dogs* ##	12				
2002	Eve Bunting	*Blackwater*	9				
2001	Jack Gantos	*Joey Pigza Swallowed the Key* ♪	9				
2000	Joan Lowery Nixon	*Spirit Seeker*	12				
1999	Jerry Spinelli	*Crash* ‡‡,£££,¿¿¿,oo	9				
1998	Nancy Farmer	*The Ear, the Eye, and the Arm* x	9				
1997	Sharon Creech	*Walk Two Moons* ~~,¿	12				
1996	Lois Lowry	*The Giver* x,♦♦♦,‡,¶¶,¶¶¶,ii,¿¿¿,¿	12				

☐ Juvenile Nonfiction   ☐ Juvenile Fiction   ■ Fiction   ■ Nonfiction

Virgina Readers Choice Award ‥			Age	Own	Recommend	To Read	Want
Year	Author	Title					
1995	Caroline B. Cooney	*Flight #116 is Down* ¶¶,¿	12				
1994	Mary Downing Hahn	*Dead Man in Indian Creek* £££,oo	9				
1993	Jerry Spinelli	*Maniac Magee* •••,¿¿¿	9				
1992	Joan Lowery Nixon	*A Family Apart*	12				
1991	Michelle Magorian	*Good Night, Mr. Tom* ~~~					
1990	Gary Paulsen	*Hatchet* ‡‡,££,£££,¿,ΩΩ	9				
1989	Joan Lowery Nixon	*The Other Side of Dark* ♪,♪♪,‡‡,33,¿	12				
1988	Judi Miller	*Ghost in My Soup*	15				
1987	John Bellairs	*The Curse of the Blue Figurine*	9				
1986	Paula Danziger	*The Cat Ate My Gym Suit*	12				
1985	No award given						
1984	Ellen Raskin	*The Westing Game* •••	12				
High School							
2011							
2010							
2009	Jeannette Walls	*The Glass Castle* ~					
2008	Scott Westerfeld	*Uglies* x,Ω,ΩΩΩ,‡,¶¶¶,ii	12				
2007	Jodi Picoult	*My Sister's Keeper* ~,~~,#,ΩΩΩ,Σ					
2006	Jaclyn Moriarty	*The Year of Secret Assignments*	12				
2005	R. K. Cusick	*The House Next Door*	12				
2004	Sampson Davis, Rameck Hunt, and George Jenkins	*The Pact: Three Young Men Make a Promise and Fulfill a Dream*	12				
2003	Louise Rennison	*Angus, Thongs and Full-Frontal Snogging* ii	12				
2002	Heather Quarles	*A Door Near Here* £	12				
2001	Jacqueline Woodson	*If You Come Softly* Σ	9				
2000	Jack Canfield	*Chicken Soup for the Teenage Soul* ♪♪,•••,ΩΩ	15				
1999	Liz Berry	*The China Garden*	15				
1998	Phyllis A. Whitney	*Daughter of the Stars*					

Year	Author	Title	Age	Own	Recommend	To Read	Want
1997	Sharon M. Draper	*Tears of a Tiger* [3]	15				
1996	Ossie Davis	*Just Like Martin*	8				
1995	Eve Bunting	*Jumping the Nail*	12				
1994	Stella Pevsner	*How Could You Do It Diane?*					
1993	Stephanie S. Tolan	*Plague Year* ¶¶¶	12				
1992	William Duncan	*Don't Look Behind You*	12				
1991	Julie Reece Deaver	*Say Goodnight Gracie* ···,[3]	15				
1990	Avi	*Wolf Rider: A Tale of Terror*	12				
1989	Eve Bunting	*Face at the Edge of the World* ♪,ºº	12				
1988	Cynthia Voigt	*Izzy Willy Nilly* ♪	12				
1987	Rosemary Wells	*The Man in the Woods*	12				
1986	Mollie Hunter	*The Third Eye*	12				
1985	S. E. Hinton	*The Outsiders*	12				

Evergreen Award—Washington ···

The Washington Young Adult Review Group (WASHYARG) sponsors the Evergreen Young Book Award. Each voter for this award must be in grades 7–12, read two or more titles from the nominated list, and cast only one vote per ballot. More information about the latest winner can be found at www.kcls .org/evergreen.

Year	Author	Title	Age	Own	Recommend	To Read	Want
2011							
2010							
2009	Susan Beth Pfeffer	*Life As We Knew It* #,Σ,ii	12				
2008	Stephenie Meyer	*Twilight* #,♦♦♦,♫♫,Ω,ΩΩ,ΩΩΩ,‡,‡‡‡,¶,¶¶,¶¶¶, ii,¿¿¿,º,∩∩,3,¡,Σ	15				

....
☐ Juvenile Nonfiction   ▨ Juvenile Fiction   ■ Fiction   ■ Nonfiction

Evergreen Award—Washington ···			Age	Own	Recommend	To Read	Want
Year	Author	Title					
2007	Eoin Colfer	*The Supernaturalist* ##	12				
2006	Christopher Paolini	*Eragon* #,##,♦♦♦,♪♪,Ω,‡,¶,33,∩,¿¿¿,ο,¿, ∩∩,οο,3,··	12				
2005	Meg Cabot	*All-American Girl* ii	12				
2004	Ann Brashares	*The Sisterhood of the Traveling Pants* ~~,‡,‡‡,Σ,¶,ii,3	15				
2003	Meg Cabot	*The Princess Diaries* 3	12				
2002	Laurie Halse Anderson	*Speak* ~~,‡‡‡,ii,¿,οο,3	15				
2001	Louis Sachar	*Holes* ·,···,##,♦♦♦,♪♪,iii,∩,¿¿¿,¿,∩∩	9				
2000	Jack Canfield	*Chicken Soup for the Teenage Soul* ♪♪,∩∩,··	15				
1999	John Gilstrap	*Nathan's Run*					
1997	Caroline B. Cooney	*Driver's Ed* ‡,ii,3	12				
1996	John Grisham	*The Client* ♪♪	15				
1995	John Grisham	*The Pelican Brief*	15				
1994	Julie Reece Deaver	*Say Goodnight Gracie* 3,···	15				
1993	Avi	*The True Confessions of Charlotte Doyle* ···,33	12				
1992	John Saul	*Creatures*	12				
1991	Orson Scott Card	*Seventh Son*	12				

Golden Archer Award—Wisconsin ∩

The Golden Archer Award was originally sponsored by the University of Wisconsin-Oshkosh. In December of 1994, the sponsorship was assumed by the Wisconsin Educational Media and Technology Association (formerly WEMA). The awards are now given in three age level categories—primary, intermediate, and middle/junior high. The nominations list is created by the committee based on titles that are selected and read by students in Wisconsin. The winners in the middle/junior high category are listed here. To view winners from 1974 to the present, please see www.wemtaonline.org/se3bin/clientgenie.cgi.

Year	Author	Title	Age	Own	Recommend	To Read	Want
2011							
2010							
2009	Jeff Kinney	*Diary of a Wimpy Kid: Greg Heffley's Journal*	9				
2008	J. K. Rowling	*Harry Potter and the Half Blood Prince* #,♪♪	9				
2007	Carl Hiaasen	*Hoot* £££,¿¿¿	9				
2006	Christopher Paolini	*Eragon* #,##,♦♦♦,♪♪,Ω,‡,¶,33,•••,¿¿¿,◦,¿, ∩∩,∞,3,••	12				
2005	J. K. Rowling	*Harry Potter and the Order of the Phoenix* #,♪♪	9				
2004	Ben Mikaelson	*Touching Spirit Bear* ♪,£££,¶¶,¶¶¶,33,∩∩	9				
2003	Anthony Horowitz	*Stormbreaker* ♪,‡‡,∞	9				
2002	J. K. Rowling	*Harry Potter and the Goblet of Fire*	9				
2001	Louis Sachar	*Holes* •,•••,##,♦♦♦,♪♪,iii,•••,¿¿¿,¿,∩∩	9				
2000	J. K. Rowling	*Harry Potter and the Sorcerer's Stone* ♦♦♦,♪♪,‡,∞	9				
1999	Gary Paulsen	*Brian's Winter* ‡‡,ii,3	12				
1998	Lois Lowry	*Number the Stars*	9				
1997	Gary Paulsen	*Harris and Me* ‡‡,∞	12				

Soaring Eagle Book Award—Wyoming ∩∩

Sponsored by the Wyoming Library Association and the Wyoming State Reading Council, the Soaring Eagle Book Award helps Wyoming students in grades 7–12 become acquainted with the best contemporary authors, become aware of the qualities that make a good book, choose the best rather than the mediocre, set a goal to read at least three good books, and honor an author whose books Wyoming students have enjoyed. The Web address is www.ccpls .org/html/soaringeagle.html.

Year	Author	Title	Age	Own	Recommend	To Read	Want
2011							
2010							
2009	Ellen Hopkins	*Crank* ∩∩∩,¶,··	12				
2008	Stephenie Meyer	*Twilight* #,♦♦♦,♫♫♫,Ω,ΩΩ,ΩΩΩ,‡,‡‡‡,¶,¶¶,¶¶¶,ıiı,•••,¿¿¿,o,3,¡,Σ	15				
2007	Christopher Paolini	*Eldest* #,♫♫,±±	12				
2006	Ben Mikaelson	*Touching Spirit Bear* ♫,£££,¶¶,¶¶¶,33,∩	9				
2005	Christopher Paolini	*Eragon* #,##,♦♦♦,♫♫,Ω,‡,¶,33,•••,∩,¿¿¿,o,¿,oo,3,••	12				
2004	Darren Shan	*Cirque Du Freak: A Living Nightmare (Cirque Du Freak #1)*	12				
2003	Louis Sachar	*Holes* •,•••,##,♦♦♦,♫♫,iıı,•••,∩,¿¿¿,¿	9				
2002	J. K. Rowling	*Harry Potter and the Prisoner of Azkaban* ♫♫	9				
2001	Misty Bemall	*She Said Yes*					
2000	David J. Pelzer	*A Child Called It: One Child's Courage to Survive* ∩∩∩	12				
1999	Jack Canfield	*Chicken Soup for the Teenage Soul* ♫♫,•••,••	15				
1998	W. R. Philbrick	*Freak the Mighty* ♦♦♦,♫,¶¶	9				
1997	Gary Paulsen	*Hatchet* ‡‡,££,£££,¿,••	9				
1996	Joan Lowery Nixon	*Whispers from the Dead* ¶¶,¶¶¶					
1995	Michael Crichton	*Jurassic Park* ♫♫,‡‡,¶¶¶,oo	12				
1994	Glora Miklowitz	Desperate Pursuit					

Year	Author	Title	Age	Own	Recommend	To Read	Want
1993	Robert McClung	Hugh Glass Mountain Man	12				
1992	Michael Blake	Dances with Wolves	12				
1991	Richard Peck	Princess Ashley ¶¶¶	12				
1991	Bill Wallace	Trapped in Death Cave	9				
1990	Isabel Allende	Of Love and Shadows	12				
1990	Eve Bunting	Someone is Hiding on Alcatraz Island	9				
1989	Judy Blume	Superfudge	8				

Juvenile Nonfiction   Juvenile Fiction   Fiction   Nonfiction

Key to Footnotes

List Name	Symbol
Abraham Lincoln Award—Illinois' High School Readers' Choice Award	ΩΩΩ
Aesop Prize	††
Agatha Award	&&
Alex Award	~
American Indian Youth Services Literature Award	♥♥♥
Americas Award	♥♥
Andre Norton Award	xx
Arthur Ellis Crime Award	&&&
Asian/Pacific American Librarians Association (APALA)	♦
Beehive Award—Utah	33
Black-Eyed Susan Award—Maryland	Σ
Boston Globe—Horn Award	***
California Young Reader Award	♪
Canadian Library Association Book Award	$$$
Carnegie Award	**
Carter G. Woodson Award	♠♠♠
Colorado Blue Spruce Award	♪♪
Cybils—Teen Bloggers Award	###
Delaware Diamonds	♪♪♪
Edgar Allan Poe Award	▼
Evergreen Award—Washington	•••
Florida Teens Read Award	Ω
Garden State Teen Book Award—New Jersey	ii
Gateway Readers Award—Missouri	¶
Geoffrey Bilson Award for Historical Fiction	&
Georgia Peach Teen Award	ΩΩ
Golden Archer Award—Wisconsin	∩
Golden Duck—Clement Award	x
Golden Sower Award—Nebraska	¶¶

Grand Canyon Reader Award—Arizona	♦♦♦
Green Earth Book Award	♥
Green Mountain Book Award—Vermont	•
Heartland Award	~~
Indiana High School Book Award	‡
Iowa High School Award	‡‡
IRA Award	~~~
Ira Lee Bennett Hopkins Promising Poetry Award	♠
Jefferson Cup	%%%
Kentucky Bluegrass Award	‡‡‡
Land of Enchantment Book Award—New Mexico	iii
Leslie Bradshaw Award—Oregon	¿¿
Locus Fantasy Prize	vv
Los Angeles Times Book Award for Young Adult Fiction	!
Lupine Award—Maine	o
Maud Hart Award—Minnesota	£££
Michael L. Printz Award	!!
Minnesota Book Award	££
Mythopoeic Fantasy Award	vvv
National Book Award for Young People's Literature	*
Nevada Young Reader's Award	¶¶¶
Norma Fleck Book Award for Nonfiction	%
North Carolina School Library Media Association	±
Oklahoma Book Award	±±±
Pennsylvania Young Readers' Choice Award Winners	¿¿¿
Phoenix Award	$
Pura Belpre Award	♦♦
Rhode Island Teen Award	o
Robert F. Sibert Medal	♠♠
Schneider Family Book Award	!!!
Scott O'Dell Historical Fiction Award	^
Sequoyah Award—Oklahoma	¿

Snow Willow Award	%%
Soaring Eagle Book Award—Wyoming	∩∩
South Carolina Association of School Librarians Young Adult Book Award	oo
Spur Storyteller Award	xxx
Teen Buckeye Book Award—Ohio	±±
Tennessee Volunteer Book Award	3
The Flume—New Hampshire Teen Reader's Choice Award	i
Thumbs Up! Award—Michigan	£
Virgina Readers Choice Award	••
Western Heritage Award	†
White Pine Award	$$
Will Eisner Comic Industry Award	†††
YALSA Teen Top Ten Award	#
Young Reader's Choice Award	##

Blank Lists

These next pages can be used to record your own lists. The first column can be used for dates and rankings. Each page contains a place to enter the list name. This gives the option of continuing a list from a previous page and making it as long as needed, or starting a new list. Examples of lists include:

- Book club lists, past and present
- Your own personal favorites list, such as a top 100
- Books to read in the next year
- Other notable or award lists that aren't mentioned previously in this journal
- Finalists from book awards

List Name:

Year	Author	Title	Age	Own	Recommend	To Read	Want

☐ Juvenile Nonfiction   ▨ Juvenile Fiction   ■ Fiction   ■ Nonfiction

List Name:

Year	Author	Title	Age	Own	Recommend	To Read	Want

List Name:

Year	Author	Title	Age	Own	Recommend	To Read	Want

Juvenile Nonfiction   Juvenile Fiction   Fiction   Nonfiction

List Name:

Year	Author	Title	Age	Own	Recommend	To Read	Want

List Name:

Year	Author	Title	Age	Own	Recommend	To Read	Want

Juvenile Nonfiction　Juvenile Fiction　Fiction　Nonfiction

List Name:

Year	Author	Title	Age	Own	Recommend	To Read	Want

List Name:

Year	Author	Title	Age	Own	Recommend	To Read	Want

Juvenile Nonfiction   Juvenile Fiction   Fiction   Nonfiction

List Name:

Year	Author	Title	Age	Own	Recommend	To Read	Want

To Read

It is not true that we have only one life to live;
if we can read, we can live as many more lives
and as many kinds of lives as we wish.
— S. I. Hayakawa

The greatest gift is the passion for reading.
It is cheap, it consoles, it distracts, it excites,
it gives you knowledge of the world and
experience of a wide kind. It is a moral
illumination.
—Elizabeth Hardwick

A capacity and taste for reading gives access
to whatever has already been discovered by
others.
—Abraham Lincoln

Use this list to keep track of books you want to read. The notes field is great for recording who recommended a given book, where you might find it, and why you want to read it. Your list can be a compilation of all your desired books, or only those not mentioned elsewere.

Title:
Author:
Notes:

Title:
Author:
Notes:

Title:
Author:
Notes:

Title:
Author:
Notes:

Title:
Author:
Notes:

Title:
Author:
Notes:

Title:

Author:

Notes:

Title:

Author:

Notes:

Title:

Author:

Notes:

Title:

Author:

Notes:

Title:

Author:

Notes:

Title:

Author:

Notes:

Title:

Author:

Notes:

Title:

Author:

Notes:

Title:

Author:

Notes:

Title:

Author:

Notes:

Title:

Author:

Notes:

Title:

Author:

Notes:

Title:

Author:

Notes:

Title:

Author:

Notes:

Title:

Author:

Notes:

Title:

Author:

Notes:

Title:
Author:
Notes:

Title:
Author:
Notes:

Title:
Author:
Notes:

Title:
Author:
Notes:

Title:
Author:
Notes:

Title:
Author:
Notes:

Title:
Author:
Notes:

Title:
Author:
Notes:

Title:

Author:

Notes:

Title:

Author:

Notes:

Title:

Author:

Notes:

Title:

Author:

Notes:

Title:

Author:

Notes:

Title:

Author:

Notes:

Title:

Author:

Notes:

Title:

Author:

Notes:

Title:

Author:

Notes:

Title:

Author:

Notes:

Title:

Author:

Notes:

Title:

Author:

Notes:

Title:

Author:

Notes:

Title:

Author:

Notes:

Title:

Author:

Notes:

Title:

Author:

Notes:

Title:

Author:

Notes:

Title:

Author:

Notes:

Title:

Author:

Notes:

Title:

Author:

Notes:

Title:

Author:

Notes:

Title:

Author:

Notes:

Title:

Author:

Notes:

Title:

Author:

Notes:

| Title: |
| Author: |
| Notes: |

| Title: |
| Author: |
| Notes: |

| Title: |
| Author: |
| Notes: |

| Title: |
| Author: |
| Notes: |

| Title: |
| Author: |
| Notes: |

| Title: |
| Author: |
| Notes: |

| Title: |
| Author: |
| Notes: |

| Title: |
| Author: |
| Notes: |

Journal Pages

All that mankind has done, thought, gained, or been, it is all lying in magical preservation in the pages of books.

—Thomas Carlyle

A well-composed book is a magic carpet on which we are wafted to a world that we cannot enter in any other way.

—Caroline Gordon

We read books to find out who we are. What other people, real or imaginary, do and think or feel is an essential guide to our understanding of what we ourselves are and may become.

—Ursula K. Le Guin

Use the next pages to record everything you read. The last column can be used to record the date a book was read or the page number of a journal entry corresponding to that book. This is a great place to keep track of all the books you've read, whether you journal about them or not.

Titles	Date/ Page #

Titles	Date/ Page #

Titles	Date/ Page #

Titles	Date/ Page #

Date:	○ hard copy ○ e-book ○ audiobook	Recommend?
Book Title:		
Author:		
Reason for Reading:		
Recommended by:		
Comments & Thoughts:		

Date:	○ hard copy ○ e-book ○ audiobook	Recommend?
Book Title:		
Author:		
Reason for Reading:		
Recommended by:		
Comments & Thoughts:		

Date:	○ hard copy ○ e-book ○ audiobook	Recommend?
Book Title:		
Author:		
Reason for Reading:		
Recommended by:		
Comments & Thoughts:		

Date:	○ hard copy ○ e-book ○ audiobook	Recommend?
Book Title:		
Author:		
Reason for Reading:		
Recommended by:		

Words to Define (include definitions and page numbers):

Passages to Remember (include page numbers):

Comments & Thoughts:

Date:	○ hard copy ○ e-book ○ audiobook	Recommend?
Book Title:		
Author:		
Reason for Reading:		
Recommended by:		
Comments & Thoughts:		

Date:	○ hard copy ○ e-book ○ audiobook	Recommend?
Book Title:		
Author:		
Reason for Reading:		
Recommended by:		
Comments & Thoughts:		

Date:	○ hard copy ○ e-book ○ audiobook	Recommend?
Book Title:		
Author:		
Reason for Reading:		
Recommended by:		
Comments & Thoughts:		

Date:	○ hard copy ○ e-book ○ audiobook	Recommend?
Book Title:		
Author:		
Reason for Reading:		
Recommended by:		
Comments & Thoughts:		

Date:	○ hard copy ○ e-book ○ audiobook	Recommend?
Book Title:		
Author:		
Reason for Reading:		
Recommended by:		
Comments & Thoughts:		

Date:	○ hard copy ○ e-book ○ audiobook	Recommend?
Book Title:		
Author:		
Reason for Reading:		
Recommended by:		
Comments & Thoughts:		

Date:	○ hard copy ○ e-book ○ audiobook	Recommend?

Book Title:

Author:

Reason for Reading:

Recommended by:

Words to Define (include definitions and page numbers):

Passages to Remember (include page numbers):

Comments & Thoughts:

Date:	O hard copy O e-book O audiobook	Recommend?
Book Title:		
Author:		
Reason for Reading:		
Recommended by:		
Comments & Thoughts:		

Date:	O hard copy O e-book O audiobook	Recommend?
Book Title:		
Author:		
Reason for Reading:		
Recommended by:		
Comments & Thoughts:		

Date:	O hard copy O e-book O audiobook	Recommend?
Book Title:		
Author:		
Reason for Reading:		
Recommended by:		
Comments & Thoughts:		

Date:	○ hard copy ○ e-book ○ audiobook	Recommend?
Book Title:		
Author:		
Reason for Reading:		
Recommended by:		
Comments & Thoughts:		

Date:	○ hard copy ○ e-book ○ audiobook	Recommend?
Book Title:		
Author:		
Reason for Reading:		
Recommended by:		
Comments & Thoughts:		

Date:	○ hard copy ○ e-book ○ audiobook	Recommend?
Book Title:		
Author:		
Reason for Reading:		
Recommended by:		
Comments & Thoughts:		

Date:	○ hard copy ○ e-book ○ audiobook	Recommend?

Book Title:

Author:

Reason for Reading:

Recommended by:

Words to Define (include definitions and page numbers):

_____
_____
_____
_____
_____
_____
_____
_____
_____
_____
_____

Passages to Remember (include page numbers):

_____
_____
_____
_____
_____
_____
_____
_____
_____
_____
_____
_____
_____

Comments & Thoughts:

Date:	○ hard copy ○ e-book ○ audiobook	Recommend?
Book Title:		
Author:		
Reason for Reading:		
Recommended by:		
Comments & Thoughts:		

Date:	○ hard copy ○ e-book ○ audiobook	Recommend?
Book Title:		
Author:		
Reason for Reading:		
Recommended by:		
Comments & Thoughts:		

Date:	○ hard copy ○ e-book ○ audiobook	Recommend?
Book Title:		
Author:		
Reason for Reading:		
Recommended by:		
Comments & Thoughts:		

Date:	○ hard copy ○ e-book ○ audiobook	Recommend?
Book Title:		
Author:		
Reason for Reading:		
Recommended by:		
Comments & Thoughts:		

Date:	○ hard copy ○ e-book ○ audiobook	Recommend?
Book Title:		
Author:		
Reason for Reading:		
Recommended by:		
Comments & Thoughts:		

Date:	○ hard copy ○ e-book ○ audiobook	Recommend?
Book Title:		
Author:		
Reason for Reading:		
Recommended by:		
Comments & Thoughts:		

Date:	○ hard copy ○ e-book ○ audiobook	Recommend?

Book Title:

Author:

Reason for Reading:

Recommended by:

Words to Define (include definitions and page numbers):

Passages to Remember (include page numbers):

Comments & Thoughts:

Date:	○ hard copy ○ e-book ○ audiobook	Recommend?

Book Title:

Author:

Reason for Reading:

Recommended by:

Comments & Thoughts:

Date:	○ hard copy ○ e-book ○ audiobook	Recommend?

Book Title:

Author:

Reason for Reading:

Recommended by:

Comments & Thoughts:

Date:	○ hard copy ○ e-book ○ audiobook	Recommend?

Book Title:

Author:

Reason for Reading:

Recommended by:

Comments & Thoughts:

Date:	○ hard copy ○ e-book ○ audiobook	Recommend?
Book Title:		
Author:		
Reason for Reading:		
Recommended by:		
Comments & Thoughts:		

Date:	○ hard copy ○ e-book ○ audiobook	Recommend?
Book Title:		
Author:		
Reason for Reading:		
Recommended by:		
Comments & Thoughts:		

Date:	○ hard copy ○ e-book ○ audiobook	Recommend?
Book Title:		
Author:		
Reason for Reading:		
Recommended by:		
Comments & Thoughts:		

Date:	○ hard copy ○ e-book ○ audiobook	Recommend?

Book Title:

Author:

Reason for Reading:

Recommended by:

Words to Define (include definitions and page numbers):

Passages to Remember (include page numbers):

Comments & Thoughts:

Date:	○ hard copy ○ e-book ○ audiobook	Recommend?
Book Title:		
Author:		
Reason for Reading:		
Recommended by:		
Comments & Thoughts:		

Date:	○ hard copy ○ e-book ○ audiobook	Recommend?
Book Title:		
Author:		
Reason for Reading:		
Recommended by:		
Comments & Thoughts:		

Date:	○ hard copy ○ e-book ○ audiobook	Recommend?
Book Title:		
Author:		
Reason for Reading:		
Recommended by:		
Comments & Thoughts:		

Date:	○ hard copy ○ e-book ○ audiobook	Recommend?
Book Title:		
Author:		
Reason for Reading:		
Recommended by:		
Comments & Thoughts:		

Date:	○ hard copy ○ e-book ○ audiobook	Recommend?
Book Title:		
Author:		
Reason for Reading:		
Recommended by:		
Comments & Thoughts:		

Date:	○ hard copy ○ e-book ○ audiobook	Recommend?
Book Title:		
Author:		
Reason for Reading:		
Recommended by:		
Comments & Thoughts:		

Date:	○ hard copy ○ e-book ○ audiobook	Recommend?
Book Title:		
Author:		
Reason for Reading:		
Recommended by:		

Words to Define (include definitions and page numbers):

Passages to Remember (include page numbers):

Comments & Thoughts:

Date:	○ hard copy ○ e-book ○ audiobook	Recommend?
Book Title:		
Author:		
Reason for Reading:		
Recommended by:		
Comments & Thoughts:		

Date:	○ hard copy ○ e-book ○ audiobook	Recommend?
Book Title:		
Author:		
Reason for Reading:		
Recommended by:		
Comments & Thoughts:		

Date:	○ hard copy ○ e-book ○ audiobook	Recommend?
Book Title:		
Author:		
Reason for Reading:		
Recommended by:		
Comments & Thoughts:		

Date:	○ hard copy ○ e-book ○ audiobook	Recommend?
Book Title:		
Author:		
Reason for Reading:		
Recommended by:		
Comments & Thoughts:		

Date:	○ hard copy ○ e-book ○ audiobook	Recommend?
Book Title:		
Author:		
Reason for Reading:		
Recommended by:		
Comments & Thoughts:		

Date:	○ hard copy ○ e-book ○ audiobook	Recommend?
Book Title:		
Author:		
Reason for Reading:		
Recommended by:		
Comments & Thoughts:		

Date:	◯ hard copy ◯ e-book ◯ audiobook	Recommend?
Book Title:		
Author:		
Reason for Reading:		
Recommended by:		

Words to Define (include definitions and page numbers):

Passages to Remember (include page numbers):

Comments & Thoughts:

Date:	O hard copy O e-book O audiobook	Recommend?
Book Title:		
Author:		
Reason for Reading:		
Recommended by:		
Comments & Thoughts:		

Date:	O hard copy O e-book O audiobook	Recommend?
Book Title:		
Author:		
Reason for Reading:		
Recommended by:		
Comments & Thoughts:		

Date:	O hard copy O e-book O audiobook	Recommend?
Book Title:		
Author:		
Reason for Reading:		
Recommended by:		
Comments & Thoughts:		

Date:	○ hard copy ○ e-book ○ audiobook	Recommend?
Book Title:		
Author:		
Reason for Reading:		
Recommended by:		
Comments & Thoughts:		

Date:	○ hard copy ○ e-book ○ audiobook	Recommend?
Book Title:		
Author:		
Reason for Reading:		
Recommended by:		
Comments & Thoughts:		

Date:	○ hard copy ○ e-book ○ audiobook	Recommend?
Book Title:		
Author:		
Reason for Reading:		
Recommended by:		
Comments & Thoughts:		

Date:	○ hard copy ○ e-book ○ audiobook	Recommend?

Book Title:

Author:

Reason for Reading:

Recommended by:

Words to Define (include definitions and page numbers):

Passages to Remember (include page numbers):

Comments & Thoughts:

Date:	○ hard copy ○ e-book ○ audiobook	Recommend?
Book Title:		
Author:		
Reason for Reading:		
Recommended by:		
Comments & Thoughts:		

Date:	○ hard copy ○ e-book ○ audiobook	Recommend?
Book Title:		
Author:		
Reason for Reading:		
Recommended by:		
Comments & Thoughts:		

Date:	○ hard copy ○ e-book ○ audiobook	Recommend?
Book Title:		
Author:		
Reason for Reading:		
Recommended by:		
Comments & Thoughts:		

Date:	○ hard copy ○ e-book ○ audiobook	Recommend?
Book Title:		
Author:		
Reason for Reading:		
Recommended by:		
Comments & Thoughts:		

Date:	○ hard copy ○ e-book ○ audiobook	Recommend?
Book Title:		
Author:		
Reason for Reading:		
Recommended by:		
Comments & Thoughts:		

Date:	○ hard copy ○ e-book ○ audiobook	Recommend?
Book Title:		
Author:		
Reason for Reading:		
Recommended by:		
Comments & Thoughts:		

Date:	○ hard copy ○ e-book ○ audiobook	Recommend?

Book Title:

Author:

Reason for Reading:

Recommended by:

Words to Define (include definitions and page numbers):

Passages to Remember (include page numbers):

Comments & Thoughts:

Date:	○ hard copy ○ e-book ○ audiobook	Recommend?
Book Title:		
Author:		
Reason for Reading:		
Recommended by:		
Comments & Thoughts:		

Date:	○ hard copy ○ e-book ○ audiobook	Recommend?
Book Title:		
Author:		
Reason for Reading:		
Recommended by:		
Comments & Thoughts:		

Date:	○ hard copy ○ e-book ○ audiobook	Recommend?
Book Title:		
Author:		
Reason for Reading:		
Recommended by:		
Comments & Thoughts:		

Date:	○ hard copy ○ e-book ○ audiobook	Recommend?
Book Title:		
Author:		
Reason for Reading:		
Recommended by:		
Comments & Thoughts:		

Date:	○ hard copy ○ e-book ○ audiobook	Recommend?
Book Title:		
Author:		
Reason for Reading:		
Recommended by:		
Comments & Thoughts:		

Date:	○ hard copy ○ e-book ○ audiobook	Recommend?
Book Title:		
Author:		
Reason for Reading:		
Recommended by:		
Comments & Thoughts:		

Date:	○ hard copy ○ e-book ○ audiobook	Recommend?
Book Title:		
Author:		
Reason for Reading:		
Recommended by:		

Words to Define (include definitions and page numbers):

Passages to Remember (include page numbers):

Comments & Thoughts:

Date:	○ hard copy ○ e-book ○ audiobook	Recommend?
Book Title:		
Author:		
Reason for Reading:		
Recommended by:		
Comments & Thoughts:		

Date:	○ hard copy ○ e-book ○ audiobook	Recommend?
Book Title:		
Author:		
Reason for Reading:		
Recommended by:		
Comments & Thoughts:		

Date:	○ hard copy ○ e-book ○ audiobook	Recommend?
Book Title:		
Author:		
Reason for Reading:		
Recommended by:		
Comments & Thoughts:		

Date:	○ hard copy ○ e-book ○ audiobook	Recommend?
Book Title:		
Author:		
Reason for Reading:		
Recommended by:		
Comments & Thoughts:		

Date:	○ hard copy ○ e-book ○ audiobook	Recommend?
Book Title:		
Author:		
Reason for Reading:		
Recommended by:		
Comments & Thoughts:		

Date:	○ hard copy ○ e-book ○ audiobook	Recommend?
Book Title:		
Author:		
Reason for Reading:		
Recommended by:		
Comments & Thoughts:		

Date:	○ hard copy ○ e-book ○ audiobook	Recommend?
Book Title:		
Author:		
Reason for Reading:		
Recommended by:		

Words to Define (include definitions and page numbers):

Passages to Remember (include page numbers):

Comments & Thoughts:

Date:	○ hard copy ○ e-book ○ audiobook	Recommend?
Book Title:		
Author:		
Reason for Reading:		
Recommended by:		
Comments & Thoughts:		

Date:	○ hard copy ○ e-book ○ audiobook	Recommend?
Book Title:		
Author:		
Reason for Reading:		
Recommended by:		
Comments & Thoughts:		

Date:	○ hard copy ○ e-book ○ audiobook	Recommend?
Book Title:		
Author:		
Reason for Reading:		
Recommended by:		
Comments & Thoughts:		

Date:	○ hard copy ○ e-book ○ audiobook	Recommend?
Book Title:		
Author:		
Reason for Reading:		
Recommended by:		
Comments & Thoughts:		

Date:	○ hard copy ○ e-book ○ audiobook	Recommend?
Book Title:		
Author:		
Reason for Reading:		
Recommended by:		
Comments & Thoughts:		

Date:	○ hard copy ○ e-book ○ audiobook	Recommend?
Book Title:		
Author:		
Reason for Reading:		
Recommended by:		
Comments & Thoughts:		

Date:	○ hard copy ○ e-book ○ audiobook	Recommend?

Book Title:

Author:

Reason for Reading:

Recommended by:

Words to Define (include definitions and page numbers):

Passages to Remember (include page numbers):

Comments & Thoughts:

Date:	○ hard copy ○ e-book ○ audiobook	Recommend?
Book Title:		
Author:		
Reason for Reading:		
Recommended by:		
Comments & Thoughts:		

Date:	○ hard copy ○ e-book ○ audiobook	Recommend?
Book Title:		
Author:		
Reason for Reading:		
Recommended by:		
Comments & Thoughts:		

Date:	○ hard copy ○ e-book ○ audiobook	Recommend?
Book Title:		
Author:		
Reason for Reading:		
Recommended by:		
Comments & Thoughts:		

Recommendations

Make books your companions; let your book-shelves be your gardens: bask in their beauty, gather their fruit, pluck their roses, take their spices and myrrh. And when your soul be weary, change from garden to garden, and from prospect to prospect.

—Ibn Tibbon

There is no friend as loyal as a book.

—Ernest Hemingway

Never trust anyone who has not brought a book with them.

—Lemony Snicket, *Horseradish: Bitter Truths You Can't Avoid*

Use this list to record books you'd like to recommend to others.	**Own**
Book:	
Author:	
Recommend to:	

Book:	
Author:	
Recommend to:	

Book:	
Author:	
Recommend to:	

Book:	
Author:	
Recommend to:	

Book:	
Author:	
Recommend to:	

Book:	
Author:	
Recommend to:	

Book:	
Author:	
Recommend to:	

Book:	
Author:	
Recommend to:	
Additional Notes:	

Use this list to record books you'd like to recommend to others.	**Own**
Book:	
Author:	
Recommend to:	

Book:	
Author:	
Recommend to:	

Book:	
Author:	
Recommend to:	

Book:	
Author:	
Recommend to:	

Book:	
Author:	
Recommend to:	

Book:	
Author:	
Recommend to:	

Book:	
Author:	
Recommend to:	

Book:	
Author:	
Recommend to:	

Additional Notes:

Use this list to record books you'd like to recommend to others.	**Own**
Book:	
Author:	
Recommend to:	

Book:	
Author:	
Recommend to:	

Book:	
Author:	
Recommend to:	

Book:	
Author:	
Recommend to:	

Book:	
Author:	
Recommend to:	

Book:	
Author:	
Recommend to:	

Book:	
Author:	
Recommend to:	

Book:	
Author:	
Recommend to:	
Additional Notes:	

Use this list to record books you'd like to recommend to others.	**Own**
Book:	
Author:	
Recommend to:	

Book:	
Author:	
Recommend to:	

Book:	
Author:	
Recommend to:	

Book:	
Author:	
Recommend to:	

Book:	
Author:	
Recommend to:	

Book:	
Author:	
Recommend to:	

Book:	
Author:	
Recommend to:	

Book:	
Author:	
Recommend to:	
Additional Notes:	

Use this list to record books you'd like to recommend to others.	**Own**
Book:	
Author:	
Recommend to:	

Book:	
Author:	
Recommend to:	

Book:	
Author:	
Recommend to:	

Book:	
Author:	
Recommend to:	

Book:	
Author:	
Recommend to:	

Book:	
Author:	
Recommend to:	

Book:	
Author:	
Recommend to:	

Book:	
Author:	
Recommend to:	
Additional Notes:	

Use this list to record books you'd like to recommend to others.	**Own**
Book:	
Author:	
Recommend to:	

Book:	
Author:	
Recommend to:	

Book:	
Author:	
Recommend to:	

Book:	
Author:	
Recommend to:	

Book:	
Author:	
Recommend to:	

Book:	
Author:	
Recommend to:	

Book:	
Author:	
Recommend to:	

Book:	
Author:	
Recommend to:	
Additional Notes:	

Use this list to record books you'd like to recommend to others.	**Own**
Book:	
Author:	
Recommend to:	

Book:	
Author:	
Recommend to:	

Book:	
Author:	
Recommend to:	

Book:	
Author:	
Recommend to:	

Book:	
Author:	
Recommend to:	

Book:	
Author:	
Recommend to:	

Book:	
Author:	
Recommend to:	

Book:	
Author:	
Recommend to:	

Additional Notes:

Use this list to record books you'd like to recommend to others.	**Own**
Book:	
Author:	
Recommend to:	

Book:	
Author:	
Recommend to:	

Book:	
Author:	
Recommend to:	

Book:	
Author:	
Recommend to:	

Book:	
Author:	
Recommend to:	

Book:	
Author:	
Recommend to:	

Book:	
Author:	
Recommend to:	

Book:	
Author:	
Recommend to:	
Additional Notes:	

Use this list to record books you'd like to recommend to others.	**Own**
Book:	
Author:	
Recommend to:	

Book:	
Author:	
Recommend to:	

Book:	
Author:	
Recommend to:	

Book:	
Author:	
Recommend to:	

Book:	
Author:	
Recommend to:	

Book:	
Author:	
Recommend to:	

Book:	
Author:	
Recommend to:	

Book:	
Author:	
Recommend to:	
Additional Notes:	

Use this list to record books you'd like to recommend to others.	**Own**
Book:	
Author:	
Recommend to:	

Book:	
Author:	
Recommend to:	

Book:	
Author:	
Recommend to:	

Book:	
Author:	
Recommend to:	

Book:	
Author:	
Recommend to:	

Book:	
Author:	
Recommend to:	

Book:	
Author:	
Recommend to:	

Book:	
Author:	
Recommend to:	
Additional Notes:	

Use this list to record books you'd like to recommend to others.	**Own**
Book:	
Author:	
Recommend to:	

Book:	
Author:	
Recommend to:	

Book:	
Author:	
Recommend to:	

Book:	
Author:	
Recommend to:	

Book:	
Author:	
Recommend to:	

Book:	
Author:	
Recommend to:	

Book:	
Author:	
Recommend to:	

Book:	
Author:	
Recommend to:	
Additional Notes:	

Use this list to record books you'd like to recommend to others.	**Own**
Book:	
Author:	
Recommend to:	

Book:	
Author:	
Recommend to:	

Book:	
Author:	
Recommend to:	

Book:	
Author:	
Recommend to:	

Book:	
Author:	
Recommend to:	

Book:	
Author:	
Recommend to:	

Book:	
Author:	
Recommend to:	

Book:	
Author:	
Recommend to:	
Additional Notes:	

Loaner Lists

A book, too, can be a star, a living fire to lighten the darkness, leading out into the expanding universe.

—Madeleine L'Engle

Books are the ultimate Dumpees: put them down and they'll wait for you forever; pay attention to them and they always love you back.

— John Green, *An Abundance of Katherines*

Books Loaned: Use this list to keep track of your personal lending library. Record the title of the book, who borrowed it, when it was borrowed, and when it was returned.

Borrowed | Returned

Title:

Loaned to:

Title:

Loaned to:

Title:

Loaned to:

Title:

Loaned to:

Title:

Loaned to:

Title:

Loaned to:

Title:

Loaned to:

Title:

Loaned to:

Title:

Loaned to:

Title:

Loaned to:

Title:

Loaned to:

Books Loaned: Use this list to keep track of your personal lending library. Record the title of the book, who borrowed it, when it was borrowed, and when it was returned.

Borrowed | Returned

Title:

Loaned to:

Title:

Loaned to:

Title:

Loaned to:

Title:

Loaned to:

Title:

Loaned to:

Title:

Loaned to:

Title:

Loaned to:

Title:

Loaned to:

Title:

Loaned to:

Title:

Loaned to:

Title:

Loaned to:

Books Loaned: Use this list to keep track of your personal lending library. Record the title of the book, who borrowed it, when it was borrowed, and when it was returned.

Borrowed | Returned

Title:

Loaned to:

Title:

Loaned to:

Title:

Loaned to:

Title:

Loaned to:

Title:

Loaned to:

Title:

Loaned to:

Title:

Loaned to:

Title:

Loaned to:

Title:

Loaned to:

Title:

Loaned to:

Title:

Loaned to:

Books Loaned: Use this list to keep track of your personal lending library. Record the title of the book, who borrowed it, when it was borrowed, and when it was returned.

Borrowed | Returned

Title:

Loaned to:

Title:

Loaned to:

Title:

Loaned to:

Title:

Loaned to:

Title:

Loaned to:

Title:

Loaned to:

Title:

Loaned to:

Title:

Loaned to:

Title:

Loaned to:

Title:

Loaned to:

Title:

Loaned to:

Books Loaned: Use this list to keep track of your personal lending library. Record the title of the book, who borrowed it, when it was borrowed, and when it was returned.

	Borrowed	Returned

Title:

Loaned to:

Title:

Loaned to:

Title:

Loaned to:

Title:

Loaned to:

Title:

Loaned to:

Title:

Loaned to:

Title:

Loaned to:

Title:

Loaned to:

Title:

Loaned to:

Title:

Loaned to:

Title:

Loaned to:

Books Loaned: Use this list to keep track of your personal lending library. Record the title of the book, who borrowed it, when it was borrowed, and when it was returned.

| | Borrowed | Returned |

Title:

Loaned to:

Title:

Loaned to:

Title:

Loaned to:

Title:

Loaned to:

Title:

Loaned to:

Title:

Loaned to:

Title:

Loaned to:

Title:

Loaned to:

Title:

Loaned to:

Title:

Loaned to:

Title:

Loaned to:

Books Loaned: Use this list to keep track of your personal lending library. Record the title of the book, who borrowed it, when it was borrowed, and when it was returned.

Borrowed | Returned

Title:

Loaned to:

Title:

Loaned to:

Title:

Loaned to:

Title:

Loaned to:

Title:

Loaned to:

Title:

Loaned to:

Title:

Loaned to:

Title:

Loaned to:

Title:

Loaned to:

Title:

Loaned to:

Title:

Loaned to:

Books Loaned: Use this list to keep track of your personal lending library. Record the title of the book, who borrowed it, when it was borrowed, and when it was returned.

Borrowed · Returned

Title:

Loaned to:

Title:

Loaned to:

Title:

Loaned to:

Title:

Loaned to:

Title:

Loaned to:

Title:

Loaned to:

Title:

Loaned to:

Title:

Loaned to:

Title:

Loaned to:

Title:

Loaned to:

Title:

Loaned to:

Books Loaned: Use this list to keep track of your personal lending library. Record the title of the book, who borrowed it, when it was borrowed, and when it was returned.

| | Borrowed | Returned |

Title:

Loaned to:

Title:

Loaned to:

Title:

Loaned to:

Title:

Loaned to:

Title:

Loaned to:

Title:

Loaned to:

Title:

Loaned to:

Title:

Loaned to:

Title:

Loaned to:

Title:

Loaned to:

Title:

Loaned to:

Books Loaned: Use this list to keep track of your personal lending library. Record the title of the book, who borrowed it, when it was borrowed, and when it was returned.

Borrowed | Returned

Title:

Loaned to:

Title:

Loaned to:

Title:

Loaned to:

Title:

Loaned to:

Title:

Loaned to:

Title:

Loaned to:

Title:

Loaned to:

Title:

Loaned to:

Title:

Loaned to:

Title:

Loaned to:

Title:

Loaned to:

Books Loaned: Use this list to keep track of your personal lending library. Record the title of the book, who borrowed it, when it was borrowed, and when it was returned.

	Borrowed	Returned

Title:

Loaned to:

Title:

Loaned to:

Title:

Loaned to:

Title:

Loaned to:

Title:

Loaned to:

Title:

Loaned to:

Title:

Loaned to:

Title:

Loaned to:

Title:

Loaned to:

Title:

Loaned to:

Title:

Loaned to:

Books Loaned: Use this list to keep track of your personal lending library. Record the title of the book, who borrowed it, when it was borrowed, and when it was returned.

Borrowed | Returned

Title:

Loaned to:

Title:

Loaned to:

Title:

Loaned to:

Title:

Loaned to:

Title:

Loaned to:

Title:

Loaned to:

Title:

Loaned to:

Title:

Loaned to:

Title:

Loaned to:

Title:

Loaned to:

Title:

Loaned to:

Resources

The best moments in reading are when you come across something—a thought, a feeling, a way of looking at things—which you had thought special and particular to you. Now here it is, set down by someone else, a person you have never met, someone even who is long dead. And it is as if a hand has come out and taken yours.

—Alan Bennett, *The History Boys: A Play*

References and Resources

***Note to parents: please monitor the websites your teen visits.

Other Places to Find Great Book Lists

Teen Library Sites

Most public libraries have lists for teens. The libraries mentioned here have exceptional resources for teens and their parents.

Appleton Public Library	teen.apl.org/bklists/index.asp
Austin Public Library—Connected Youth	www.connectedyouth.org/books
Bettendorf Public Library	www.bettendorflibrary.com/teens
Boulder Public Library	www.boulderteens.org
Cumberland Public Library	www.cumberland.lib.nc.us/ccplyouth/teensindex.htm
Denver Public Library—Evolver	teens.denverlibrary.org
Evanston Public Library	www.epl.org
Hasting Public Library—Teen Domain	www.hastings.lib.ne.us/teen.html
Hennepin County Library—Teen Links	www.hclib.org/teens
Internet Public Library—Teen Space	www.ipl.org/div/teen/browse/rw7600
Los Angeles Public Library—Teen Web	www.lapl.org/ya/stuff/index.html
Mi-—Continent Public Library	opac.mcpl.lib.mo.us/uhtbin/cgisirsi/x/HEADQTRS/0/1/1223/X
Peninsula Library—Teen Lists	www.plsinfo.org/recommend/readinglists/teen_titles.html
Public Library of Charlotte & Mecklenburg County	www.plcmc.org/readers_club/features/featuresList.asp
San Jose Library—Teen Web	www.sjlibrary.org/gateways/teens/booklists
Seattle Public Library	www.spl.org/default.asp?pageID=audience_teens
Skokie Public Library	www.skokielibrary.info/s_teens/tn_books/index.asp
Sno-Isle Libraries Teen Book Lists	www.sno-isle.org/page/?ID=3148
Sussex County Library	www.sussexcountylibrary.org/teens.htm
Tulsa Public Library	teens.tulsalibrary.org
Wayne Public Library	www.waynepubliclibrary.org/teens

Teen Reading Sites

All Together Now	atn-reading-lists.wikispaces.com
Cooperative Children's Book Center	www.education.wisc.edu/ccbc/books/ detailLists.asp?idBookListCat=4
Favorite Teenage Angst Books	www.grouchy.com/angst
Flamingnet	flamingnet.com
Guys Read	www.guysread.com
Reader's Robot	www.tnrdlib.bc.ca/rr.html
Reads4Teens	reads4teens.org
Teen Reads	www.teenreads.com
YA Books Central	www.yabookscentral.com
YALSA—Young Adult Library Services Association	www.ala.org/ala/mgrps/divs/yalsa/yalsa.cfm

Publications

CM Magazine—Canadian Book Review	www.umanitoba.ca/cm/index.html
Teen Ink—Magazine, website, and books written by teens	www.teenink.com
Polyphony H.S.—A student-run national literary magazine for high school writers and editors	www.polyphonyhs.com
Booklist Online	www.booklistonline.com

Young Adult Literature Blogs

A Chair, A Fireplace & A Tea Cozy	yzocaet.blogspot.com/index.html
A Pile o' Books	apileobooks.weebly.com/index.html
A True Reality	atruereality.blogspot.com
All Five Stars	fivestarreading.blogspot.com
Alley of Books	alleyofbooks.blogspot.com
And Another Book Read	andanotherbookread.blogspot.com
Bean Bag Books	beanbagbooks.blogspot.com
Becky's Book Reviews	blbooks.blogspot.com
Between the Lines	www.betweenthelines.com.au
Book Bopper	bookbopper.blogspot.com
Booked Books	booked-books.blogspot.com

Bookends	bookends.booklistonline.com
Bookluver-Carol's Reviews	www.bookluver-carol.blogspot.com
Books by Their Cover	booksbytheircover.blogspot.com
Books Make Great Lovers	www.booksaremylove.blogspot.com
Bookworm Readers	bookwormbooklovers.blogspot.com
Bookwyrm Chrysalis	yafantasy.com
Charlotte's Library	charlotteslibrary.blogspot.com
Cynsations	cynthialeitichsmith.blogspot.com/index.html
Eat Sleep Dance Read	eatsleepdanceread.blogspot.com
Em's Bookshelf	emsbookshelf.blogspot.com
Frenetic Reader	freneticreader.blogspot.com
GreenBeenTeenQueen	www.greenbeanteenqueen.com
Hope's Bookshelf	princess2293.blogspot.com
In Bed with Books	inbedwithbooks.blogspot.com
Kids Lit	kidslit.menashalibrary.org/category/teen
La Femme Readers	lafemmereaders.blogspot.com
Lauren's Crammed Bookshelf	laurenscrammedbookshelf.blogspot.com
Mrs. Magoo Reads	www.mrsmagooreads.com
No Flying, No Tights	www.noflyingnotights.com/index2.html
Oops...Wrong Cookie	oopswrongcookie.blogspot.com
Persnickety Snark	persnicketysnark.blogspot.com
Pop Culture Junkie	aleapopculture.blogspot.com
Rainbow Project	rainbowlist.wordpress.com/rl-2009
Reader Rabbit	readerrabbit.blogspot.com
Readergirlz	www.readergirlz.com/issue.html
Reading Junky's Reading Roost	readingjunky.blogspot.com
Reading Rants!	www.readingrants.org
Rhiannon Hart	rhiannon-hart.blogspot.com
Seven Impossible Things Before Breakfast	blaine.org/sevenimpossiblethings
Sparrow Review	sparrowreview.blogspot.com
Squeaky Books	squeakybooks.blogspot.com
Stop, Drop & Read	orientaldesires.blogspot.com
Tales of a Ravenous Reader	lushbudgetproduction.blogspot.com

Teen Tuesday	teentuesday.blogspot.com
Temppatt	temppatt.blogspot.com
The Book Muncher	thebookmuncher.blogspot.com
The Book Obsession	bookworm0440.blogspot.com
The Book Vault	the-book-vault.blogspot.com
The Compulsive Reader	thecompulsivereader.blogspot.com
The Magic of Ink	inkmagic.blogspot.com
The Page Flipper	thepageflipper.blogspot.com
The Story Siren	www.thestorysiren.com
The Ya Ya Yas	theyayayas.wordpress.com
Tower of Books	towerofbooks.wordpress.com
Under the Covers	www.lisachellman.com/blog
Welcome to My Tweendom	tweendom.blogspot.com
Wondrous Reads	cityofbooks.blogspot.com
Word for Teens	wordforteens.blogspot.com
Y.A. New York	www.yanewyork.com
YA Blog News	yablognews.blogspot.com
YA Fresh	yafresh.blogspot.com
YAreads.com	www.yareads.com
Young Adult Book Bloggers	youngadultbookbloggers.blogspot.com

Resources for Parents

Moms Inspire Learning Simple resources and strategies to inspire lifelong learning, reading, and leading	www.momsinspirelearning.com/2009/07/picky-reading-in-search-of-the-best-ya-books.html
Boys Read Transform boys into lifelong readers	www.boysread.org/index.html
Common Sense Media	www.commonsensemedia.org
LitLover Resources for starting a teen book club, including discussion questions and activities	www.litlovers.com/litkids.htm
Read Kiddo Read	readkiddoread.com/home

Teen Book Club Suggestion Sites

Leon County Library	www.leoncountyfl.gov/LIBRARY/youth-child/teensbookclublist.asp
Shoulder to Shoulder Parent/teen book club	www.shouldertoshoulderminnesota.org/?q=node/44
DearReader.com Receive an email each day with a five-minute excerpt of the current book club selection	www.dearreader.com

Author Websites

Adele Geras	www.adelegeras.com
Aidan Chambers	www.aidanchambers.co.uk
Alex Flinn	www.alexflinn.com
Alyson Noel	www.alysonnoel.com
Amelia Atwater-Rhodes	www.tdos.org
An Na	www.anwriting.com
Ann Brashares	www.randomhouse.com/teens/sisterhoodcentral
Ann Rinaldi	www.annrinaldi.com
Anna Myers	annamyers.info/books
Anne McCaffrey	www.annemccaffrey.net
Annette Curtis Klause	www.childrensbookguild.org/klause.htm
Anthony Horowitz	www.anthonyhorowitz.com
Autumn Cornwell	www.autumncornwell.com
Avi	www.avi-writer.com
Ben Mikaelsen	www.benmikaelsen.com
Carl Deuker	members.authorsguild.net/carldeuker
Carl Hiaasen	www.carlhiaasen.com
Carolee Dean	www.caroleedean.com
Carolyn Meyer	www.readcarolyn.com
Catherine Atkins	www.catherineatkins.com
Cecilia Galante	www.ceciliagalante.com
Celia Rees	www.celiarees.co.uk
Cherie Bennett	www.cheriebennett.com
Chris Crutcher	www.chriscrutcher.com

Chris Crutcher	www.chriscrutcher.com
Chris Lynch	ChrisLynchBooks.com
Christopher Golding	www.christophergolding.com
Christopher Paolini	www.alagaesia.com
Christopher Paul Curtis	www.christopherpaulcurtis.com
Coe Booth	www.coebooth.com
D. L. Garfinkle	www.dlgarfinkle.com
David Almond	www.davidalmond.com
David Levithan	www.davidlevithan.com
David Lubar	www.davidlubar.com
Dean Hughes	www.deanhughes.net
Deb Caletti	www.debcaletti.com
Diane Duane	www.youngwizards.net
Dianne Gray	www.prairievoices.com
Donna Jo Napoli	www.donnajonapoli.com
E. Lockhart	www.theboyfriendlist.com
Eoin Colfer	www.eoincolfer.com
Francesca Lia Block	www.francescaliablock.com
Gail Carson Levine	GailCarsonLevineBooks.com
Gail Giles	www.gailgiles.com
Garret Freymann-Weyr	www.freymann-weyr.com
Garth Nix	www.garthnix.co.uk
Gary Paulsen	www.randomhouse.com/features/garypaulsen
Gary Soto	www.garysoto.com
Gordon Korman	www.gordonkorman.com
Gregory Maguire	www.gregorymaguire.com
Han Nolan	www.hannolan.com
Hannah R. Goodman	www.hannahrgoodman.com
Holly Black	www.blackholly.com
J. K. Rowling	www.jkrowling.com
J. R. R. Tolkien	www.tolkiensociety.org
Jacqueline Woodson	www.jacquelinewoodson.com
James Patterson	www.jamespatterson.com

Jane Yolen	www.janeyolen.com
Jean Craighead George	www.jeancraigheadgeorge.com
Jean Ure	www.jeanure.com
Jennifer Armstrong	www.jennifer-armstrong.com
Jerry Spinelli	www.jerryspinelli.com
Joan Bauer	www.joanbauer.com
Joe Craig	www.joecraig.co.uk
John Flanagan	www.rangersapprentice.com
John Green	www.sparksflyup.com
Jordan Sonnenblick	www.jordansonnenblick.com
Judy Blume	www.judyblume.com
Julia Alvarez	www.juliaalvarez.com
Julia DeVillers	www.girlwise.com
K. L. Going	www.klgoing.com
Kenneth Oppel	www.kennethoppel.ca
Laurie Faria Stolarz	www.lauriestolarz.com
Laurie Halse Anderson	www.writerlady.com
Lemony Snicket	www.lemonysnicket.com
Libba Bray	www.libbabray.com
Lois Duncan	loisduncan.arquettes.com
Lois Lowry	www.loislowry.com
Lorie Ann Grover	www.loorieanngrover.com
Louis Sachar	www.louissachar.com
Louisa May Alcott	www.louisamayalcott.org
M. E. Kerr	www.mekerr.com
Madeleine L'Engle	www.madeleinelengle.com
Marcus Sedgwick	www.marcussedgwick.com
Mariah Fredericks	www.mariahfredericks.com
Markus Zusak	www.markuszusak.com
Marlene Perez	www.marleneperez.com
Maureen Johnson	www.maureenjohnsonbooks.com
Meg Cabot	www.megcabot.com
Megan McCafferty	www.meganmccafferty.com

Mel Glenn	www.melglenn.com
Melissa de la Cruz	www.melissa-delacruz.com
Nancy Farmer	www.nancyfarmerwebsite.com
Nancy Garden	www.nancygarden.com
Natasha Friend	www.natashafriend.com
Neal Shusterman	www.storyman.com
Ned Vezzini	www.nedvezzini.com
Neil Gaiman	www.neilgaiman.com
Nikki Grimes	www.nikkigrimes.com
Orson Scott Card	www.hatrack.com/osc/about.shtml
Patricia McCormick	www.pattymccormick.com
Patrick Jones	www.connectingya.com
Paul Fleischman	www.paulfleischman.com
Paul Zindel	www.paulzindel.com
Paula Danziger	www.scholastic.com/titles/paula
Peter Abrahams	www.peterabrahams.com
Peter Dickinson	www.peterdickinson.com
Philip Pullman	www.philip-pullman.com
Rick Riordan	www.rickriordan.com
Robert Lipsyte	www.robertlipsyte.com
Rosemary Graham	www.rosemarygraham.com
S. E. Hinton	www.sehinton.com
Sarah Dessen	www.sarahdessen.com
Scott O'Dell	www.scottodell.com
Scott Westerfeld	www.scottwesterfeld.com
Shane Collins	www.subway19.tk
Shannon Greenland	www.shannongreenland.com
Shannon Hale	www.squeetus.com
Shannon Hale	www.squeetus.com
Sharon Creech	www.sharoncreech.com
Sharon G. Flake	www.sharongflake.com
Sharon M. Draper	www.sharondraper.com
Shelley Hrdlitschka	www.shelleyhrdlitschka.com

Shelly Stoehr	www.shelleystoehr.com
Sherman Alexie	www.fallsapart.com
Sid Fleischman	www.sidfleischman.com
Sonia Levitin	www.sonialevitin.com
Sonya Sones	www.sonyasones.com
Stephanie S. Tolan	www.stephanietolan.com
Stephenie Meyer	www.stepheniemeyer.com
Steve Kluger	www.stevekluger.com
Susan Vaught	www.susanvaught.com
Suzanne Collins	www.suzannecollinsbooks.com
Suzanne Fisher Staples	www.suzannefisherstaples.com
T. A. Barron	www.tabarron.com
Teena Booth	www.teenabooth.com
Terry Davis	www.terrydavis.net
Terry Pratchett	www.terrypratchettbooks.com
Tim Bowler	www.timbowler.co.uk
Ursula K. Le Guin	www.ursulakleguin.com
Vivian Vande Velde	www.vivianvandevelde.com
Walter Dean Myers	walterdeanmyersbooks.com
Will Hobbs	www.willhobbsauthor.com

Literary Terms

Written by Molly Lundquist of LitLovers.com

LitLovers is a full-service website devoted to book clubs and individual readers. The site offers a wealth of resources: reading guides, book recommendations, online lit courses, how-tos, recipes, and games—all to enhance reading and the book club experience. Molly Lundquist, the LitLovers founder, spent years as a corporate speechwriter and later as a college English instructor. LitLovers combines her passions for reading, writing, and teaching.

Allegory (see Symbol)

Archetype (see Symbol)

Characters—individuals who populate a book and act out the storyline or plot. There are major and minor characters, as well as a protagonist (hero or heroine) and antagonist (rival to protagonist).

Characterization—the method by which authors create characters. Writers choose among five different "shapes," or types, of characters and also decide whether characters develop or change.

Round—psychologically and emotionally complex characters with fully developed inner lives.

Flat—two dimensional, underdeveloped characters with scant attention paid to inner lives.

Stock—stereotypes, such as dumb blonde or jock, miserly man, handsome rake, or femme fatale. Authors use both round and flat (even stock) characters in the same story—there isn't time or space enough to develop all characters equally.

Dynamic—characters who change during the course of the story; they grow, mature, and learn about the world and their role in it. Dynamic characters are main characters (thought not all main characters are dynamic).

Static—characters who remain unchanged by the end of the story. Static characters make up secondary and minor characters.

Cliché—an expression that becomes trite with overuse. Clichéd writing is unoriginal and predictable, often following a formulaic plot.

Climax (see Plot)

Comedy—today, a humorous narrative; traditionally, a drama that begins with disorder but ends with order restored and happiness on the part of all characters. Shakespeare's *As You Like it* is a comedy.

Conflict—the struggle between opposing forces in a story. Conflict creates interest and suspense within a plot (suspense is what keeps you turning the page). Authors use two types of conflict, often within the same story:

External—conflict outside characters that acts upon them: character vs. character; character vs. community, society, or nature; or nation vs. nation.

Internal—conflict within a character, an emotional or psychological state of mind in which a character wars against him/herself.

Denouement (see Plot)

Epic—traditionally, a long narrative poem recounting the adventures of a (mythological) hero who reflects the history and wider values of his culture (*The Iliad* and *The Odyssey*); today, a term that often refers to any narrative incorporating a wide, historical sweep of a given society.

Fantasy—fiction that takes place in a non-existent world, such as a fairyland. Tolkein's Lord of the Ring series is a good example, as is C. S. Lewis's The Chronicles of Narnia and J. K. Rowling's Harry Potter series.

Figure of speech—a word or phrase that points to something other than its literal meaning, that connotes rather than denotes. Figures of speech heighten meaning by creating an emotional response from the reader. (See Metaphor and Simile.)

Flashback (see Plot Devices.)

Foreshadowing (see Plot Devices)

Genre—French for type or kind; used in literature to distinguish between poetry, drama, and prose. Or comedy, tragedy, epic poetry, and romance. Or fiction and nonfiction. Sub-genres refer to action, detective/mystery, fantasy, gothic, romance, science fiction, spy, thriller, or western. Or biography, memoir, history, and current events. "Genre" is a fluid word.

Gothic—type of fiction originated by Horace Walpole in the eighteenth century centering on magic, mystery, and spooky medieval buildings. Today, it refers to a dark, foreboding mystery and an unknown terror. Emily Bronte's *Wuthering Heights*, Daphne DuMaurie's *Rebecca,* and even Steven King's *The Shining* are a few examples.

Graphic novels—books in a comic/cartoon format, either fiction or nonfiction. They differ from comic books in that they are sold in bookstores rather than newsstands or comic book shops. Subject matters, often hefty or serious, may revolve around current or historical events. One of the first graphic novels was *Maus* (1986–1991) by Art Spiegelman, which consists of two volumes recounting the Holocaust. A more recent example is *Persepolis* (2000) by Marjane Satrapi, which is about the author's childhood in Iran.

Imagery—the use of descriptive words, phrases, or figures of speech (similes or metaphors) that appeal to a reader's sensory perceptions. Images convey the mood, or atmosphere, of a work.

Irony—a different reality than what is intended or expected. There are four basic types of irony:

Verbal—what is said is not what is meant. Sarcasm is a form of verbal irony.

Situational—what happens is the opposite of what is expected or desired; unintended consequences.

Dramatic—readers know things that the characters do not. Readers are "in the know."

Cosmic—bad things happening to good people; a working out of fate.

Manga—cartoon or comic-book narratives whose modern form originated in Japan during the mid- to late twentieth century. Common topics include romance, action-adventure, science fiction, mystery, horror, and historical drama. In the United States, this genre may be referred to as Amerimanga. Manga comics often appear in serial form and may then be collected into a book format. Successful managa may be converted into an anime (animated) film.

Magical realism—fiction based on the life of ordinary individuals but interspersed with supernatural or magical beings and occurrences. Magical realism was developed by South American writers, primarily Gabriel Garcia Marquez and Jorge Borges, and employed by North American writers like Alice Hoffman. (See Realism.)

Melodrama—a work of fiction depending on sensationalism—heightened drama—to achieve its effects; heavy dependence on plot with little character development. Characters in a melodrama tend to be sharply drawn in terms of good or evil—with heavy dependence on plot.

Metaphor—a figure of speech that compares one object to another without using the word "like" (as in a simile). "He is a snake" as opposed to "he is like a snake." (see Simile and Figure of speech).

Mood—the underlying atmosphere created in a literary work; it may be dark or somber, light and airy, mocking or earnest, satiric or sincere, dismissive or admiring. Mood is created by descriptive imagery, choice of diction, character dialog, and subject matter.

Mystery (detective or crime story)—a crime is committed and the hero/heroine must uncover the perpetrator. Mystery novels exemplify the underlying philosophy of realistic fiction in that the world is knowable (rather than mysterious and unknowable) through the close observation of empirical facts. A sub-genre of fiction.

Narrator (see Point of View)

Novel—a prose form devoted to the realistic, everyday lives of ordinary people. The novel evolved in the late 17th century from

French romances—fanciful stories centered on the nobility and interventions of supernatural beings. (See Realism and Romance.)

Paranormal—stories involving supernatural beings and occurrences or phenomena outside the realm of scientific explanation. Tales of werewolves, vampires, ghosts, and apparitions are good examples of this genre.

Paranormal romance—paranormal stories that focus on romantic relationships and tortured lovers, often werewolves or vampires.

Perspective (see Point of View)

Plot—the events or action in a story; plot is what happens to the characters. A classic plot has a basic "architecture"; think of it as a pyramid:

Exposition (ground to the left of the pyramid)—background information, usually placed at the beginning of a story. Provided either by a narrator or through dialogue.

Rising action (left side of the pyramid)—the working through of the plot's conflict.

Climax (apex of the pyramid)--when the conflict reaches its highest point of tension or suspense; the crisis, or turning point, in the action.

Falling action (right side of the pyramid)—also known as denouement, the dropping off of tension as the conflict resolves itself.

Conclusion (ground to the right)—a wrap-up of the story's plot lines, perhaps an epilogue or afterword.

Plot devices—techniques writers use to help further events of the story.

Flashback—a backward look at events prior to the story's present time frame as a way of explanation; sometimes provided by a narrator as a sort of reverie by a character.

Foreshadowing—a dramatic hint (an event, perhaps) of what is to come later in the story; often used to lay the groundwork for an ending so that it doesn't feel manipulative or "tacked on."

Suspended revelation—a device whereby the author withholds information from readers to create interest and suspense. Mysteries are completely dependent on suspended revelation, but all fiction uses it. It's like fishing—the author lets the line out gradually, bit by bit, and then reels us in at the end.

Cliff hanger—a dramatic, suspenseful moment at the end of a chapter. The reader is left "hanging" until the action is resolved in the next chapter or later.

Point of view—narrative perspective; who tells the story. POV is one the most important decisions an author makes—who tells the story determines the reader's sympathy and how much information readers are given. There are two basic points of view: first person and third person. But it's more complicated:

First-person—a character within the story: the "I" of the story. We can know only as much as the "I" character knows.

Third-person—a narrator who is external to the story, not a character. There are three types of narrators:

Omniscient—all knowing; reveals the behavior and thoughts of all characters; there is no single, privileged character.

Limited Omniscient—limited knowledge; reveals the behavior and thoughts of primary characters only—leading readers to identify more closely with them.

Objective—impersonal; reveals characters only through dialog and behavior; has no access to their inner thoughts.

Realism—fiction based on the life of ordinary individuals with strict adherence to everyday, accepted reality (no interference of supernatural elements). (See Novel and Romance.)

Romance—today, a sub-genre of fiction in which a man and woman overcome obstacles in their attraction to one another and come together at the end; traditionally, a long French narrative (prose or poetry), featuring noblemen and women. Romances, incorporating supernatural elements, gradually evolved into the realistic prose novel. (See Novel and Realism.)

Saga—a tale of family adventure over generations.

Science fiction—futuristic fiction that revolves around adventures in planetary space; often based on scientific explorations into astrophysics, such as other dimensions, parallel universes, extra-terrestrial life, and time warps. A sub-genre of fiction.

Setting—the context of the story's events. Authors choose settings carefully in order to set mood, establish theme, or use as a symbolic element. There are four basic types of settings.

Location—indoors/outdoors, rural/urban, geographical area

Time—time of day, season, year, historical era

Culture—religious values, social mores, political beliefs, philosophical outlook

Physical—weather, topography (mountains, bodies of water), architecture.

Simile—a figure of speech that compares one object to another: "her lips are like roses." (See Metaphor.)

Style—the choice of words (diction) and their arrangement into sentences that is particular to an author. Style reflects how authors attempt to express their ideas. Sentences, for instance, may be long and convoluted like Faulkner or short and pithy like Hemingway. Style can also affect mood.

Subplot—a secondary and lesser plot; used to shed light on the main plot, either through contrast or comparison. Sometimes a subplot serves as a diversion from the primary plot to relieve tension.

Subtext—what is not stated explicitly in the text. Subtext reveals a deeper, alternate meaning underlying the words written on the page.

Suspense—the anxious anticipation on the reader's part to see how the plot plays out and how characters resolve their issues. It's what keeps readers turning the pages.

Symbol—an object, person or event that represents something other than itself. There are four types of symbols:

Conventional—found in our daily lives: wedding ring (unending love); flag (love of country); dove (peace or hope). There are hundreds of conventional symbols.

Literary—used to deepen or extend a story's meaning. Literary symbols are suggestive, meaning different things—rather than definitive, meaning only one thing.

Allegory—a definitive, one-to-one correspondence, used often in religious works such as Bunyan's *Pilgrim's Progress* in which a pilgrim named Christian seeks salvation. On the path he meets characters called Hopeful, Goodwill, and Mr. Worldly.

Archetype—universal patterns that have timeless recognition: light = goodness, safety, enlightenment; dark = evil, mystery, fear; water = life force, birth/rebirth, or purity. A hero's journey follows the same pattern in all cultures (a call to action, through adversity, to victory), and the Cinderella motif (debasement to triumph) is found in hundreds of ancient folktales throughout the globe.

Theme—a central, underlying idea explored by an author; generally implicitly stated. A theme serves as a unifying principle: characters, plot, and imagery all express the working out of this central idea.

Thriller—highly dramatic, plot-driven novel characterized by fast-paced action and a clever hero who must thwart the plans of heinous villains. A sub-genre of fiction.

Tragedy—today, a narrative that ends in death or unrelenting sadness; traditionally, a drama that moves from order to disorder and ends with the downfall of the main character due to an inherent flaw (pride or lack of self-knowledge). Sophocles' *Oedipus Rex* is a tragedy, as are Shakespeare's *Othello, Hamlet,* and *King Lear*.

Urban lit—also known as "street lit," explores the dark, gritty environment of inner-city life. Primarily written by and for African Americans, urban lit began as an outgrowth of the Black Power movement in the 1970s and, some believe, has continued in its new form as hip-hop music, as well as print—an example being Sister Souljah's *The Coldest Winter Ever* (1999).

Author   Page   Author   Page